THE URBANIZATION
OF PEOPLE

THE URBANIZATION OF PEOPLE

THE POLITICS OF DEVELOPMENT, LABOR MARKETS, AND SCHOOLING IN THE CHINESE CITY

ELI FRIEDMAN

Columbia University Press   *New York*

Columbia University Press
Publishers Since 1893
New York   Chichester, West Sussex
cup.columbia.edu
Copyright © 2022 Columbia University Press
All rights reserved

Library of Congress Cataloging-in-Publication Data
Names: Friedman, Eli, author.
Title: The urbanization of people : the politics of development, labor
markets, and schooling in the Chinese city / Eli Friedman.
Description: New York : Columbia University Press, [2022] |
Includes bibliographical references and index.
Identifiers: LCCN 2021043573 (print) | LCCN 2021043574 (ebook) |
ISBN 9780231205085 (hardback) | ISBN 9780231205092 (trade paperback) |
ISBN 9780231555838 (ebook)
Subjects: LCSH: Education and state—China. | Children of migrant
laborers—Education—China. | Migrant labor—China—Social conditions. |
Urbanization—China. | Urban policy—China. | China—Population policy. |
China—Social conditions—2000–
Classification: LCC LC94.C5 F75 2022 (print) | LCC LC94.C5 (ebook) |
DDC 379.51—dc23/eng/20211116
LC record available at https://lccn.loc.gov/2021043573
LC ebook record available at https://lccn.loc.gov/2021043574

COVER DESIGN: Julia Kushnirsky
COVER IMAGE: Eli Friedman

For Julia

CONTENTS

PREFACE

I
t was winter in Beijing, and children in the courtyard of Shusheng School were playing in a mound of coal. I had just traveled for an hour and a half from Beijing's imposing and ordered core out to the derelict periphery of Chaoyang District for my first ever visit to a migrant school. While I was expecting poor conditions, I could not help but be taken aback by the state of disrepair and apparent lack of investment in physical plant. Coal was the school's source of warmth in the winter and was now doubling as playground equipment.

I had come on an exploratory visit to investigate teachers' working conditions in urban China's migrant schools. I had learned of these schools—generally fully privatized, often without official licensing, and almost exclusively populated by the children of rural-to-urban internal migrants—in my earlier research on labor politics. As a labor sociologist, I had an intuition that viewing these schools as a workplace would likely capture important social dynamics of urban life beyond the employment relationship. Whereas my earlier work was largely concerned with workers in the manufacturing sector, I believed that focusing on reproductive labor would more effectively illuminate the social hierarchies embedded in China's migrant labor regime. As I spoke with teachers in Beijing over the following weeks, I learned of the astonishingly bad working conditions they faced: woefully inadequate facilities, long hours, pay below minimum wage, and huge class sizes.

But I found that teachers were often more concerned with a workplace problem I couldn't have anticipated: the uneven abilities of their students. I quickly found that it was the norm for schools to have annual turnover rates of 25–30 percent of the student body. Children moved from school to school and from city to countryside and back again with astonishing regularity. Parents were overburdened with the struggle to eke out a living, and much reproductive labor typically associated with the family—not least of which was emotional availability—was pushed onto the teachers. As I visited school after school, first in Beijing and then in Guangzhou and Chengdu, I realized that these conditions were national in scope.

I began to doubt that I could restrict the study to the workplace as my focus was increasingly pulled out of the school. I found that in order to explain the stresses faced by teachers in China's migrant schools, I needed a better account of the process of capitalist urbanization. I could not understand high levels of student turnover, pathetically low wages, or the intense emotional burden faced by teachers without grasping parents' position in the labor market, the structure of the educational system at the national level, constantly evolving population control policies, and the perpetual pressure of spatial peripheralization derived from urban redevelopment. Furthermore, it became clear that for many working-class migrants, the question of urbanization was for them a problem of uniting work opportunities with familial relations in space and time. Could they actually work *and* live in the city? These struggles with schooling revealed a radical disjuncture in China's cities between

the triumphant global urbanism of capital and the highly segmented and contingent urbanization of rural migrants. My initial intuition that the migrant school would capture important
sociological aspects of life in the city was correct, but exploited
and emotionally exhausted teachers now appeared as one feature of a broader process of population management and capitalist transformation. In essence, my research on China's migrant
workers shifted focus, without shifting sites, from the politics
of the workplace to the politics of social reproduction amid
rapid urbanization.

I came to accept this reorientation toward urbanization haltingly as I worried about the risk inherent in trying to enter a new
academic field. As I immersed myself in new literature, however, I came to the conclusion that there was a real opportunity
to synthesize insights from my background in labor studies with
those from education and urban studies. Despite the prevalence
of Marxist theorization in urban studies, I found a capital-
centric tendency in much of the literature. On the other hand,
the work on migration that has extensively documented forms of
social and economic exclusion in Chinese cities has been less
attuned to processes of capitalist development. It seemed to me
that a fuller account of the urbanization process needed to
attend to the various sides of the problem—the urbanization of
capital and its associated implications for labor and land markets, rural-to-urban migration, political exclusion and population control, and state development strategy more broadly—and
how they are negotiated. Given this particular intellectual trajectory, it perhaps goes without saying that the study that follows is methodologically and disciplinarily eclectic.

This book has been a long time coming. I began preliminary
research a decade ago, and writing was similarly drawn out over
a number of years. As the project evolved and gradually became

more focused, I was aided by the help and insight of countless friends, students, colleagues, and family members. I have had the real pleasure of working with a number of excellent research assistants in China and at Cornell, including Dai Rong, Zhuang Han, Angela He, Sherry Hu, Ning Li, Andi Kao, Mo Ni, Magic Peng, Luise Yang, Lindsey Yuan, Hao Zhang, and Zhou Xianqin. This book benefited immensely from my collaboration with Christine Wen, who provided extensive insight and conducted all of the interviews for the Guizhou portion of the research. My fieldwork could not possibly have succeeded without guidance and help from friends and colleagues in China including Lü Tu, He Mingxiu, Niu Zhikui, Wei Jiayu, Zhao Wei, and Zhuang Ming. Back in Ithaca, I was afforded the opportunity to work in a wonderful interdisciplinary environment in the Cornell Center for Social Sciences China Cities Project, where I learned from Jessica Chen Weiss, Panle Barwick, and Shanjun Li. Jeremy Wallace, the director of the project, deserves special mention as a key source of inspiration who I have called on time and again for his expertise on China's cities. I have benefited from a great number of colleagues around the world who have provided critical feedback on various pieces of the project, including Joel Andreas, Kam Wing Chan, Jia-Ching Chen, Greg Distelhorst, Yige Dong, Jamie Doucette, Peter Evans, Richard Freeman, Diana Fu, Lingxin Hao, Patrick Heller, Elaine Hui, Christina Kim, Neema Kudva, Sarosh Kuruvilla, Ching Kwan Lee, Zach Levenson, Mike Levien, Thung-Hong Lin, Ralph Litzinger, Andy Liu, Kate Maich, Tom McEnany, Meng Quan, Jonas Nahm, Dan Nemser, Marcel Paret, Bae-Gyoon Park, Pun Ngai, Aziz Rana, Elena Shih, Ed Steinfeld, Wang Xiying, and Marty Whyte. The manuscript has been much improved following the generous feedback from three anonymous reviewers. Lowell Frye has been a fantastic editor, expressing great enthusiasm and support for the project from the beginning and patiently and clearly walking me through the many steps of publication. I am very appreciative for Gregory McNamee's wonderful editing work and the efforts of the Columbia University Press staff who managed the design and production of the book. I would also like to acknowledge *Critical Sociology* and *Modern China* for allowing me to reprint portions of previously published articles, appearing in chapter 1 and chapter 6, respectively. I am very grateful for research support from Cornell's Center for Social Sciences, the East Asia Program, as well as my home, the School of Industrial and Labor Relations.

My greatest debt of gratitude is to my family. My mother and father, Ellen and Stuart, have continually been a source of intellectual engagement and deep ethical grounding. I remember that my parents were the very first people I told of my plan to study teachers, and I was, as always, made more confident by their unwavering encouragement. Particularly given the topic of this book, I would be remiss to not acknowledge their profound contributions with respect to reproductive labor. Without their help I quite simply cannot imagine how I would have managed to stay sane, let alone complete a book, over the past few years as my wife Julia and I struggled to negotiate intense work demands with raising two young children amid a pandemic. Similarly, my mother-in-law, Sabina, has been a source of reassurance and support, on numerous occasions dropping everything to hop on a plane to Ithaca to enjoy time with her grandchildren and rescue us from one crisis or another.

This project is considerably older than my two children, Noemi and Isaac. It may seem trite to point this out, but this has been a challenging period of history in which to raise children. And yet, as Julia and I often comment, it is impossible for us to imagine surviving crises epidemiological and social alike without them; they have taught us how to experience joy amid hardship. Although the project predates them, Noemi and Isaac have also helped me to uncover new affective contours in the research. I always understood intellectually that it was hard for the parents I interviewed to face state-produced separation from their young children, but I did not really appreciate the complexity of juvenile emotional needs or the tragedy of choosing between familial collocation and economic survival until my own children were born.

Finally, there are a million reasons why this book would not exist without Julia. There are all the normal and heroic things spouses do for each other—providing solace and happiness, dividing the emotional and physical labor of maintaining a household, and tolerating work-induced absences. But she has also made far and away the greatest intellectual contribution to the book, shaking me out of my grumpy foot-dragging on engaging seriously with biopolitics. Although it took years of sometimes anguished intellectual groping, she opened new theoretical vistas that radically changed how I see China and capitalist societies more broadly. I gratefully and lovingly dedicate this book to her.

INTRODUCTION

*Some people look down on outsiders, as soon as we speak it's,
"Outsider! Ha ha, outsider!" They can't live without outsiders.*

—Shandong migrant in Beijing

D uring the summer of 2011, the Beijing municipal government launched an offensive against the children of migrant workers. Just weeks before the beginning of the school year, bulldozers demolished at least two dozen migrant schools, putting thousands of children and their parents in a desperate situation. Anyone enrolled in these largely unlicensed and privately run schools was there because they had been excluded from the public education system, a consequence of their parents' nonlocal *hukou* (household registration). Neighboring migrant schools would not be able to absorb all of the recently displaced students, and in any event the registration period had passed long before. Parents either had to scramble to find another migrant school willing to admit them at the last moment or send their children, possibly alone, to the poverty of the village. There was widespread condemnation, both domestically and internationally, of the wanton human destruction left in the trail of these demolitions. But the government provided only the thinnest and most perfunctory of explanations: these schools were not up to standard.

Over the next three years, it became increasingly clear that these school demolitions were not an aberration, but rather an opening salvo in a campaign to expel the "low-end population." A common and ideologically entrenched cliché at the time held that China, and Beijing in particular, had too many people, and that the city's "carrying capacity" would be exceeded if public services were open to all PRC citizens.[1] Nonetheless, China's large cities have drawn in many millions of rural migrants in recent decades and continuously exceeded self-imposed population limits, while their economic expansion has been underwritten by mass inflows of this pliable and cheap labor. By 2014, however, the Beijing municipal government had deployed a whole array of techniques to apply expulsionary pressure on migrants deemed undesirable. Chief among these techniques was raising the bar of entry for public schools while continually strangling whatever space had existed for informal education. In popular discourse, this nativist crackdown came to be referred to as "population control via education" (*jiaoyu kongren* 教育控人). Although migrants had long faced evictions and various forms of exclusion in Beijing, this new strategy focused my attention on the school as an increasingly important battle line in the city's politics of urbanization.

Given the ratcheting exclusionary politics in the capital, I was surprised by significant discussion in some media in 2013–14 over the fact that the central government was moving to eliminate *hukou* barriers in pushing for "the urbanization of people."[2] This latter term was an implicit acknowledgment that the peasantry had been increasingly urbanized as workers but not as full humans, for their rights to social services such as public housing, health care, and education were abrogated upon arrival in the city. Within months of each other, the central government announced the National New Urbanization Plan, 2014–2020 (hereafter, "the plan") and the State Council Opinion on Advancing Reform of the Residency System. Much was made of the former's effort to relocate 100 million people to cities within six years, while the latter eliminated the distinction between rural and urban *hukou*.

But the pro-urbanization rhetoric did not comport with what I had been witnessing in the preceding few years. In fact, these much-ballyhooed plans were quite explicit that "extra-large cities" were to be excluded from the reform efforts. The plan delineated a social geography in which an individual's levels of human capital would correspond to their location within the national sociospatial hierarchy.[3] Building on efforts going back at least to the 1990s to relax urban *hukou* requirements in smaller cities, the plan envisioned that the bulk of the urbanization of people would occur outside the tier-one cities.[4] Those "extra-large" cities with over five million people, on the other hand, were to strictly control their population growth.[5] But the plan did not demand that these megacities close off human circulation altogether. Rather, they were encouraged to establish a "stratified *hukou* acquisition channel [*jietishi luohu tong-dao* 阶梯式落户通道] for controlling the scope and rhythm of *hukou* acquisition." This worked in tandem with the 2014 residency reform, which called for extra-large cities to establish point-based citizenship, a seemingly transparent method for quantifying and ranking human capital. In Beijing, Party Secretary Guo Jinlong's public statement hinted at the state's intentions: "permanent residents from outside of Beijing should enjoy social services *as long as they fulfill their obligations*" (emphasis added).[6]

The state conceived of these obligations as contributing to the optimization of the urban population. At this moment in history, optimization referred primarily to two interrelated aspects. The first was that aspiring urbanites would need to advance the upgrading of the local economy. Although the shift from industrialization-led to urbanization-led development had begun years earlier, Xi Jinping exerted great effort toward accelerating this trend after assuming full power in 2013. The state saw the transition to an urban-centered economy as being likely to raise wages, increase domestic consumption, and catalyze less ecologically destructive forms of growth, all key features of economic "rebalancing." In order to realize this transformation, cities wanted to selectively pull in the right kinds of labor that would allow them to realize this high-value-added, green service economy.

The second directly related aspect of population optimization was responding to the problem of a rapidly aging urban population. The so-called one child policy had been intended to raise the quality of the population by allowing families and schools to focus on fewer children.[7] But this policy, along with structural changes in the urban economy, had resulted in precipitously declining birth rates in cities. Given that city governments are largely responsible for financing health care and pensions, the aging of the population presented a serious concern. One way cities tried to address this was by pressuring young, highly educated, women to have children early, and to have two children.[8] In early 2015, at precisely the same time Shanghai was expelling those migrants deemed to be "low-end population," an official from the city's Health and Family Planning Commission publicly called for Shanghainese to propagate, arguing, "two children provided a family with the proper stability and social development."[9] But the megacities knew they could not count solely on an increasing local birth rate to buoy their working-age population, so an additional obligation of the newly admitted urban residents would be to provide an infusion of economic vitality to an increasingly geriatric demographic.[10]

There was a notable silence in state rhetoric about the tens of millions of people living in megacities who could not meet the standards for admission. This raised a series of pressing empirical questions that structured my research: What kinds of migrants could be "urbanized" in the places where they worked? Based on what had happened to migrant children in 2011–2014, it was clear that a large swath of the migrant population was unable to meet the state-determined conditions for accessing education and other services in Beijing. What would happen to those who did not qualify? And what might be the implications for emergent regimes of migration, citizenship, and class in urban China? In other words, the central questions I aim to address in this work are: How does the state manage flows of people into cities? That is, how are people being urbanized?[11] And what are the social consequences of that approach?

MULTIPLE URBANIZATIONS

The literature on China's urbanization has expanded impressively in recent decades, with important developments in our understanding of how the metaprocess of spatial relocation and concentration has shaped and been shaped by the state, capital, and labor. With respect to the former, scholars have noted for many years the outsized role of the state in shaping the urbanization process in what has been sometimes termed "state-led

urbanization."[12] That is, in contrast to liberal capitalist economies, the Chinese state has a much greater capacity to control
land, movements of people, and the flows of investment that
shape the urbanization process. You-tien Hsing, however, has
revised this framework in arguing that the state is transformed
by urbanization as much as the reverse, what she terms the
"urbanization of the local state."[13] As we will see in the project
at hand, a whole host of national problems—economic development, social welfare, stability maintenance—have increasingly
come within the purview of urban governance.

Similarly, there is no question that capital has become more
urbanized and that China's economy is increasingly urban (rather
than rural or industrial) in character.[14] The Chinese state at all
levels has of late focused on land and urbanization-led growth,
particularly following the 2008 economic crisis, as manufacturing's contribution to GDP peaked in 2012 and has fallen
significantly since.[15] In the absence of full privatization, this has
still resulted in the commodification of land, urban redevelopment and real estate speculation as well as infrastructure development on a scale unprecedented in world history.[16] In short, there
is now ample evidence not only that capital is increasingly seeking
profits via reorganization and intensified utilization of urban
space, but also that the state at various levels is actively encouraging this process and utilizing control over land as a macroeco-
nomic lever.[17]

Paralleling the literature on the urbanization of capital is
research on migrant workers. While not explicitly framed as
such, the phenomenon this body of work describes is the urbanization of labor. Labor scholars have extensively documented
the highly exploitative and informalized labor regimes rural
migrants are subjected to, as well as their general social isola-
tion in the city.[18] In referencing their political agency, Pun Ngai

and Lu Huilin have referred to "unfinished proletarianization," a condition that is heavily structured by migrants' uneven insertion into urban life.[19] The spatial separation of workers' rural social reproduction from the dynamic urban labor market has been essential to cheapening labor, which was seen by the state as their key comparative advantage in economic development.[20] This outsourcing of social expenses to the countryside is enforced first and foremost by the *hukou*, which has been the "secret" to China's astonishing growth.[21]

From the late twentieth century until the present, the urbanization of the state, capital, and labor has proceeded apace—but the urbanization of *people* has lagged. The distinction between labor and people is critical. Whereas the former refers to humans simply in their capacity for economic production, the latter encapsulates a broader sense of need, for example, access to decent housing, health care, and education, as well as social life and leisure. In the absence of such provisions, one may be a worker, but they cannot fully develop and express their humanity. A spatial concept by definition, the urbanization of people indicates a process wherein humans relocate processes of production *and* reproduction, in relative proximity to each other, from a rural to an urban space. While advancing this trend is a stated aim of the central government, important questions remain as to who will be urbanized in which spaces, why, and to what effect. The oft-repeated fact that China's urban population exceeded 50 percent in 2011, while symbolically important, is not helpful in understanding the politics and process of the urbanization of people.[22]

There is extensive literature on rural to urban migration in China that is quite relevant, even if it is not always framed as a problem of urbanization per se. A recurring theme in this research is the prevalence of various forms of exclusion, particularly for

rural to urban migrants. In addition to problems in the workplace mentioned earlier, this phenomenon manifests in a variety of spheres including labor markets, urban social geography
and housing as well as health and education.[23] The relatively
unique institutional arrangement of *hukou* is acknowledged to
play a critical role in structuring this exclusion although there
has been debate over the extent of its ongoing relevance.[24] In a
variety of institutional and social spheres, rural migrants' insertion into urban space is segmented and incomplete as citizenship has come to be characterized by a *"continuum* of statuses."[25]
This has resulted in migrant families resorting to all manner of
sociospatial triage in reproductive activities, with the emergence of a huge growing population of "left-behind children" in
the countryside, as well as split families and recurrent circular
migration.[26]

   This view puts its finger on a critical aspect of China's
urbanization, namely the spatial severing of life and work for
hundreds of millions of so-called peasant-workers. A common
thread throughout is an emphasis on the ways in which *hukou*
as well as other social and legal institutions serve to *exclude*
rural migrants.[27] While there is no doubt that this is the case,
the migrant question in urban China is not simply one of
exclusion. Rather, it is one of a simultaneous tethering *and*
repulsion: inclusion as labor and exclusion as a full social
being.[28] In order to more fully capture how this political
dynamic unfolds, it is necessary to incorporate in a holistic
manner an analysis of the urbanization of capital, labor, *and*
people, and to interrogate their interactions and imbrications
rather than approach each in a segmented manner. Although
any empirical perspective will necessarily be partial, I have
attempted throughout to situate the urbanization of people as
one moment in a broader process of state-managed capitalist

urbanization and to explore linkages between various features of the process.[29]

STUDYING SCHOOLING

There are numerous perspectives from which one could meaningfully study the urbanization of people and its social consequences: the workplace, the home, the government agency, the hospital, sites of leisure, the streets themselves. However, the school provides important insights that cannot be gleaned from other standpoints. As I will empirically demonstrate in the following chapters, schools serve as an index of a variety of social conditions: parents' levels of education, position in labor and housing markets, and access to social services; processes of urban redevelopment and spatial reconfiguration; and social resistance are all reflected in the school. This is because the school is the institution of social reproduction par excellence—and here I refer to reproduction in a double sense.

The first sense is what might be considered the affirmative, or biopolitical, function of the school. At its best, the school is a space in which children are cared for and encouraged to develop physical, cognitive, and affective capacities that will allow them to realize their potential. From the perspective of the child, the parents, and society more broadly, these capacities are necessary to become a fully functioning adult (of course the specific capacities, ideologies, and orientations that are inculcated vary widely across social settings). For capital, schooling is necessary to produce a workforce endowed with various technical and creative capacities, not to mention a degree of docility—note Foucault's comment that disciplinary power oriented toward the body "dovetails" with population-oriented biopower.[30] And it goes without saying that the state employs the education system as one of the key institutions in the exercise of biopower, through which it delivers a variety of measures aimed at producing a biologically and socially viable population. In short, this sense of the term refers to the intergenerational renewal of the population, or "social reproduction" in the Marxist sense.

The second meaning, what we might refer to as "class reproduction," is closely associated with Pierre Bourdieu.[31] It refers to the maintenance of a particular organization of social domination across time.[32] As argued in his work with Jean Claude Passeron and elsewhere, Bourdieu identifies schools as a key institution through which dominant groups are able to solidify domination—not, as much classical theory would have it, via direct political coercion or economic exploitation, but rather by establishing their particular cultural forms as legitimate.[33] Paul Willis has similarly demonstrated that cultural patterns that emerge in schools profoundly influence where students end up in the labor market.[34] One need not have a conspiratorial view of the state to understand the ideological effects of schooling, noted most famously by Louis Althusser.[35] While the state, like capital, is concerned with producing people with marketable skills, it must also be attentive to producing certain kinds of political subjects, ones willing to submit to relatively fixed forms of social hierarchy. This latter sense of reproduction is related to the first in that they both imply a process of subjectification. The former, however, emphasizes life-enhancing interventions, while the latter refers to a process of ensuring the relative stability of class domination. "Social reproduction" and "class reproduction" within the school are by no means mutually exclusive but are nonetheless distinct aspects of a social dynamic centered on shaping the capacities and subjectivities of children.

In the context of the urbanization of people in contemporary China, the school holds further special meaning. As argued by a growing number of scholars, *hukou*, while still an important institutional obstacle, is in many ways less important than it used to be.[36] Indeed, there is growing evidence that rural *hukou* holders are reluctant to transfer to urban *hukou*, since this implies trading the security of land for an uncertain, and perhaps diminishing, safety net in the city.[37] This is particularly the case in smaller, poorer cities with less robust social welfare systems. But as evidenced in my own work as well as survey research, education continues to be the greatest motivator for those who do wish to secure urban *hukou*.[38] It is not coincidental that among the various benefits associated with urban citizenship, the public school system—the primary channel for encouraging intergenerational social mobility—remains heavily fortified. As shown clearly in the work on vocational education by Terry Woronov and Minhua Ling, schooling for migrant youth in the city serves to reproduce social and economic class domination.[39] It is precisely because the education system is the most important bastion of urban privilege that it is so crucial for understanding the social meaning of China's urbanization.

I am studying schools in something of an unconventional manner. Whereas I share a common concern with education scholars over questions of access and inequality, in this study the school is utilized as a window onto a broader process of urbanization. Scholars in urban studies, on the other hand, often advance a capital-centric understanding of urbanization that is largely concerned with land, while leaving the question of human subsistence and social life on the analytical margins.[40] Migration scholars are very much concerned with the latter issues, but there is insufficient attention to how human movement proceeds in its relationship to processes of capitalist development. My aim is to lower these various blinders in linking together the study of urbanization, capitalist development, and labor markets—and the school is an ideal site to grasp the interaction of these various processes and empirically assess the social consequences.

STRUCTURING THE STUDY

The bulk of the data presented here is drawn from 206 semi-structured interviews with 245 people, including school administrators, teachers, parents of school-aged children, and civil society actors.[41] After careful consideration, I decided against formal interviews with children, as this would likely have involved discussion of a traumatic set of issues (e.g., frequent relocation, school demolitions, absentee parents, decrepit learning conditions). This was a very complex issue, one that I wrestled with over a number of years. Ultimately, I felt that the vast social distance between myself and the children of migrant workers made it impossible for me to feel confident that I could interview them without the risk of inflicting emotional harm. Nonetheless, I frequently interacted informally with children during school visits, and both parents and teachers reflected on children's experiences. The large majority of the empirical work was conducted in migrant schools (*dagong zidi xuexiao* 打工子弟学校)—private primary and middle schools in cities serving largely or exclusively nonlocal students—but I also visited and conducted interviews at several public schools to serve as reference points.

This book is largely focused on the city of Beijing. The capital city is by no means typical and should not be considered representative, but there are other good reasons to subject this hugely important case to sustained analysis. To begin with, Beijing is, in absolute terms, one of the largest migrant-receiving cities in the country, absorbing 5.4 percent of all internal migrants.[42] But more important than its demographic weight is the political meaning of the city. In Beijing's master plan (2016–2035), Xi Jinping himself has commented on the symbolic importance of the city: "Proper construction and management of the capital is an important aspect of modernizing the nation's governance system and capacity. In various respects, Beijing serves as a representative and point of reference; we must be willing to take this on and bravely push forward, to strive to do our best in Beijing to make it a model for the entire nation."[43] This is not to suggest that other cities will or can perfectly emulate Beijing—rather, that the capital's practices in population management (and beyond) delineates a norm to which other places can be compared. Indeed, I found in my own fieldwork that school officials and education NGOs in other parts of the country were able to reference how their approach differed from Beijing.

When I started my fieldwork in late 2011, there were roughly 140–150 migrant schools in Beijing, and I was faced with the challenging task of figuring out which ones to study. This was made all the more difficult because by far most schools were informal, so I could not simply get an official listing to aid me in case selection. In order to capture the range of possibility, I consulted with local experts and school administrators to select a diversity of schools. Based on students' educational attainment, physical plant, teacher and student recruitment, overall working conditions, government and/or foundation support, and various forms of official recognition, I decided to focus on three schools: high-end (Zhifan School), mid-range (Shusheng

School), and low-end (Yinghong School).[44] This allowed me to understand the range of possibility within the migrant education sector, and draw out common themes as well as differences (a more detailed and systematic account of the cases appears in the methodological appendix). Without an exhaustive database of every school, I cannot be certain that this is a representative approach, and it certainly relies on the subjective assessments of local experts and school administrators. But without comprehensive objective measures (to say nothing of the question of access), this approach was the best choice to assess the universe of possibilities within the city. Data collected in these three schools are the basis for chapters 3, 4, and 6. I also visited four public schools in Beijing to serve as points of reference. In general, these public schools had very few nonlocal students, but one in Haidian was 87 per cent nonlocal. Interviews with principals and teachers at these schools were quite useful in helping me to pin down the specificity of the migrant school. The data on school closures and demolitions in chapter 5 was indeed "selected on the dependent variable"; I specifically sought out schools that had either been shuttered or had been threatened, including Zhenhua, Jingwei, Mingxin, and Huangzhuang schools, all in Beijing.

This book presents material from a broader project that involved fieldwork and extensive interviews from sites beyond Beijing, including Guangzhou, Chengdu, and Guiyang.[45] I ultimately decided that Beijing itself was so complex that it had to be the centerpiece of the work. This focus allowed me to unpack the diverse forces at play in the migrant school and to assess the social consequences along a variety of dimensions, while keeping external factors such as education policies, economic structure, labor market conditions, and local political concerns relatively consistent.[46] Nonetheless, the research from other regions has deeply informed my perspective and has provided critical data points in formulating my conceptual apparatus. The comparison with Guangzhou highlighted the central importance of labor market dynamics in structuring the urban state's population management regime. The research in Chengdu and Guiyang allowed me to grasp the stratified but interconnected nature of the sociospatial hierarchy, with Beijing (and, to a lesser extent, Guangzhou) occupying the apex. Interurban, interregional, and urban-rural relationships are central to my understanding of how the state manages flows of people. In the conclusion, I briefly summarize some key empirical findings from Guangzhou and Guiyang and draw out the implications. In addition to the ethnographic and interview data, I employ analysis of official documents related to *hukou* and school admissions policies from dozens of cities throughout the country.

SUMMARY OF THE ARGUMENT AND CHAPTER ORGANIZATION

I began with two key questions: How does the state manage flows of people into cities? That is, how are people being urbanized? And what are the social consequences of that approach? The answer to the first question is that the state is pursuing what I refer to as a *just-in-time* approach to the urbanization of people. This means that cities at the apex of the sociospatial hierarchy have developed an administrative framework that assesses human qualities, often assigning specific numeric values, which then serves as the basis for determining whether or not the individual in question will have access to state subsidized social reproduction. This framework is oriented toward

optimization of the population, which in Beijing refers to contributing to the city's ongoing economic ascension via high
value-added labor while helping to underwrite and sustain the
social welfare of the existing, and rapidly aging, urban population. I employ the "just-in-time" concept because megacities are
attempting to secure labor in just the right quantities and of just
the right qualities, at just the right time, while dispatching with
social protections for anyone deemed surplus. At the national
level, the central government envisions a citizenship regime
in which an individual's levels of human capital correspond as
closely as possible to their position within the national sociospatial hierarchy: high-end cities for the high-end population, low-
end places for the low-end population.[47] But despite the relatively strong coordinative capacity of the twenty-first-century
PRC, this just-in-time effort cannot be realized in practice. It
is a utopian vision of population management, not an empirical
reality.

Nonetheless, and to respond to the second key question, these
political efforts have very real social consequences. Through an
analysis both of formal school admissions requirements as
well as interviews with parents trying to get their children into
public school, I argue that China's citizenship regime funnels
nominally public resources precisely to those who need them
least. In what I term the "inverted welfare state," we see that
the series of evaluative criteria, focused heavily although by no
means exclusively on labor market metrics, provide public assistance for individuals with a *preponderance* of economic, social,
and cultural capital. The education and other reproductive
needs of working-class and poor migrants are left to the whims
of the market. The inversion of the logic of the welfare state
is made even more profound when the citizenship regime is
viewed in the context of China's highly unequal economic

geography and fiscal hierarchy. Cities such as Beijing that have the most restrictive citizenship regime are also the places with the best services, whereas those places that have relaxed or eliminated *hukou* barriers provide far inferior services. This is clear with respect to Beijing's system of public education, including not only elite primary and secondary schools but also internationally recognized universities that grant preferential access to local residents. When viewed in its totality, this system suggests a strong rigidification of China's sociospatial class hierarchy.

Despite ongoing exclusion in the realm of social reproduction, tens of millions of migrants remain tethered to the megacities as workers. They simply cannot survive in their formally designated place of (rural) residence. Those who remain while being denied access to schools are extremely vulnerable, subject to myriad indignities and expulsionary pressures.[48] Even as the city continues to depend on their labor, the state has consciously used restrictions on access to education as a means to limit urban population growth. Those excluded from public education in Beijing are left to a barely regulated shadow education system, one that is fully marketized despite exclusively serving those with hardly any economic means. The consequence is what I refer to as *concentrated deprivation*, for migrant schools are the last resort for students and teachers who do not have better options. Furthermore, migrant families are constantly subjected to shifting official requirements for public school admissions, which are arbitrarily enforced and have often left people in the lurch. The state occasionally takes more coercive measures to remove those deemed unnecessary by shuttering or even demolishing migrant schools. All of these pressures result in severe trauma and emotional stress on students. Moreover, because the parents of these students are overworked as they struggle to survive, a disproportionate share of affective and reproductive labor is transferred from the family onto the shoulders of teachers. In sum, the specific approach to urbanizing people in contemporary China enhances existing forms of inequality based on class and *hukou* status, while producing a series of dislocations and oppressions for poor and working-class migrants.

The remainder of the book proceeds as follows. Chapter 1 delineates the conceptual framework for the research. It begins with a discussion and reinterpretation of biopolitics by situating the concept explicitly within a dynamic of capitalist urbanization. Based on a synthesis of Marx and Foucault, I provide a reconceptualization of population/surplus-population. This is followed by a discussion of just-in-time as developed within the Toyota Production System, while pointing to the specificity of just-in-time urbanization in contrast to manufacturing. Readers primarily interested in the empirical work may proceed directly to chapter 2, since the remainder of the book is accessible without full command of the conceptual tools. Chapter 2 details the various policies governing *hukou* and school admissions policies in Beijing and other urban areas and provides evidence to support the argument about the inverted welfare state. In chapter 3 I turn to ethnographic data in describing migrant schools in Beijing. Here I provide a ground-level view of the severe deprivation within these schools, with an account of the administrative and fiscal arrangements that produce such an outcome. Chapter 4 approaches the question of educational access for migrants from the perspective of parents, and I provide extensive interview data on their ongoing challenges in trying to secure schooling for their children in the city. Chapter 5 pairs with the previous chapter, but rather than focus on how administrative interventions push working-class migrants out of the city, here we see the "hard edge" as represented in school closures and demolitions. The final empirical section in chapter 6 shifts perspective yet again to that of teachers, a feminized workforce that often ends up absorbing the myriad affective shocks and traumas to which migrant children are subjected within the urban population management regime. I conclude with comparative glances at migrant schooling in other regions of China before suggesting some spatial extensions of the project.

1

CONCEPTUALIZING THE POLITICS OF URBANIZATION

The Just-in-Time Response

In fact, the two processes—the accumulation of men and the accumulation of capital—cannot be separated; it would not have been possible to solve the problem of the accumulation of men without the growth of an apparatus of production capable of both sustaining them and using them; conversely, the techniques that made the cumulative multiplicity of men useful accelerated the accumulation of capital.

—Michel Foucault, *Discipline and Punish*

Power, and specifically the state, aims to manage spatio-temporal distributions of the population in relationship to processes of capital accumulation. This general problem of regulating the geography of human life and work can be negotiated in myriad ways. "Just-in-time urbanization" is how I conceptualize the specific population management strategy of the Chinese state.[1]

CAPITALISM AND BIOPOLITICS

The most frequently cited definition of biopower comes from Michel Foucault's March 17, 1976, lecture at the Collège de

France: it is the power to "'make' live and 'let' die."[2] He describes a series of techniques that emerged largely in the eighteenth century in which power becomes oriented less toward repression and the right to kill (though this never disappears totally) and more toward the production and fostering of a productive population—one that must be "made to live." Biopower "dovetails" with bodily oriented disciplinary power, but for the first time it constructs the population as an object of power, as a thing to be worked on and improved.[3]

What is the relationship between biopower and capitalist development?[4] A crucial passage from *History of Sexuality* suggests that there is something uniquely capitalist about biopower: "The adjustment of the accumulation of men to that of capital, the joining of the growth of human groups to the expansion of the productive forces and the differential allocation of profit were made possible in part by the exercise of bio-power in its many forms and modes of application."[5] Furthermore, "[the task of biopower is] distributing the living in the domain of value and utility."[6] These passages make clear that biopower is not only concerned with the production and maintenance of life, but also mediates distributions of labor and capital. In other words, certain kinds of humans need to be "made to live" in particular places in the pursuit of value production.[7]

This raises a basic coordination problem that has emerged in disparate historical and national settings: How do people bring together appropriate quantities and qualities of capital and labor, in the right space and at the right time? Disjunctures in the spatiotemporal distribution of labor and capital have derived from an array of historical conditions including varying processes of dispossession and proletarianization, dynamics of capital accumulation, uneven insertion into global markets, and forms of social hierarchy and domination, among others.[8] Biopower must be understood as oriented not only toward ensuring the biological viability of the population but also toward ensuring the appropriate production and distribution of the population in relationship to the accumulation of capital. Determination of what constitutes an appropriate distribution is fundamentally a political question, and one that has historically fallen largely, although not exclusively, to the state.[9]

Much of the recent biopolitically oriented literature on capitalist development has focused on one such disjuncture, namely the urban overaccumulation of proletarianized people vis-à-vis opportunities for wage labor. Echoing David Harvey's concept of accumulation by dispossession, Tania Li has argued that capitalist accumulation has of late favored (largely rural) dispossession over (largely urban) exploitation.[10] One consequence of this is that millions of people have migrated to cities without any hope of finding viable wage labor, and are left to gather in growing slums.[11] This surplus population is superfluous to the needs to capital, treated by the state as "human waste," and seen as fit only for expulsion from urban space.[12] The old historical telos of rural surplus labor migrating to cities to be productively employed—taken as given by scholars from Marx to Lewis and beyond—is clearly no longer tenable.[13] Much literature has also commented on racialization as a key feature of the biopolitics of capitalist development, an issue to which we will return shortly.[14]

My understanding of the relationship between capitalist development and biopolitics differs markedly from much existing scholarship, in part due to China's relatively unique, labor absorbing, economic dynamism over the past several decades. To begin with, China's experience with capitalism does not comport with the vision of expansive urban surplus population excluded from formal wage labor, relegated to eking out subsistence on the margins of society. To be sure, land dispossession has been a key feature of development in China, often engendering violent resistance.[15] Informal employment has expanded in certain regions and sectors and is likely underestimated and informal housing has emerged in periurban areas.[16] Nonetheless, when compared to other large poor and middle-income countries, China is much more notable for its rapid expansion of formal employment in export-oriented manufacturing, central government efforts toward regulating labor markets, and relative dearth of slums.[17] The Chinese state, and specifically the *urban* state, is not single-mindedly oriented toward expulsion, as industrial capital has demanded vast quantities of labor. Chronic labor shortages have appeared in various regions and some capitalists have decided where to expand production at least in part based on local government ability to secure a workforce.[18] This is by no means intended as a normative affirmation of Chinese capitalism, which has been predicated on ruthless authoritarianism that has produced staggering inequalities. It is simply to note that, when compared to many other countries, recently proletarianized people in China are much more likely to be exploited via formal wage labor.[19] This empirical reality suggests that the conceptual tools we have at our disposal are inadequate to account for the question of how power sorts people in the process of urbanization.

Population and Surplus Population

Foucault's discussion of biopolitics asks an important question, and one that guides my investigation into the politics of capitalist urbanization: Who is made to live, and who is allowed to die, in which spaces and what times? But this simple question needs to be further elaborated before it can be put to work in empirical research. By injecting relationality into Foucauldian "population"—specifically by opposing it to a reconceptualized "surplus population"—we can more precisely assess the politics of urban inclusion and exclusion that is at the heart of this research.

Foucault provides a succinct definition of "population": it is that part of humanity that is made to live, that is, is constructed as a political object and subjected to various forms of life-enhancing interventions, including public hygiene, health, and education. But what is outside of the population? Foucault argues that this is where racism intervenes, that *race* delineates who is allowed to live and who is allowed to die.[20] The overwhelming focus of his work is on the former category, a decision that has opened him to critiques for overlooking the actual history of racism in the colonial encounter.[21] Scholars have for many decades analyzed the deep imbrication of racial domination and capitalist expansion, more recently from an explicitly biopolitical perspective.[22] Ruth Wilson Gilmore provides a more precise biopolitically oriented definition of racism as "state-sanctioned or extralegal production and exploitation of group-differentiated vulnerability to premature death."[23] Alexander Weheliye both affirms and expands this conceptualization to include processes of dehumanization and subjection to political violence.[24]

Although this politics of simultaneous dependence and denigration resonates with the experience of migrant workers in China's capitalist urbanization, the centrality of race must be revisited.[25] Certainly when we consider biopolitics at the global level, race is a primary line of division. China has been inserted into a global white supremacist order, in which Asians, and specifically Chinese people, have been dehumanized in the service of producing for transnational capital.[26] At the national level, the Chinese state has actively constructed an internal racial hierarchy based on Han supremacy, and it pursues colonial forms of governance in peripheral regions such as Inner Mongolia, Xinjiang, and Tibet.[27] As China's overseas investments expand throughout the world, racialization will become increasingly important, but this is as yet not a central feature of the country's urban politics or form.[28] Given my specific concern with cities, it is notable that China's urbanization has been underwritten by the (Han) state's willingness and ability to sacrifice *its own race* as it has embraced the role of "conveyor belt for capitalism."[29] And as was made clear at the outset of the book, the urban Chinese state has enacted brutal, life-denying acts against migrants who have been deemed extraneous. In sum, the postrevolutionary Chinese state, which in large part bases its legitimacy on national liberation and the "great revival of the Chinese nation," has been pushed to devise biopolitical technologies capable of inserting a division within its own race.[30]

Rather than an a priori assumption that race is constitutive of Chinese urban biopolitics, let us return to the prior question: Who is allowed to live, and who is exposed to death?[31] To begin with, we should not think of life and death in literal, biological terms. Rather, we must think of life as being a socially determined phenomenon that encapsulates and transcends mere biological existence. Indeed, this is consistent with Foucault's thinking on the matter. He lists regulatory mechanisms aimed at creating a productive population: "Health-insurance systems, old-age pensions; rules on hygiene that guarantee the optimal longevity of the population; the pressures that the very organization of the town brings to bear on sexuality and therefore procreation; child care, education, et cetera."[32] This broader, sociological understanding of the substance of life is precisely what Marxist theorists have long referred to as *social reproduction*, that is, the (gendered) maintenance and regeneration of the population at some socially determined level of subsistence. Similarly, "death" should refer not only to a literal or immediate extinguishing of biological life but also to denial of basic socially determined needs such as housing, education, health care, community, and excessive exposure to risk and premature death.[33] This conceptualization of life and death then allows us to reformulate the biopolitical question from a reproductive standpoint: access to social reproduction, be it through the auspices of nonmarket social protections or the wage, is the line of division between those who are made to live, the population, and those who are exposed to death, the surplus population.[34]

Rooting our conception of surplus population in the sphere of reproduction holds important analytical advantages over existing approaches.[35] Nearly all scholars have defined surplus population in relationship to wage labor and utility to capital, a trend rooted in Marx's initial definition: "[it is] a population which is superfluous to capital's average requirements for its own valorization, and is therefore a surplus population."[36] More recently, Tania Li has argued, "The key to their [surplus population] predicament is that their labour is surplus *in relation to* its utility for capital," and Mike Davis speaks of a "mass of humanity structurally and biologically redundant to global accumulation and the corporate matrix."[37] A first issue with these definitions is that it is not apparent how to precisely determine whether someone or some group is of utility to capital. Informal workers of all of sorts can be productive and profit-generating, and exploitation can operate through unequal market exchange rather than wage labor. Other forms of informal, domestic, and reproductive labor, often gendered and/or racialized, may not directly activate expansive capital accumulation, but they can still form a necessary social basis upon which accumulation rests.[38] Even if capitalists or the state do not want to pay for the cost of reproduction for these workers, that does not mean they are irrelevant for accumulation.

The fundamental problem with defining surplus population based on utility for capital is that it cannot adequately account for sociopolitical dynamics. In diverse historical settings, we have seen states expel potential workers, spatially and/or socially, for reasons completely unrelated to their economic utility, thereby *rendering* them surplus. Frequently such political interventions are catalyzed by racist or nativist sentiments. The urban state in China has occasionally expelled precisely those workers who make the economy function: domestic workers, sex workers, street hawkers, recyclers, taxi drivers, construction workers, and even factory workers have all been rendered surplus by expulsion from spaces of economic dynamism. In these cases, the state actively undermines social reproduction for workers who have been demanded by capital. This results in creation of a surplus population, but one produced according to a primarily political logic.[39] On the other hand, the state may decide to ensure social reproduction even for people whom capital would otherwise be unlikely to employ. The clearest example is disabled military veterans, but other politically or symbolically potent groups may similarly be the beneficiaries of life-enhancing biopower for reasons completely unrelated to their economic utility.

With this reconceptualized population-surplus population framework, we are now in a position to ask a series of theoretically informed empirical questions: Who in the city has access to reproduction? Who is excluded? And what are the mechanisms for inclusion or exclusion? This approach allows us to center politics, since the divisions between population and surplus population are economically inflected but fundamentally *political* phenomena.[40] A laborer's utility to capital, or to some particular capitalist, is, practically speaking, often not the state's sole concern. Furthermore, this highlights the relative porousness, at least in the case of China's capitalist urbanization, of the categories of population and surplus population. The urban state has developed a much more supple, dynamic set of technologies for sorting and filtering the population. A worker who was surplus yesterday may be admitted to the urban population today—or expelled tomorrow.

An Urban Specification

I have thus far discussed the biopolitics of capitalist development largely without reference to space. But I am concerned here specifically with urbanization, which while related to other processes constitutive of capitalism such as industrialization and agrarian transformation is nonetheless a distinct object of inquiry. Indeed, Foucault recognized the centrality of urbanization in the emergence of biopower, as he claims that a core political problem of eighteenth-century Europe was "the question of the spatial, juridical, administrative, and economic opening up of the town: resituating the town in a space of circulation . . . the problem of the town was essentially and fundamentally a problem of circulation."[41] But as in contemporary China, it was not a simple opening up in general; "it was a matter of *organizing* circulation, eliminating its dangerous elements, making a division between good and bad circulation, and maximizing the good circulation by diminishing the bad."[42]

But this is far too general a statement. What, from the perspective of the urban state, is good circulation, and what is bad?

Before we can specify how the urban state in China distinguishes good from bad circulation, some definitional issues with regard to "the urban" are in order. Mirroring broader discussions in the social sciences and humanities, in recent years there has been intense debate on the question of whether cities are a basically universal phenomenon or whether southern, postcolonial, and postsocialist cities demand to be studied on their own terms.[43] This is the most recent iteration of a longstanding debate over how to conceive of and explain the emergence of cities, and it is neither practical nor particularly germane to the research at hand to summarize these arguments in any detail.[44] I will simply note that I share Richard Walker's view that capitalist cities are first and foremost a space for the extraction and concentration of economic surplus and, "a primary way to make the surpluses and the power behind them visible to the world, enjoy them to the utmost and express superiority over other people."[45] Furthermore, the real object of inquiry here is not the Chinese city per se, but China's urbanization.[46] An orientation to process highlights not only the extraction and spatial concentration of surplus and related transformation of agrarian society but also the dynamic spatial politics of urban population management. A perspective that identifies a certain density and volume of aggregate urban population misses the uneven contours and trajectories of social admission and expulsion that characterizes the biopolitics of urbanization. This process-based orientation, however, does not preclude a concern with relatively fixed objects. While it would of course be foolish to conflate the state's categories with analytical categories, the administrative boundaries of the city are nonetheless of crucial importance to understanding the experience of rural-urban migration, particularly so in China.[47] So while we cannot allow such (relatively arbitrary) formal boundaries to constrain the scope of the analysis, we must also be attentive to the way in which these efforts at stabilization, objectification, and boundary drawing have real social and political effects.

A focus on cities is of the utmost importance for a study of China, since it is the decisive scale at which biopower is deployed and the population sorted. Despite the national-liberation rhetoric of the revolution, urban social reproduction in the Mao era was quite decentralized, rooted as it was in the *danwei*, or work unit.[48] Marketization in the 1990s resulted in the destruction of the certainties of the "iron rice bowl" in urban areas and decollectivization of land in the countryside.[49] Social services in both city and countryside were subjected to market forces, often with disastrous consequences.[50] A process of centralization of responsibility for social services began in the cities following the dissolution of the Mao-era, firm-based organization of social reproduction. However, a national welfare state has not been created, and obligations for the provision of most social services have been largely confined to the level of the municipality.[51] While the central state has pushed forward the construction of a national labor market, the citizenship regime is incredibly fractured, with each city controlling access to full social citizenship via *hukou* controls, as well as contingent access to public resources such as education for those without local *hukou*. One consequence of the state socialist legacy of mobility controls is that there are few countries in the world where the urban state plays as decisive a role in sorting domestic populations and providing social services as in China.

Furthermore, as has been widely remarked in the literature, China has followed a highly decentralized model of market reforms in which local governments (in both rural and urban areas) were given the incentive and capacity to pursue economic growth.[52] Referred to as "local protectionism" in China, cities became quite entrepreneurial in attracting capital, leading many to ignore their own labor and environmental regulatory responsibilities.[53] City governments are particularly reliant on land deals as a source of tax revenue, which has been a primary cause of violent land expropriation.[54] Officials often claim that these sources of revenue are essential in an environment in which the central government establishes new obligations without providing concomitant increases in fiscal transfers. One way for fiscally constrained governments to balance their budgets is to limit the growth of the population considered local, that is, those to whom the state has an obligation to provide services such as education. With the central government continually reaffirming that *hukou* policy, or the capacity to determine who has access to local services, is within the purview of local governments, China's citizenship politics are indisputably urban in character.

With this understanding of the centrality of the urban in filtering the population, we can now return to the politics of differentiating good from bad circulation.

REGULATING CIRCULATION: THE URBAN GROWTH DILEMMA

The biopolitics of capitalist urbanization are animated at a deep level by competing and sometimes contradictory impulses on the part of state and capital to alternatively admit and expel people.[55] We might think of this movement of humans as a constituent element of the implosion-explosion dialectic, a concept first elaborated by Lefebvre and more recently extended by Neil Brenner.[56] But it is important here to make a clear analytical distinction between urbanization as a process of concentration of capital as opposed to people.[57] The implosion-explosion dynamics of capital, firms, and infrastructure adheres to a different political logic than is the case for people. I assume uneven and contradiction-laden processes of spatial concentration not only for labor and capital, but also within the broad category of labor. While the question of which kinds of labor are admissible at what times is ultimately an empirical question and subject to significant subnational variation, we can identify certain general conditions that structure tendencies in state action.

Capital and labor are mutually constitutive—a cliché, but a relevant one. Capital can reduce but never eliminate its dependence on labor, and cities must admit populations if they are to grow economically. Labor-intensive manufacturing is still the most reliable route to development, even in the twenty-first century. In order to attract such industry, urban governments must be able to pull in large volumes of cheap and docile labor. As was shown to be the case over the past several decades, this capacity has proven decisive in allowing China to industrialize and post historically unprecedented rates of growth year after year. Even in the postindustrial city, all kinds of low-end work undergird the circulation and accumulation of capital, from workers in transportation and infrastructure to caregivers, restaurant workers, street sweepers, construction workers, security guards, and countless others who make cities run. As for the upper tiers of the labor market, cities cannot count on recruiting these workers from within their own jurisdictions. Translocal labor populates all kinds of elite industries, including finance, entertainment, media, higher education, and the legal profession. The implosion dynamic draws people in from far beyond the formal bounds of the city.

Admission of newcomers is not without its drawbacks from the perspective of the state. Given that the wage rarely constitutes the full cost of labor power, the state is almost always on the hook for some of the costs of social reproduction of the workforce, particularly for those workers who are underpaid. Politically, urban elites often fear that new arrivals will undermine the social fabric of the community, bringing with them crime, drugs, and disease. Nativist fears of social dissolution or political chaos looms large in the consciousness of the urban state— particularly so in China, where concerns about the "carrying capacity" (*chengzaili* 承载力) of cities are a key feature of state discourse. The state's perception of economic and political pressures owing to excess accumulation of people constitutes what I call the "overpopulation crisis."[58] It is precisely this sense of crisis that has led cities like Beijing to employ various methods to eject migrants.

Expulsion of undesirable populations, while perhaps effectively responding to nativist, xenophobic, or racist sentiment, engenders other problems for capital and the state. With a tighter labor market, capital is likely to face rising wages and more assertive workers. While these dynamics are sectorally uneven, inability to pin down a sufficient quantity of labor could lead capital to flee to areas in which labor is more abundant. This in turn would lead to falling tax revenue for the state. This "profitability crisis" may then push the state back in the direction of admitting populations.

The urban growth dilemma refers to the competing imperatives faced by the state in managing economic expansion and the urbanization of people (see figure 1.1). Overaccumulation of people in the cities raises the specter of a fiscal crunch and social chaos. But every attempt to address the overpopulation

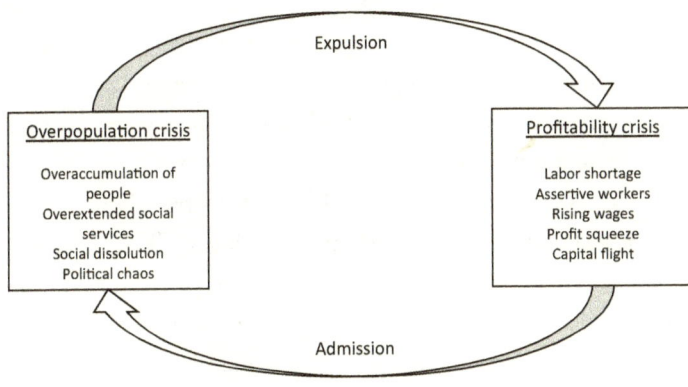

FIGURE 1.1 The urban growth dilemma.

crisis simultaneously hastens a profitability crisis by depriving capital of its lifeblood, labor. These are crisis *tendencies* and not necessarily discrete and diachronic events. While cities face widely heterogeneous local political arrangements, as well as a differential capacity to respond, this tension is a central motor force of the politics of urbanization.

The question then becomes: How specifically have Chinese cities responded to this dilemma? How can we conceptualize the strategies they have employed as they attempt to overcome the political problem of spatiotemporal disjunctures in the distribution of labor and capital?

JUST-IN-TIME URBANIZATION

My answer, in short, is that Chinese cities are pursuing a "just-in-time" (JIT) approach to urbanization. David Harvey has commented, "In the long run, therefore, the supply of both quantities and qualities of labor power stands to be reasonably elastic, though constrained by social costs, long time-horizons for certain kinds of adjustment, and important irreversibilities."[59] But the state can strive to shrink this time-horizon and to counter these irreversibilities. This is a key aspect of population management initiatives, and the Chinese state has at its disposal the planet's most advanced techniques. A central claim of this work is that Chinese megacities are pursuing a JIT approach to urbanization in an attempt to overcome the political and economic problems posed by the urban growth dilemma.[60] Much as with Foucault's understanding of the panopticon,[61] JIT urbanization is a utopian strategy—one that can never be realized as imagined, but nonetheless with very real consequences.

In what ways does this constitute a JIT approach? Taiichi Ohno, the person most responsible for the development of the Toyota Production System (TPS), provides the following definition: "Just-in-time means that, in a flow process the right parts needed in assembly reach the line at the time they are needed and only in the amount needed."[62] When considering urbanization, of course, the "parts" in question are not auto components but workers. So rather than think about how companies organize the production and movement of commodities through the supply chain, here we are concerned with how cities (and especially China's wealthy megacities) regulate the movement of labor into urban space. While the analogy with auto production is imperfect in a number of respects, the basic impulse remains the same: megacities are attempting to develop a technocratic apparatus capable of regulating the flow of workers into and out of the city.

Aside from these general similarities, there are some more specific parallels between JIT production and JIT urbanization. To begin with, there is a similar focus on a reduction of warehousing. JIT production sees warehousing of parts as wasteful and costly, since it requires additional expenditures on space as well as labor to maintain the stores. "Warehousing" of people is also costly and includes housing as well as other costs associated with social reproduction. JIT urbanization aims not just for economic efficiency but also to address the potential political problems associated with warehousing people. As is well established in the literature, Chinese urban elites have long subscribed to a neo-Malthusian worldview that associates overpopulation with political chaos.[63] By keeping surplus populations at bay in the countryside or smaller towns, megacities intend to draw in workers on a strictly as-needed basis, thereby serving both economic and political ends.

A second parallel is a concern with the reduction of waste.[64] Both approaches are oriented toward reducing costs and improving productivity "through the elimination of various wastes such as excessive inventory and excessive workforce."[65] Michelle Yates postulates the emergence of the "human-as-waste" under late capitalism, suggesting that the tendency to exclude or undermine living labor presents a historical limit to capitalist accumulation.[66] But again, China is somewhat different in that capital actually has employed hundreds of millions of people. In this case, a human who was "waste" yesterday may be a viable worker today. The point, from the perspective of JIT urbanization, is to eliminate any responsibility on the part of capital or the urban state to underwrite social reproduction for that person during a "waste moment." When workers are rendered superfluous, even temporarily, the state reserves the right to expunge them.

A final related similarity is the tendency to maintain flexibility through dualization. While more associated with TPS and Japanese employment relations in general rather than JIT in particular, workforce flexibility is central to achieving

JIT production.[67] Toyota and other Japanese firms were at the forefront in dividing the industrial workforce into a stable, unionized core, which enjoyed strong job security and generous benefits, and a contingent, temporary workforce that could be utilized and discarded with minimal friction. JIT urbanization envisions a core group of citizens who enjoy a variety of rights (most notably for this study, the right to public education), surrounded by a contingent workforce that may be included in certain spheres of social and political life and not others. This latter group experiences access to social services as a revocable privilege rather than a right.[68] This rupture in the citizen-worker nexus gives cities greater flexibility in deploying the right kinds of labor power at the right time, without having to bear the costs associated with maintenance and reproduction of workers.[69] Furthermore, as denizens, these expendable workers have no right to political representation or participation in the city.

There are also some important differences between JIT production and JIT urbanization, a brief discussion of which will be useful in highlighting the specificity of the latter. The fundamental difference owes to the different character of the commodities in question. According to Yasuhiro Monden, "it is the principle aim of the Toyota Production System to control over-production—to ensure that all processes make products according to the sales velocity of the market."[70] But cities' biopolitical capacity, that is, the ability to regulate the production, maintenance, and circulation of people, is inevitably much more constrained than is the case in auto production. As Michael Storper and Richard Walker have noted, "workers cannot be industrially produced as are true commodities."[71] The Chinese state has developed an highly competent biopolitical machinery, the chief example of which are notorious birth control policies that were aimed at controlling overproduction of people.[72] But despite megacities' position at the apex of the Chinese political economy, they do not have the capacity to actively control the production of workers, to say nothing of determining the appropriate quantities, qualities, and circulation thereof. Cities are dependent on the hinterlands to produce workers for them, and unlike the lead firm in JIT production, they exercise little control over their suppliers. While cities certainly try to regulate the flow of people according to demand in the market, they cannot directly control production.[73]

Related to this is the issue of differentiating good from bad circulations, which refers to managing qualities. Quality assurance is central to any form of material production, and JIT is no exception. But differentiating and managing *human* qualities is significantly more complex than for auto parts, given humanity's infinite qualitative diversity. As has been widely studied in recent years, managing the *suzhi* (human quality) of the population has become a central concern of the Chinese state, and in particular its education system.[74] Elites have linked *suzhi* improvements directly to market value and possibilities for national economic development, while, "some bodies are recognized as having more value than others and therefore more deserving of the rights of citizenship."[75] As we will see in the following chapters, urban governments have developed a dizzying array of metrics for assessing the qualities of potential citizens, which include things such as education, age, and skillset, as well as history of paying local taxes, donating blood, and abiding by laws, including but not limited to adherence to birth control policies. All of this is to say that JIT urbanization involves a much more complex, and certainly less reliable, process of information management and quality assurance than is the case for JIT production.

Finally, there are important political consequences that follow from the fact that the object of JIT urbanization is people rather than things. Workers' place-specific sociality and frequent demands for respect and autonomy pose a host of problems that are irrelevant for JIT production. Since there will always be a coordination problem between the production of potential wage laborers and the demands of the labor market, inevitably some workers will be underutilized—and given nearly universal market-dependence, this can create social friction. In short, workers are not merely objects, and their subjectivity and need for community and survival pose a challenge to JIT principles. Precisely because of this, the state's vision of labor market management remains in the realm of utopia rather than empirical reality. Chimerical though it may be, the *pursuit* of frictionless technocracy embodied in JIT urbanization has enormous social consequences.

CONCLUSION

Dominant Marxist approaches have focused on how people who are deemed surplus to the needs of capital can be subjected to life-denying forms of exclusion and expulsion. This view, however, does not comport with the reality of contemporary Chinese cities, where we have seen the state expel workers who are in fact critical to sustaining capital. A Foucauldian or biopolitical approach would lead us to look for *racism* as the axis of social differentiation that allows the state to subject people to social death. While this view is helpful in injecting politics into the analysis of surplus population, race is not the decisive form of social hierarchy structuring urban China's biopolitics. JIT urbanization is the *specific* political strategy Chinese megacities have employed to mediate competing imperatives to draw in certain kinds of labor while reducing their own obligations to socially reproduce those very workers, and sociospatial hierarchy is the "racism" that legitimates dehumanization and disposability of a segment of the dominant race. The state machinery aims to deliver the right labor in the right quantities at the right time, a regime that is manifestly imbued with profound inequities and an austere indifference to social need.

2

URBAN DEVELOPMENTALISM
AND THE INVERTED
WELFARE STATE

Wherever the parents are working, they need to let children into school. Wherever they're living, they need to let them into school. It should be like this.

—Mr. Fan, Father in Beijing's Liwanzhuang

In response to the tensions wrought by the urban growth dilemma, the state has developed a variety of techniques that aim to quantify human qualities. Although the utopia of subjecting labor to just-in-time principles can never be realized, there are real social consequences. The distribution of nominally public services is characterized by an inversion of the logic of means testing: there is a *negative* association between need and ability to access public goods. In other words, the greater an applicant's access to social, economic, and cultural capital, the greater the likelihood that applicant will be able to get his or her children access to quality public education. The techniques for sorting the population, when seen in the context of China's spatial administrative hierarchy and uneven development, constitute an emergent "inverted welfare state," which holds major implications for the country's structure of inequality.

FROM INDUSTRIALIZATION
TO URBANIZATION

Beginning in the late twentieth century, China embarked on a process of capitalist transition that led to an historically unprecedented, generation-long economic expansion. Marketization began with rural land reforms in the late 1970s, which led to significant increases in output.[1] But the locus of growth quickly shifted from agriculture to industry. Early successes of the town and village enterprises suggested that the countryside would continue to be at the forefront of reform, while heavy industry in urban areas remained dominated by state-owned enterprises.[2] By the early 1990s, export-oriented manufacturing had come to be the primary driver of growth, particularly in the country's southeast. Initially contained in the spatially circumscribed special economic zones, this undeniably capitalist system of production found its ultimate validation in stupendous rates of economic growth. From the opening up of additional coastal cities in the 1980s to the establishment of Shanghai's vast Pudong New Area in 1990, gradually more spaces and people were opened up to foreign investment, capitalist labor practices, and export-oriented manufacturing. Places where local private enterprise had developed in a more bottom up manner, as in Zhejiang Province, had encountered years of political challenges from a central state still nervous about full-blown marketization.[3] By the 1990s, these regions were hailed as heroic trailblazers in the new economy, rather than as politically contentious capitalist roaders. With free enterprise established as ideologically correct, the state-owned sector was then subjected to liquidation, privatization, and mass layoffs with the remaining SOEs increasingly pushed to operate according to market principles.[4] This attack on the planned economy generated massive worker resistance, but high levels of growth were maintained throughout, albeit with a high degree of spatial unevenness.[5]

A number of crucial factors facilitated this unprecedented economic expansion but China's key comparative advantage was its large, cheap, well-educated, and politically kneecapped workforce.[6] On the eve of marketization in 1978, only 18 percent of China's population was classified as urban leaving 785 million people in rural areas.[7] China's overall level of development was still quite low, with a GDP per capita of just over USD $150.[8] This population was relatively healthy and well-educated, thanks to investments in human development in the Mao era.[9] As for this emergent working class's docility and exploitability, China had no labor laws whatsoever until 1994. The only legally permissible union, the All China Federation of Trade Unions, is not a worker-based organization, but rather is subordinate to the Communist Party and has almost never demonstrated a willingness to take action against employers.[10] Offering this workforce up to global capital has been a primary method by which the state has attracted astonishing levels of FDI, which fueled a generation of high speed growth.

This deep pool of exploitable labor was produced and maintained, crucially, via state controls on mobility.[11] During the era of the command economy, demobilization of labor was necessary to allow the state to extract surplus from rural areas to invest in heavy industry and the "iron rice bowl" in urban areas.[12] This exploitative relationship was predicated on keeping peasants in rural areas, for the system would collapse if too many people moved to cities to take advantage of the relatively generous provisions of the *danwei* (work unit) system. But such an exclusionary regime could not satisfy the demands of the emergent labor-intensive private industry that characterized the export-oriented economy. Particularly in regions of coastal China where this model of development was dominant, people with rural *hukou* received temporary rights to occupy urban space as long as they were granted permission by employers. Circulatory migration was the dominant model, which meant that urban governments—and by extension employers in their jurisdictions—did not have to underwrite the costs of social reproduction.[13] Teenage workers appeared in the cities, relatively healthy and well-educated. The millions of workers in manufacturing as well as construction were likely to be located in cheap, on-site dorms largely severed from urban social life.[14] By the time they reached their mid-twenties, most returned to the village to start their own families. Nearly all of the costs of social reproduction, including schooling, health care, and old age care, were borne by the countryside. As in the Mao era, development was predicated on exploitation of the peasantry, but now rural labor was provisionally allowed into urban space. China's cheap labor strategy was thus built on the spatial severing of the moments of (urban) production from (rural) reproduction.

Over the course of the first decade of the twenty-first century, this model began to show signs of stress. To begin with, areas in coastal China started to report significant labor shortages in 2004, leading to much debate as to whether China had exhausted its supply of rural surplus labor.[15] Pinning down a sufficient workforce came to be an increasingly major challenge for many labor-intensive industries, pushing some of them to relocate abroad or to interior provinces.[16] China's export-oriented model had generated massive trade surpluses, primarily owing to trade with the United States, and its current account surplus grew to a peak of USD $421 billion in 2008.[17] In addition to the political friction that these surpluses generated, this left China's economy uncomfortably dependent on foreign consumers, a point that was emphasized during the 2008 economic crisis. During that crisis, tens of millions of migrant workers were thrown out of work, and despite frequent protests over unpaid wages they often had no choice but to return to the countryside.[18] A massive stimulus package propped up growth, but at the expense of dramatically increasing the debt to GDP ratio. Although Wen Jiabao had stressed the need to increase domestic consumption since 2004, China's already extremely low levels of domestic consumption (as a share of GDP) declined somewhat during the latter half of the 2000s (see figure 2.1).[19] The idea of economic "rebalancing"—that is, addressing class and regional disparities, increasing domestic consumption, moving up the value chain, reducing debt levels, and generating more ecologically sustainable growth—was accepted as orthodoxy by the end of Hu Jintao's administration in 2012.

The Shift to the City

Xi Jinping assumed full leadership of the country in 2013, and he quickly acted to promote urbanization as the primary means for advancing economic rebalancing. In March 2014, the State Council unveiled the National New Urbanization Plan (2014–2020), which was hailed as a blueprint for China's shift to urbanization-driven development. The plan was animated by the belief that urbanization would reduce inequality, increase domestic consumption, and promote higher-value-added production and ecologically sustainable development. The nation's political

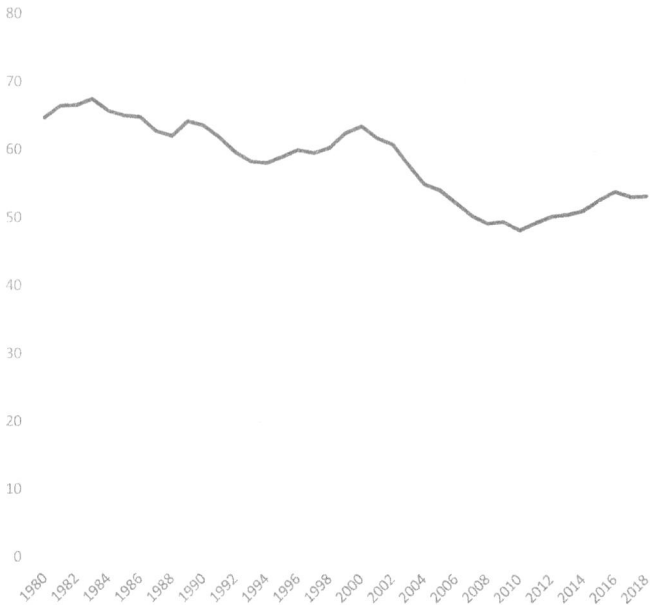

FIGURE 2.1 Household final consumption expenditure (% of GDP).
Source: World Bank Open Data, https://data.worldbank.org/indicator
/NE.CON.TOTL.ZS?locations=CN (accessed May 2, 2020).

leadership maintained that urbanization would drive the "Kuznets curve" experienced in the Global North in the twentieth century, with the expectation that greater urbanization-led development would result in decreased inequality.[20] A key assumption built into the plan was that anticipated increases in the average output per worker would translate into higher wages and greater consumption capacity.

To some extent, the plan described an urban-centered capitalism that was already coming into existence. Industrialization-led development was on the wane, with industry's share of GDP plateauing in the mid-1990s and beginning a marked decline from 2006 (see figure 2.2). As You-tien Hsing argues, land had already moved to the center of the politics of development, and the fortunes of the urban economy, municipal budgets, and a huge number of urban residents came to be tied to real estate markets.[21] By 2013, seven of the wealthiest ten people in Beijing were in property development, and in 2014 behemoth developers Vanke and Wanda were among the ten largest private companies in China.[22] This shift in the basis of growth is reflected in the rapid growth of finance, real estate, and construction in the late 2000s and into the 2010s (see figure 2.3). This is by no means to claim that traditional manufacturing and extractive industries had become irrelevant to Chinese capitalism, but rather to note

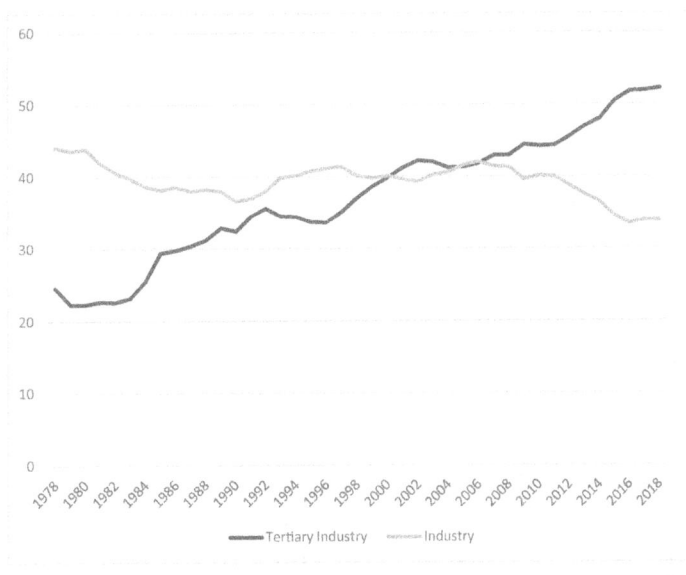

FIGURE 2.2 Percent contribution to GDP.

Source: China Statistical Yearbook 2019,
http://www.stats.gov.cn/tjsj/ndsj/2019/indexeh.htm

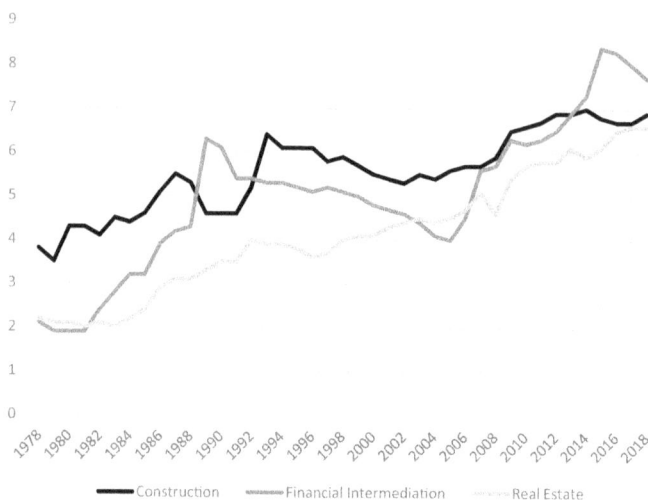

FIGURE 2.3 Percent contribution to GDP.
Source: China Statistical Yearbook 2019,
http://www.stats.gov.cn/tjsj/ndsj/2019/indexeh.htm

that marketization of land in China's cities was clearly increasing the relative weight of urbanization as a driver of growth.

However, urbanization is not, and can never be, merely the concentration of capital, expansion of a dense built environment, and increasing property values. In China, the urbanization of *people*, the migration, resettlement, and organization of social reproduction in the city, has never been a foregone conclusion. In contrast to much literature on overurbanization and surplus populations in the Global Southern city, economists have referred to China as "under-urbanized," in that there are fewer urban residents than would be expected based on its level of development.[23] Although more than half of China's total population was considered urban by 2011, the obstacles to human movement into cities remained formidable, and the number of people living in cities without urban *hukou* continued to grow (see figure 2.4). The central government became increasingly concerned that these obstacles could hinder the development of the postindustrial consumer-driven economy.

A sign of change in central policy came in 2013 when the phrase "urbanization of people" (*ren de chengzhenhua* 人的城镇化) entered the official lexicon. The mere existence of this state-approved phrase served as an implicit acknowledgment: the urbanization of capital, the state and even the aesthetic and

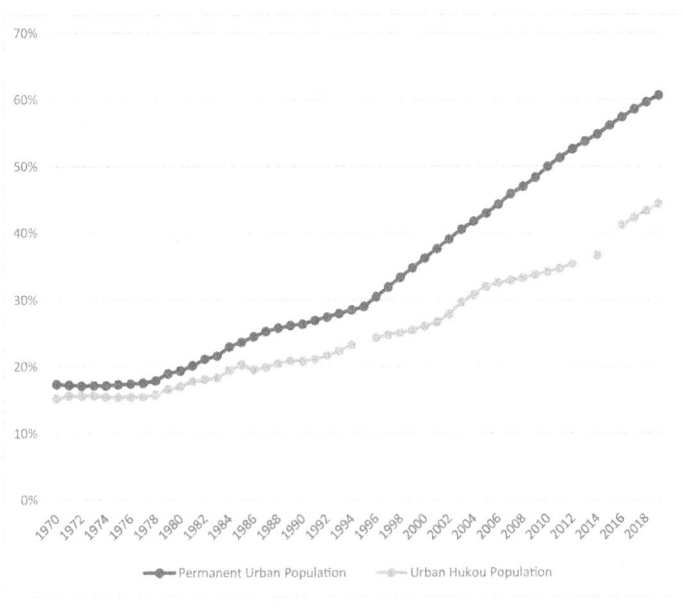

FIGURE 2.4 Urban permanent residents and urban *hukou* holders as share of total population.

Sources: China Data Online, National Statistics, Population and Employment, Population of China; Percentage of Urbanization by Household Registered 2016–2019, 中华人民共和国国民经济和社会发展统计公报 (Zhonghua Renmin Gongheguo Guomin Jinji he Shehui Fazhan Tongji Gongbao) 2016–2019.

symbolic orders were well on their way.[24] But even though hundreds of millions of people occupied the physical space of cities and were legally incorporated as workers, they continued to be repelled in other respects. The urbanization of people, then, refers to the central government's stated desire to increase the proportion of people not only working but also consuming and permanently residing in cities. In discussing the National New Urbanization Plan, Xi Jinping repeatedly stressed that "the urbanization of people is the core."[25] As people permanently relocated to the cities, the state imagined that their *suzhi* (human quality) would be improved, output would increase, and a new high-consuming middle class would serve as the social basis of a prosperous and ecologically sustainable society.

In line with this new developmental orientation, a number of policy shifts in 2014 suggested a relaxation of *hukou* restrictions. In addition to encouraging people to move to cities, with the stated goal of a national urbanization rate of 60 percent by 2020, the new plan aimed to reduce the percentage of people living in cities without local *hukou*.[26] The plan was also quite forthcoming in acknowledging that "the urbanization of land has been faster than the urbanization of people" and the fact that serious inequalities had emerged over the previous decades: "Disparities in access to public services between local and migrant populations have produced ever more apparent contradictions in cities' dual structure. The model of primarily relying on unequal public services to minimize expenses and promote rapid urbanization is not sustainable."[27]

In July 2014, the State Council released the "Opinion on Promoting Reform of the Residency System," a document intended to complement the move to urban-led development. The key feature of the opinion was a call to "unify the rural and urban *hukou* registration system" and "comprehensively implement a residential permit system."[28] The former was hailed as an indication of the end of the apartheid-like features of the system that made transferring from rural to urban *hukou* particularly difficult.[29] The residential permit was intended to replace the "temporary resident permit," a designation that allowed migrants to stay and work in the city while denying them access to social services. The residential permit, on the other hand, was supposed to allow for migrants to enjoy similar (though not necessarily identical) rights to those of people with local *hukou*. As had been the case a decade prior, some analysts asked if this was the end of *hukou*-based discrimination.[30]

RECONFIGURING THE SOCIOSPATIAL HIERARCHY

A closer analysis of these and related policies points to an important nuance: the government was encouraging certain kinds of people to move to certain kinds of cities. Item six of the urbanization plan is titled "promoting the transfer of rural to urban hukou for *those who meet certain conditions*" (emphasis added).[31] As had been the case previously, the central government did not dictate to the municipalities any specifics as to the conditions for accessing local *hukou*. But the types of conditions that were generally applicable included "number of years of employment, number of years of residence, and number of years of participation in urban social insurance," adding that both employment and residence should be "stable and legal." Crucially, the central government did not promise any fiscal restructuring to accommodate these new arrivals.

Although the center did not directly dictate conditions for admission to various kinds of cities, the urbanization plan clearly reflected the state's long-standing fears about overpopulation in the largest cities:[32]

> Townships and small cities should comprehensively relax restrictions for attaining local *hukou*; cities with a population of 500,000–1 million residents should relax restrictions in an orderly manner; large cities with a population of 1–3 million should reasonably relax restrictions; large cities with a population of 3–5 million should reasonably establish conditions for attaining local *hukou*; extra-large cities with a population of more than 5 million should strictly control the scope of their population.[33]

It is clear is that the central government did not envision significant *hukou* liberalization in large cities—precisely the places with the most developed economies and most generous social welfare provision. The urbanization plan employed an official term for this stratified citizenship regime: the "differentiated *hukou* acquisition policy" (*chabiehua luohu zhengce* 差别化落户政策).

The central state's injunction to severely curtail population growth in the largest cities suggested a major political challenge. Indeed, China's migrants are significantly overrepresented in large cities, with a clear positive correlation between city size and the percent of population constituted by migrants (see figure 2.5).[34] If we look more specifically at the cities with an urban district population (*chengqu renkou* 城区人口) of over 5 million, that is, those that are supposed to "strictly control" population growth, the problem becomes even more glaring. According to data from the 2015 *China Urban Construction Yearbook*, there were relatively few of these extra-large cities: Beijing, Shanghai, Tianjin, Guangzhou, Shenzhen, Nanjing, and Chongqing.[35] But these cities alone are likely absorb more than one-quarter of all migrants.[36] Although population

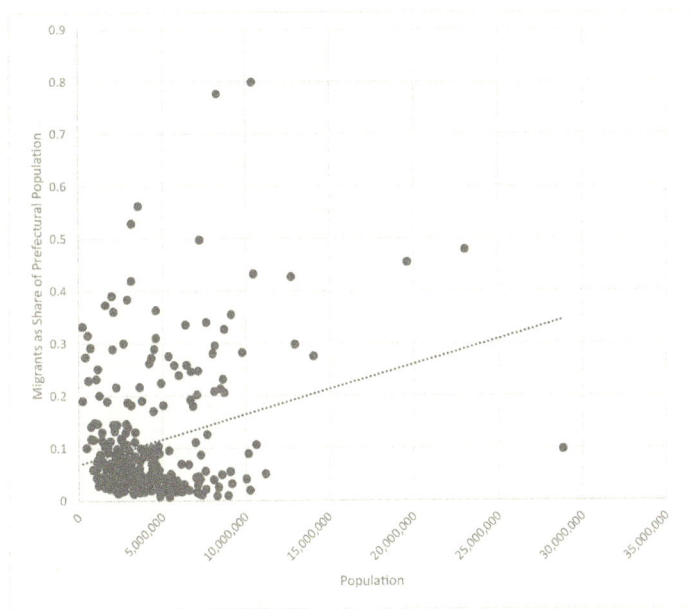

FIGURE 2.5 Migrant share of population. These data refer to "entering population" (*qianru renkou* 迁入人口) and include migrants both to urban districts (*qu* 区) as well as rural counties (*xian* 县).

Source: China Population Census, 2010. Self-calculated.

growth was certainly slowing in the megacities by 2014, these cities would still need to deploy powerful methods to meet their population control goals.

Point-Based *Hukou* Admission

An increasingly important feature of just-in-time (JIT) urbanization has been the center's promotion of point-based *hukou* acquisition (*jifen ruhu* 积分入户). These plans, modeled to some extent on the "blue stamp" *hukou* programs from the 1990s, have been implemented in the extra-large cities as well as smaller wealthy cities in the Pearl River Delta, Yangzi River Delta, and Jingjinji (Beijing-Tianjin-Hebei) megalopolises.[37] Shanghai implemented an early version of point-based *hukou* application in the mid-2000s, and Guangdong Province created a policy framework for its many migrant-receiving cities in 2011.[38] Although the programs are most common in Guangdong, several other municipalities have since devised their own schemes. While there is significant variation between various cities' approaches, the basics are the same. Any citizen is eligible for consideration—there are no place-based exclusions. Applicants accrue points based on various characteristics, and after meeting some point threshold they are then allowed to apply for local *hukou* (though application by no means guarantees acceptance).[39]

By the end of 2015, point-based *hukou* schemes existed in only a limited number of cities. Programs had been unveiled in the Guangdong cities of Guangzhou, Shenzhen, Dongguan, Zhuhai, and Zhongshan. Elsewhere, Tianjian and Shanghai had plans in place, while Beijing did not announce its plan until the end of 2016, with Chengdu following suit in 2017. The State Council's opinion had said that cities with a population over 5 million should establish point-based schemes. On the other hand, the opinion says that cities with a population of 3–5 million "can" establish point-based systems. Both Zhuhai and Zhongshan have fewer than 3 million people, but given their location in the Pearl River Delta they have a relatively high proportion of migrants. Clearly, there is no prohibition on smaller cities developing such schemes, even if they are not required to do so.

The point-based programs are emerging as a key institution to enhance the state's population management capacity. Value in the labor market is the most important, though by no means the only, metric determining how the state sorts those worthy of subsidized reproduction from those deemed surplus. While there is important variation between cities, the basic labor-market orientation of the plans is reflected in the State Council's 2014 opinion, which states that cities should "emphasize resolving *hukou* for people who have been in the city for a long time, have strong employability, and can adapt to urban industrial transformation and upgrading, and the competitive urban environment." In Beijing's "Measure on Point-Based Hukou Management," one of the four primary considerations is "ensuring the human resources to improve the central functions of the capital city."[40]

The single most important way that labor market value is operationalized in these plans is by distributing points based on educational attainment.[41] Although each city assigns different values for different types of degrees, in general the higher the academic accomplishment the more points an applicant can accrue. Guangzhou assigns points for technical degrees, while Shanghai's system favors those with PhDs as well as graduates of the prestigious "211" universities.[42] Across the board, cities assign points for various kinds of skills that are in demand in the local labor market.

In addition to the focus on education, the point-based plans contain a variety of other provisions that are oriented toward including people with high levels of cultural and economic capital. As is recommended in the State Council's opinion, applying for local *hukou* will almost always require that migrants can produce labor contracts and leases. Most cities assign points based on the amount of income tax applicants have paid within the municipality. For instance, Guangzhou and Tianjin both assign points for applicants who have paid at least 100,000 yuan in income taxes over the previous three years, whereas Shenzhen has an elaborate system with eight tiers that awards progressively more points for more income tax paid. Shenzhen, Tianjin, and Dongguan also award points for business taxes paid if the applicant is the owner or a shareholder. Following educational credentials, payments into the tax system are the most reliable route to accumulate points.[43] Paying into local social insurance plans is also a critical component in accumulating points, since most cities assign points for the number of years that applicants have paid into the local pension fund. Beijing requires that applicants have paid into local social insurance for seven years in order to be able to apply.

Beyond contributions to the local tax base, simply owning property can be beneficial. Beijing awards one point for every year of residence in a house that the applicant owns, whereas renters accumulate only half a point per year of residence. People in informal housing accumulate no points. In Chengdu, applicants receive ten points for owning a home, whereas renters receive only one point. Dongguan and Shenzhen further distinguish between people who own their apartment outright as opposed to those who have a mortgage, with the former type of applicant receiving 50 percent more points than the latter. More straightforwardly, Dongguan awards four points (to a maximum of 100) for every 100,000 yuan invested locally. On the other hand, Shenzhen, Tianjin, and Chengdu deduct points for people with poor credit.[44]

There are other non-economic metrics cities use to secure the right kind of population. Most cities deduct significant points for any run-in with the law, and even noncriminal legal violations can result in big deductions.[45] Chengdu bars applicants who have any criminal offenses or those who have participated in "organizations or activities banned by the state."[46] Having children born in violation of birth control policies results in major deductions in Zhongshan, Dongguan, Shenzhen, and Chengdu. And people over forty-five are either barred completely from applying or receive point demerits for each year over that age. In Beijing's plan, this stipulation is explained as an effort to "optimize the population's age structure." Finally, applicants can accrue points for winning various forms of state-sponsored awards (e.g., "model worker").

Talent Programs

In the absence of, or sometimes parallel to, point-based *hukou* admission, many cities and provinces have established "green card" or "fast track" policies explicitly aimed at attracting talent.[47] In 2018 Beijing announced a preferential residence application program for "high-level domestic talents," including "skilled personnel in science and technology, creative people in culture and art, financial management talents, [and] patent holders of new inventions." But the competition to attract highly educated workers in profitable industries has been particularly intense in provincial capitals and other large wealthy cities outside of the traditional powerhouses of Beijing, Shanghai, Guangzhou, and Shenzhen. Chengdu exemplified this trend when in 2017 the city introduced a "talent green card" that would grant special privileges to human talents (*rencai* 人才) in home purchases, medical care, low interest rate loans, and even free visits to the local panda research center.[48] Xi'an unveiled a program that would allow university graduates to apply for a local *hukou* simply by uploading photos of their student ID and national ID cards.[49]

Benefits for highly educated young people have not been limited to administrative prioritization but have also included housing subsidies. In Hainan, the government followed a set of severe restrictions on property purchases by non-*hukou* holders with the announcement of a "one million talent plan" that would open a special *hukou* application and home-purchasing channel for people who qualify as talented. The provincial government's website asserted, "When talented individuals come to Hainan they don't have to worry that they can't buy a home, or can't afford to buy."[50] In an effort to retain skilled workers, the city of Wuhan built tens of thousands of subsidized "talent apartments" that were available only to recent university graduates.[51] As with all of the other plans discussed here, education credentials and labor market value were the key metrics in determining levels of talent, although they are not (outwardly, at least) point-based. While children's access to public schools has not been emphasized in these plans, that is because it is simply a right attendant to acquiring housing and local *hukou*. Similar preferential policies, all of which provide direct state subsidies to social reproduction, appeared in numerous cities, including Changsha, Nanjing, and Tianjin.

In 2018, just a few months after justifying the eviction of tens of thousands of migrant workers by citing urban overpopulation, the Beijing municipal government took things a step further in establishing new "green card" policies aimed at sourcing the right quantities and qualities of labor *globally*. Under this plan, a close analog of which existed in Shanghai, foreigners qualifying as human talent would enjoy permanent residency, access to local schools, the right to purchase homes and cars, and even cash incentives of up to 1 million yuan.[52] The *People's Daily* was enthusiastic about these green card policies: "China's door will open wider and wider. More superior human talents will settle in China, inevitably paying powerful human capital dividends for China's future development."[53] Although the number of slots for international human talent remained small in number, it served as yet another instantiation of the underlying political logic of the urban state.

Implications for the Sociospatial Hierarchy

In fact, the number of slots for point-based *hukou* admission for Chinese citizens also appears to be quite small. Guangzhou and Shenzhen offered a paltry 3,000 and 4,600 respectively in 2010.[54] By 2017, Shenzhen increased its quota to 10,000, equivalent to 0.1 percent of the city's non-*hukou* population of 7.9 million (as of the end of 2016). Zhongshan approved only 27,515 applicants in the eight years following the 2009 rollout.[55] In the three years following the 2017 implementation of Beijing's point-based plan, 12,000 applications were approved (including applicants' dependents, a total of over 20,000 new *hukou* were granted).[56] It is thus clear that the point systems are not a means for extending citizenship rights on a mass scale. Rather, it is a mechanism for pulling in and pinning down specific kinds of labor and creating an ethical framework of self-improvement to discipline the millions who in reality have no chance at securing the rights to state-subsidized social reproduction.[57]

It is worth emphasizing the profound inequity embedded in such an approach to bestowing full citizenship rights. To begin with, the demand for a labor contract excludes vast swathes of the citizenry. Informality in China has been grossly underreported, and Philip Huang estimated in 2009 that there were 168 million informal workers in urban areas.[58] Efforts to formalize labor markets have had uneven success, with working-class migrants less likely to benefit from greater legal protections.[59] Furthermore, the proportion of migrant workers signing labor contracts *dropped* from 42.8 percent in 2009 to 35.1 percent in 2016.[60]

It is extremely unlikely for workers without a contract to meet another nearly universal demand of the point-based *hukou* schemes, namely, proof of social insurance payments. Many workers (regardless of registration status) find that unscrupulous employers fail to make required insurance payments. According to official statistics, in 2014 only 16.7 percent of migrant workers overall, and a mere 3.9 percent of workers in construction, participated in "old age insurance."[61] Similarly, a formal housing lease is not a straightforward proposition. Migrants continue to be largely excluded from subsidized housing in the cities, and there is little chance for most of them to be able to afford commodity housing.[62] As a result, millions of working-class migrants continue to be housed in informal "villages in the city." In addition to housing-based exclusion, lack of higher education qualifications will immediately disqualify millions of people with rural *hukou*. Given that only 8 percent of the rural workforce had some upper secondary education in 2010, the vast majority of migrants will be severely disadvantaged, if not immediately disqualified, from a successful *hukou* application in one of the megacities.[63] The consequence of all of this is that it is precisely those least likely to be able to secure adequate livelihoods through wage labor who are most likely to be excluded from *hukou* and its attendant access to nominally public services.

It must also be noted that the labor market-centric *hukou* admission regime has important implications for ethnic inequality. While there are no categorical bans or point demerits for ethnic minorities, widespread racial discrimination in the labor market has the effect of imposing a likely insurmountable obstacle to *hukou* acquisition for most non-Han applicants in megacities. Anecdotal evidence of labor market discrimination against minorities, particularly Tibetans and Uyghurs, is widespread.[64] A growing literature has also identified that minorities are subject to disproportionate rates of poverty, though there is debate as to whether this is attributable to ethnicity as opposed to other factors such as location and education.[65] But Margaret Maurer-Fazio's large-scale field experiment has shown a significant effect for ethnicity in job applications in the urban private sector, with Mongolians, Tibetans, and Uyghurs much less likely to receive a callback than their Han counterparts.[66] The formally race-blind character of *hukou* programs will serve to reinforce already existing ethnic hierarchy as refracted through the labor market. Race is not the primary axis of biopolitics in China's megacities, and it certainly is the case that rural Han are, from the standpoint of absolute demographic weight, the group that stands to lose the most. Nonetheless, it is important from an ethical standpoint to note the racial implications of point-based *hukou* admissions.

In sum, this is a politics that seeks to *manage* the problem of circulation rather than closing off circulation altogether, to extend conditions for social reproduction to the right kinds of labor while dispensing with life-enhancing interventions for those deemed surplus. Point-based plans are an effort to formalize and make transparent (indeed, transparency is emphasized in the language of these official documents) the highly unequal methods large cities have used for distributing rights to local services for many years. And there is no doubt that these plans are emerging as key administrative tools in cities' efforts to get the right kind of labor power delivered, in the right quantity, and at the right time. In conjunction with the more coercive measures to expel undesirable migrants, this suggests an urbanization strategy imbued with the logic of JIT.

The problem, however, is that such a technocratic vision of perfect control over human movement can never be realized in practice, particularly in a country which already has a national labor market. By attending to one side of the urban growth dilemma, avoiding overpopulation, the state would simultaneously deprive capital of a cheap workforce. But while a national labor market has been institutionalized, citizenship is still constituted at the local level. To put it another way, China has realized freedom of movement for labor but not people. The consequence is there are nearly 300 million migrants who are moving "out of plan." How are these people included and excluded in urban social space, and what politics emerge from this contradictory tethering to the city? More specifically, for those who are living in the city but have no chance of securing local *hukou*, how do they go about getting access to education for their children?

ACCESSING EDUCATION WHEN MIGRATING "OUT OF PLAN"

The question of how to integrate people living in cities without local *hukou* is an increasingly pressing social problem. Even if the central government's optimistic forecasts are realized, hundreds of millions of people will continue to live outside their area of *hukou* registration. Children of primary and middle-school age constitute a significant share of this population, growing from 9.98 million in 2009 to 13.67 million in 2015.[67] Beijing alone had 687,000 migrants aged fourteen and younger in 2015.[68] The parents of these children have been subjected to a seemingly ad hoc system in which some people are allowed to access public education some of the time. However, as with *hukou* applications, the seemingly impartial bureaucratic arrangements urban governments use to make this determination in fact follow a consistent logic of funneling this nominally public good to those who need it least. As noted earlier, governments have quite consciously used the carrot of public school access as a method for luring human talent.

As with much social policy, the messaging from the center on education for migrant children is generally commendable if vague. Following a 2001 decision from the State Council, official policy for the children of migrant workers has been referred to as "the two primaries" (*liangweizhu* 两为主).[69] This means that receiving areas are *primarily* responsible for the education of migrant children and that these children should *primarily* be placed in public schools. In 2003, the Ministry of Education reaffirmed this in an official opinion and called on local governments to include migrant children in budgeting and city planning, to reduce or eliminate additional fees, and to provide support and oversight for private migrant schools.[70] However, questions about conditions for enrollment and specific budgetary arrangements remained in the hands of local officials.

Following these central directives, the city of Beijing made important progress in placing an increasing share of migrant students in public schools. According to an official estimate, in 2001 only 12.5 percent of migrant children in Beijing were enrolled in public schools.[71] In 2004 the city banned the widespread practice of charging nonlocal children additional fees (*jiedufei* 借读费). In the same proclamation, the government said that in the event of a migrant school closure or demolition, district education departments "should" assign students to new schools. According to official reports, by 2015 public school enrollment of migrant children had increased to 78 percent.[72] This is likely an optimistic number, since students in the most informal situations are also the least likely to be counted. Regardless of the specific number, the general trend is clear.

During this process, however, migrant children have never been given the *right* to public education in Beijing (or any other place where they do not have *hukou*). In 2004, the Beijing government established a system for public school admissions that came to be known as the "five permits." In order to be considered for a place in a public school, parents would need to produce: a labor contract, proof of local housing in the form of a deed or lease, a temporary residence permit (*zanzhuzheng* 暂住证), *hukou* for the entire family, and proof that there are no guardians in the parents' place of *hukou* registration. This last requirement is particularly vexing, since it requires parents to take time away from work to travel to their place of *hukou* registration, where they will likely have to pay a bribe to a local official to produce a logically incoherent document (i.e., one demonstrating that this condition *doesn't* exist). If parents are able to collect all of these documents, they can then submit an application, which it must be emphasized, by no means guarantees access to a public school. Finally, despite the practice having been banned, migrant parents whom I interviewed in Beijing without exception believed that they would have to pay school administrators exorbitant bribes of 20,000–100,000 yuan in order to get into a public school, with better schools requiring higher bribes.[73]

The consequence of these arrangements is that a large segment of the population is still excluded from public education. These parents are then faced with an impossible choice. The first option, and by far the more popular one nationally, is to keep their children in the village where they *are* guaranteed access to public education, although it is generally of poor quality. According to one widely cited survey, 58 percent of rural children live without one parent, whereas 26 percent are living apart from both parents.[74] Tens of millions of these "left-behind children" are testament to the fact that China's spatially uneven development and fractured citizenship regime have eviscerated the rural family structure.[75] The second option is to send their children to local migrant schools that are completely, or almost completely, dependent on tuition for funding their activities. Left-behind children and migrant children outside of their hometown together now constitute a massive population of 100 million.[76]

As more and more migrants began bringing their children with them to the city in the 1990s, the number of private migrant schools grew rapidly in Beijing. In recognition of the growing presence of informal migrant education, in 2005 the Beijing Education Committee issued the "Notification on Strengthening Management of Floating Population Self-Run Schools." This notification established the principle of "supporting some [schools], approving some, and eliminating some," suggesting an effort to either bring migrant schools under government management or to eliminate them. This goal was not immediately realized, and data from a survey released in 2009 found that more than half of migrant schools in the city were still unregistered but remained in operation.[77] By 2012 most people working in the field estimated there were 140–150 migrant schools in the city, roughly two-thirds of which were unlicensed.[78] But the general trend over the course of the 2000s and 2010s was clearly toward restricting the growth of informal schooling. By 2018 the best available estimate put the number of migrant schools at 107, down from a peak of 300 in 2006.[79]

We see two interrelated trends occurring over the course of the 2000s and 2010s: a higher percentage of migrant children in Beijing are being accepted into public schools even as the space for informal education is gradually eliminated (albeit unevenly, and in fits and starts).[80] At a high enough level of abstraction, this seems unobjectionable, inasmuch as it suggests a process of formalization and extension of public services to those without local *hukou*. The reality was not nearly so benign. As the share of migrant children included in public schools increased, those excluded were subjected to an increasingly brutal regime aimed at denying access to basic social reproduction with the hopes of driving them from the city. Whether it was the mass school demolitions of 2011, followed by more sporadic demolitions and closures in subsequent years, or the mass housing evictions of 2017, those dependent on informal social reproduction encountered an increasingly hostile state that was, often against the objections of capitalists, rendering this population surplus.[81]

It was at precisely this same time that the state began ratcheting demands for inclusion in public schools. The rules governing admission to public schools became highly exclusionary in 2014, and many parents who expected to be able to get their children into schools were left scrambling. I will discuss at length how migrant parents responded to these changes in chapter 4, but here I will mention a few examples of how the state was consciously employing the method of "population control via education."[82] Some districts implemented a new rule that parents need to live and work in the same area where they were applying for school admission—a major problem for the countless migrants who live in peripheral areas but work in the urban core. In some districts, both the mother and father had to live and work within the district. Other districts added new length of residence requirements or demanded proof of paying into social insurance within the district. The government also set up a new and reportedly confusing online registration system in which parents had to complete a series of steps within a designated time window. And there was much anecdotal evidence that parents who managed to gather all the appropriate materials would be given new and seemingly arbitrary demands upon each return visit to the registration offices. Although the "five permits" rule was still formally in place, one report found dozens of different pieces of documentation that parents had been asked to produce.[83] These rule changes were nothing less than a concerted effort to foreclose public schooling for more and more migrants while eliminating informal options—a coercive intervention to optimize the structure of the population in accordance with the perceived needs of the city.

An Aside on the Ideology of Overpopulation

Beijing simply has too many people, and it would be beyond the capacity of the city to provide public services to migrants.[84] So runs an argument mobilized again and again by the state and its defenders as justification for the exclusionary education system. It is simply not rooted in reality. Based on the government's own data, Beijing and other wealthy megacities like it are in a better position to expand access to social services than they have ever been.

As can been seen clearly in figure 2.6, the total number of students in Beijing's primary schools fell significantly in the late 1990s and early 2000s. Even with the increase in students from 2006, likely owing in part to the relative relaxing of public school admission for migrants mentioned before, enrollment is

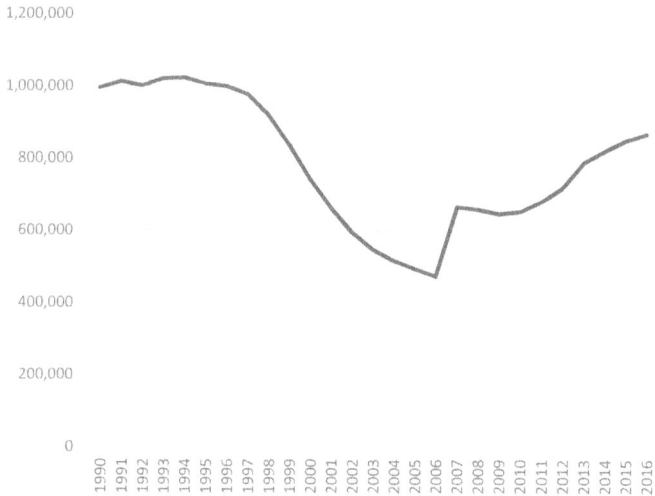

FIGURE 2.6 Total students enrolled in Beijing primary schools.

Source: Beijing Tongji Nianjian, 2017.

well below where it was in the mid-1990s. It should also be noted that these data collapse public and private school enrollments. This is significant because private school enrollments were increasing at precisely this time (see figure 2.7), suggesting that the government was fiscally responsible for a falling share of total enrollees. Furthermore, the increase in private school enrollees almost certainly is based on underreporting, since the tens of thousands of students in unlicensed private schools would not be captured.

The city's lowered enrollment come at a time when its fiscal capacity has been growing explosively (see figure 2.8). Between 1994 and 2016, while the total number of primary school students dropped by 156,086, the city's tax revenue experienced an astonishing thirty-seven-fold increase. It is thus apparent that

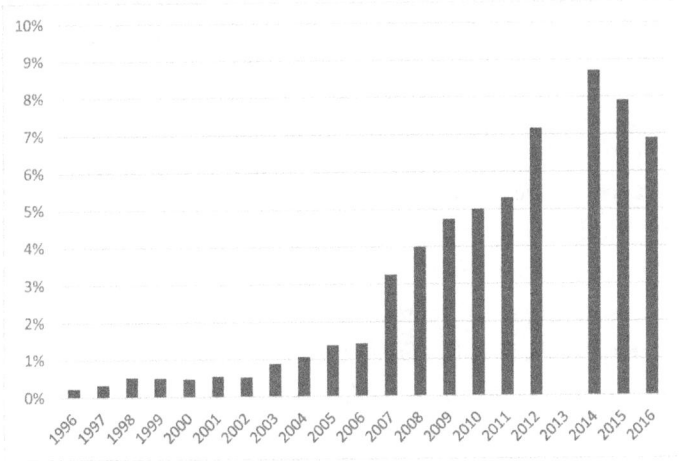

FIGURE 2.7 Percent students enrolled in private school, Beijing.

Source: Beijing Tongji Nianjian, 2017.

Note: Data for private school enrollees in 2013 was listed as 1.77 percent. This data point was highly anomalous and is almost certainly a mistake or due to some methodological irregularity. Thus, I have decided to exclude this observation.

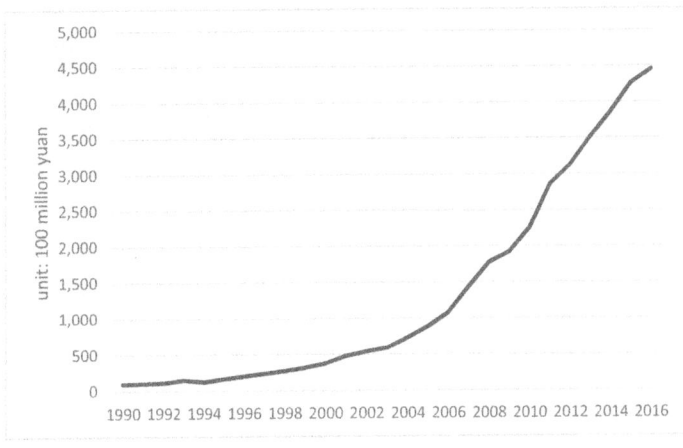

FIGURE 2.8 Beijing tax revenue.

Source: Beijing Tongji Nianjian, 2017.

the city has simply decided to use their expanding resources for other purposes, not least of which is increased spending for those considered part of the population.

Beijing is in many ways exceptional, most important with respect to the brutality directed at those who fail to gain entrance to the public system. But there is a key similarity nationwide: wealthy cities have devised techniques to extend public education to precisely those migrants who are *most* capable of securing social reproduction via market mechanisms. In this respect, Beijing has fallen behind a number of other cities that are now deploying point-based technologies in determining public school admissions for migrants. A brief overview of these emergent systems is critical to understand the politics of the urbanization of people more broadly.

POINT-BASED SCHOOL ENROLLMENT

More or less in tandem with the extension of point-based *hukou* schemes have emerged point-based public school enrollment procedures for nonlocal *hukou* holders. Although these plans were not yet operational in my field sites while I was conducting research, they have become increasingly widespread. Not coincidentally, they quickly became popular in major migrant-receiving cities in the Pearl River Delta and Yangzi River Delta. After being piloted in Guangdong's Zhongshan in 2010, numerous neighboring cities adopted similar plans, including Guangzhou, Shenzhen, Dongguan, Zhongshan, and the Yangzi River Delta cities of Suzhou, Kunshan, Ningbo, and Changzhou, among others.[85] Notably, Beijing did not have point-based school enrollment as of 2018. The basic mechanics of point-based school enrollments are the same as for *hukou*: applicants without local *hukou*, in this case the parents of the child, accrue points based largely on their perceived value to the locality and stability of employment, residence, and tax contributions. These metrics allow education departments to rank applicants, and then distribute the allotted number of places starting from the top of the applicant pool and working their way down. As with *hukou* applications, there are specific yearly quotas that cannot be exceeded. One major difference from *hukou* administration is that district-level governments have the right to establish their own frameworks for distributing points, since the districts are of greater importance in financing education. These frameworks often differ markedly within a given city.

As noted, the metrics employed in point-based school admissions are broadly similar to those of the point-based *hukou* system. Especially important is length of time legally residing, working, and paying taxes and social insurance within the district. Many districts have required lengths of stay before applicants can even be considered. Most urban districts will allot more points for more time in residence (up to a certain limit), as well as more points for more money paid into social insurance or the local tax system. For instance, in Guangzhou's Panyu District, applicants receive one point for every 1,000 yuan they have paid in personal income tax over the previous five years.

Cities have also used point-based school enrollments as a means of bolstering real estate markets. This is apparent in that those who own their homes accumulate more points than renters. Also in Panyu District, a standard rental lease is assigned five points, whereas home ownership is assigned twenty five points. Neighboring Zhongshan doubled the number of points assigned for owning a house in the city for the 2015 admissions cycle, with the government claiming that those who owned property are more likely to stay in the city over the long term.

Districts in Shenzhen such as Nanshan have highly elaborated point ladders, in which newly constructed homes are awarded four more points than "secondhand" homes, and owners with 51 percent or more equity in their homes accumulate more points (as many as ten) than those with 50 percent or less. In Nanshan, renters also face a complex point ladder, but even the highest step is assigned half the points of the bottom of the home ownership ladder. In cities around the country, those in informal housing receive no points or are excluded from applying altogether.

Applicants' labor market value is a central component of point-based school enrollments, but it is somewhat less so than is the case for *hukou* applications. Many districts in Guangzhou and beyond do assign significant points for parents' level of education or "urgently needed skills." While supposed value in the labor market is one of the most significant point-generators in many districts, it is important to note that this is not uniformly the case. In Guangzhou, three of eight districts do not offer points based on parents' level of education. Of the fifty-four districts nationwide with point-based enrollment in 2016, twenty-eight offered some kind of reward for parents' level of education or skill certifications. In these twenty-eight districts, this is generally an important source of points, and it can make the difference between a successful and failed application. But tenure of residence, employment, and payments into social security are a more consistently important metric nationally. Even in Guangzhou's Zengcheng District, where education is a factor, applicants are awarded ten points for a bachelor's degree, but they can also earn ten points for simply being employed in the district in any profession for five years. On average, then, point-based school enrollment places somewhat less emphasis on labor market value than is the case for *hukou* applications.

As with the *hukou* applications, adherence to the law and state-determined morality is an important metric. Most important in this respect is compliance with birth control policies. Panyu District requires documentation from the birth control agency in order to be considered for application, whereas in neighboring Zengcheng District there is a descending point ladder for those who are born within the birth control policy, those born outside of the plan but who have paid off their fines, those born outside of the plan but who have only paid a portion of the fines, and those born outside of the plan who have not paid their fines (receiving no points at all). Many districts deduct points for criminal violations, as in Zhongshan where any criminal offense within the past five years results in a 100-point deduction (which would almost certainly result in the application's being rejected). In some cases, seemingly innocuous transgressions such as traffic violations can result in deductions. For instance, in Kunshan, an applicant would lose five points for any traffic violation in the previous year, a total equivalent to the number of points assigned for having a degree from a technical college. In nearly every case, applicants can gain significant points for having won one of a variety of official commendations or honors.

Urban governments have also used point-based enrollment to valorize heteronormative family arrangements. While there is unevenness in this respect, many districts offer points that can only be accessed by heterosexual couples in which both of the parents reside and work in the same place. In Guangzhou, Panyu District and Baiyun District offer instructive examples. Giving a clear advantage to heterosexual couples in which both parents are present, Panyu allows both the mother's and father's levels of education and payments to social insurance to be used to accumulate points (up to the given limit for each category). Baiyun has accepted a seemingly onerous requirement for even being *considered* for application: "The husband and wife must live in the district continuously for two years (or the husband and wife have both lived in the district together for more than one year, and in total they have five years or more of continuous residence)." The same requirements hold not just for residence, but also for working and paying social insurance. Some jurisdictions, such as Jinwan District in Zhuhai, do not require both parents to be present, and applicants must choose which parent will represent them in points assessment. Given that China's uneven development has imposed structural constraints on maintaining nuclear families, even families adhering to the heteronormative ideal will face immense challenges.[86] Queer family arrangements are in violation of the moral order of the state, with the children's social reproduction consequently left to the vagaries of the market.

While on average point-based public school enrollment favors the wealthiest applicants, there are a very small number of countervailing stipulations where points are assigned to applicants who, on average, would be more likely to need social protection. Panyu District and Huadu District in Guangzhou assign points for ethnic minorities, albeit only half the number of points accruing to a bachelor's degree. And Haizhu District gives seven points to applicants with rural *hukou*, just below the eight points one receives for owning a house within the district. These point allotments are exceptional, and they certainly fall well short of what would be necessary to realize a significant redistributive effect.

It should also be noted that point-based enrollment, even for those whom it is designed to benefit, by no means results in educational equality with full *hukou*-possessing residents. Point-based enrollments are generally available only to students entering either primary or middle school. If a child moves to the city during year two of primary school, they must wait until middle school to have another chance at enrolling through this mechanism. Furthermore, regardless of how many points a family can accumulate, they are still excluded from sitting for the high school and university entrance exams. Thus, preferential admissions to the most prestigious universities still requires *hukou* in nearly every large city—certainly those with top-tier universities. There is little pretense that, even in the best-case scenario, point-based public school enrollment will do much to counteract educational inequality. But there are real political implications of these plans: migrants who have not made the cut for full citizenship are subjected to yet another regime of assessment, quantification, and ranking if they wish to access public education in the city.

THE INVERTED WELFARE STATE

The central government's desire to address the migrant question and advance the urbanization of people is real; indeed, this may be the single most important social issue they face. Most of the rhetoric and many of the concrete policy initiatives seek to better integrate people into cities, to reduce *hukou* barriers, to equalize educational opportunities, and to ensure more balanced forms of development. The problem, however, is that the center has explicitly left the implementation of *hukou* and educational policies to city-level and in some cases district-level governments. China's highly localized patchwork of policies for *hukou* admission and granting provisional access to education actually adhere to a relatively consistent logic: that of a *negative means test* in which access to services is dependent on a preponderance of resources.

But that is not the end of the story. This generalized pattern of negative means tests, when seen in the context of the country's highly uneven patterns of capitalist development and inequitable fiscal capacities, presents a staggering image of emergent sociospatial hierarchy. The cities that are wealthiest, and theoretically most able to bear the fiscal responsibility of increased social spending, have the highest bar of entry for those applying for *hukou* and for contingent admission to public schools.[87] Furthermore, the elite institutions of higher education, which are the most reliable mechanisms for upward socioeconomic mobility, are all located in large, highly restricted cities. In general, the larger the city the better the social services, and the harder it is for migrants to access state-subsidized social reproduction. The "inverted welfare state," then, is the regime produced by a generalized pattern of negative means tests combined with the country's highly uneven patterns of capitalist development and inequitable fiscal capacities that funnel public resources to the pinnacle of the spatial administrative hierarchy.[88] The implications for educational exclusion and rigidification of the class structure are legion.

Some further explication and empirical evidence will be useful in fleshing out this argument. Few would be surprised to learn that there is a clear and positive correlation between city size and GDP per capita (figure 2.9), a pattern that is by no means unique to China. The reasons underlying this are complex and the subject of debate, but the source of this phenomenon is not particularly important.[89] Much more germane to this study is simply the empirical fact that the richest cities are the most difficult ones for migrants to access. Even if there is evidence that China has moved away from urban bias in its fiscal structure, as of 2017 the trend line remained steep: on average, moving from a city with 5 million inhabitants to one with 10

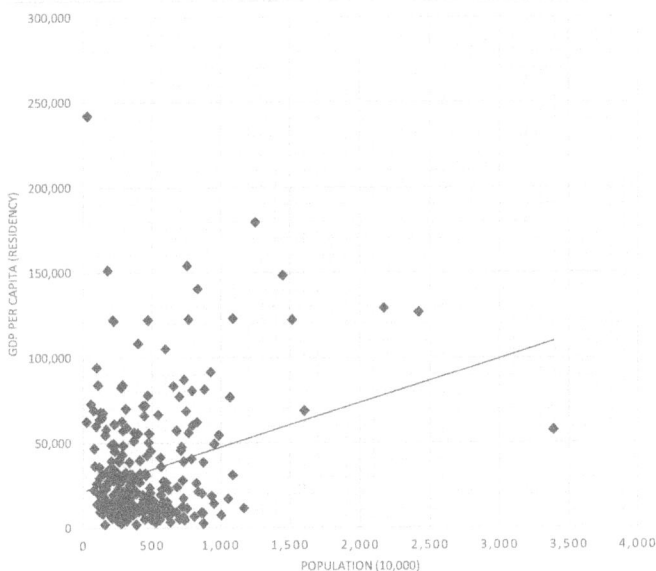

FIGURE 2.9 GDP per capita and city population, 2017.

Source: China Data Online (China City Statistics).

million results in a 38 percent increase in GDP per capita.[90] With this as background, the 2014 National New Urbanization Plan's injunction for population control to become increasingly stringent the larger the city appears in new light. If implemented, the clear implication of the plan is that migrants should be actively denied the possibility of relocating to the wealthiest cities.

As if being relegated to underdeveloped spaces in the national hierarchy were not enough, there is the further problem that social services in these cities are *also* underresourced in comparison to their big city counterparts. As can be seen in figure 2.10, there is a clear positive correlation between city size

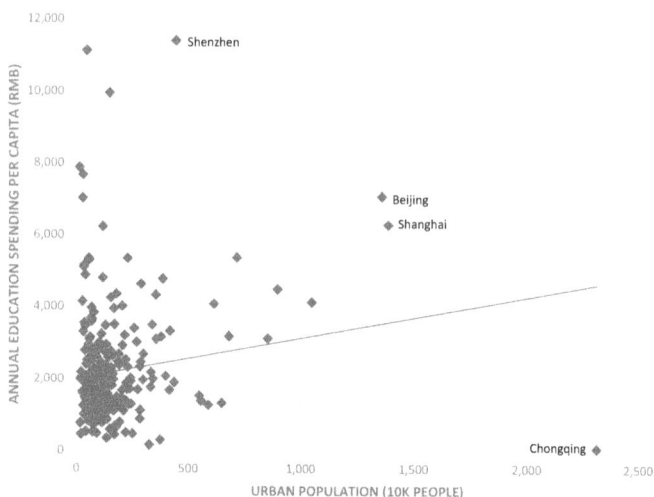

FIGURE 2.10 Education spending in urban China, 2017.
Source: *China Data Online* (China City Statistics).

and annual education spending per capita. Beijing sits well above the line, although it pales in comparison with migration-magnets Dongguan and Shenzhen.[91] If we look specifically at primary school financing, the Beijing municipal government spends 25,793.55 yuan per student per year, 2.7 times that of the national average of 9,557.89.[92] Increased education spending in the megacities cannot be attributed to the higher cost of land, as public schools do not pay for land. Rather, they are able to spend more money to attract better teachers, invest in the hard infrastructure of the schools, and provide a greater diversity of educational experiences.

One way to address this inequality would be to centralize education financing to ensure greater equality in spatial distribution.

Unfortunately, the recent trend has been precisely the opposite: education spending has been increasingly *de*centralized as local governments (i.e., provincial or below) have taken on a larger share of education financing (see figure 2.11). Although I have not been able to secure national education financing data disaggregated at the municipal or district level, the central-local disparity alone suggests widening regional inequality. Indeed, increased regional inequality has been the general trend since fiscal decentralization took off in the 1980s.[93] Central government efforts to date have done little to counter market trends, and wealthier cities continue to be able to offer far superior services.[94]

Although somewhat beyond the purview of this study, the final step in this deeply unequal educational landscape comes

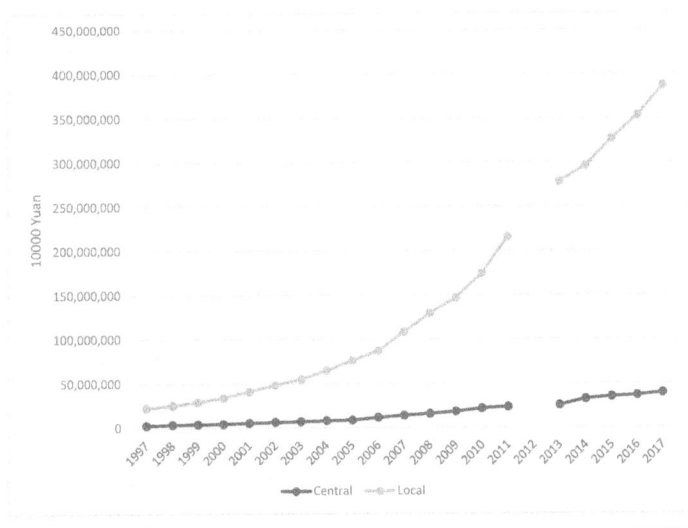

FIGURE 2.11 Central and local education expenditures.

Data for 2012 were unavailable. *Source*: China Statistical Yearbook, assorted years.

with university admissions. As is well known, and hotly debated within China, universities reserve a relatively large number of spots for their local population. This means that applicants applying to universities located in their city of *hukou* registration have a much easier time gaining admission than those applying from elsewhere. The reason this exacerbates educational inequality is because the elite universities are, not coincidentally, in large cities where gaining *hukou* is the most difficult. In 2014 Peking University and Tsinghua University enrolled students from Beijing at per capita rates of 14 and 12.5 times that of students from the rest of the country, respectively. Similarly, Shanghai's prestigious Fudan University and Shanghai Jiaotong University enrolled locals at per capita rates of 21.1 and 64 times that of students from elsewhere.[95] Nor are such disparities restricted to the super-elite institutions: Tianjin University granted admission to locals at a rate 50.8 times that of nonlocals.[96] Even if we focus on admission rates for Beijing and Shanghai residents, cities relatively similar in terms of average wealth and levels of education, we see great disparities. Beijing locals have enrollment rates that are 5.5 times and 10.1 times those of their Shanghainese counterparts at Peking University and Renmin University, respectively. On the other hand, Shanghainese enrollment rates at their local flagships of Fudan University and Jiaotong University are 7.8 and 47.7 times those of people from Beijing. There are of course myriad factors at play here beyond *hukou* status, including family wealth, quality of primary and secondary education, parents' education, and locality preferences, to name a few. Nonetheless, even descriptive statistics are highly suggestive that locality matters significantly.[97] Access to elite tertiary education, a crucial step in locking in class advantages across generations, is thus similarly regulated by the logic of the inverted welfare state.

CONCLUSION

By 2014, the central government had explicitly reoriented its development strategy toward urbanization-driven growth while advocating for the urbanization of people. But as we have seen, the important caveat is that people were to be urbanized in spaces that correspond to their assessed quality. *Just-in-time urbanization* designates the utopian strategies megacities have employed to secure labor in the right qualities and quantities at the right time, in an effort to optimize the population and upgrade the economy. Those excluded from *hukou* membership in the city must submit to a *negative means test* to try to gain access to public schools, in which there is a negative association between need and access. Finally, when situated within China's broader economic geography, I have characterized this regime as the *inverted welfare state*, an arrangement in which the quality of social reproduction one can access corresponds to their existing levels of human capital.

Theoretically, this argument allows us to revisit an earlier debate on market transition and the bases of inequality in postsocialist societies.[98] With the emergence of point-based citizenship and school enrollments, it is apparent that the value of political capital has experienced a relative decline from the rigid exclusion of the Mao era. China has constructed a national labor market, and urban citizenship is relatively porous, as even the best-barricaded cities have sought to admit the right human capitals. But it would be clearly mistaken to conclude that state socialist forms of status hierarchy have disappeared, or are being continually corroded by market forces.[99] Indeed, there is a pernicious interaction of status and market-based inequalities that do not close off human circulation altogether even as they foreclose access to public goods in the cities for the overwhelming majority of nonlocals. In other words, the specific form of market inequality we see in contemporary China is not antagonistic to, but rather presupposes, state socialist inequality. This suggests that even if *hukou* were to be abolished tomorrow, poor people would be released into a market with wildly unequal access to cultural capital accumulation, and China's high levels of educational and economic inequality would likely persist. Status and class must be addressed together, for they are in fact deeply imbricated.

As might be imagined, the state's pursuit of JIT urbanization paired with the political economy of the inverted welfare state has already come at immense social cost. Tens of millions of migrant families have been excluded from social protections in the city—the only place where they can find employment adequate to survival. Those denied access to public schools by the battery of administrative procedures are left with no choice but to turn to the market for meeting their educational needs. A market for migrant education has indeed sprung into existence in Beijing, but it is one that is hardly regulated and fails spectacularly at responding to social need.

3

THE MIGRANT SCHOOL

Concentrated Deprivation

When we have parent-teacher conferences, we tell the parents, "regardless of whether the children's scores are high, our teachers are doing their best." Because the conditions in our school aren't up to speed, teachers don't have teaching materials, and the facilities are insufficient, they have to rely just on their mouth to educate the children.

—Principal Ma, Yinghong School

The essence of the inverted welfare state, detailed at length in the previous chapter, is to extend nominally public goods to those who need them least. In order to secure access to public education in China's wealthiest megacities, nonlocal people must demonstrate their utility to the local state, a utility in which individual labor market value is a crucial metric. But there is another vast segment of urban residents who supply the devalued labor that makes the city run while remaining excluded from all forms of state-subsidized social reproduction, their children relegated to shadow informal schooling. These tens of millions of migrants have been urbanized as labor but not as full human beings, their social reproduction remaining precarious and tied to the vagaries of the market.

Beijing's migrant schools, the privatized organizations that have emerged in all major Chinese cities to respond to the increasing tendency toward family migration, are spaces of *concentrated deprivation*. Anyone who can gain access to the public system will do so, including both students and teachers. The public system hovers over the private, snapping up individuals from the surplus population deemed likely to enhance their test score metrics, while the problem of default collective exclusion remains. Migrant schools are left to serve the least well-prepared, least well-resourced families, and they must do so in an almost totally privatized environment that lacks resources as well, as Principal Ma put it earlier.[1] The precarity experienced by parents in the labor and housing markets is refracted into the schools, resulting in astonishingly high levels of student turnover. Social entropy is therefore institutionalized in the migrant school, with profound consequences for the pedagogical environment. Civil society organizations have intervened in some cases to provide financial and other forms of support. While these efforts are meaningful in individual cases, they remain a drop in an ocean of service denial. With parents tethered to the city as labor but excluded as full people, their social reproduction needs are left to the whims of a barely regulated market and a capricious urban state.

PRODUCING INFORMAL EDUCATION

The emergence of the migrant school must be situated within the changing regimes of accumulation and migration described in the previous chapter. As noted, in the early twenty-first century there was an increased trend for migrants to stay in cities longer and to migrate as a family.[2] One consequence was that the number of "brought-along children" (*suiqian zinü* 随迁子女) increased rapidly. Although largely excluded from secondary and tertiary education in the cities (particularly the largest, wealthiest cities), the general increase in family migration in this period of time resulted in increasing demands from nonlocals for compulsory schooling (grades 1–9) in their receiving areas (see figure 3.1).

Growth in the number of migrant children in cities occurred within a context of broader national education reform. Following a 1985 central government reform, schools of all kind came to be subject to greater market pressures, and fully private

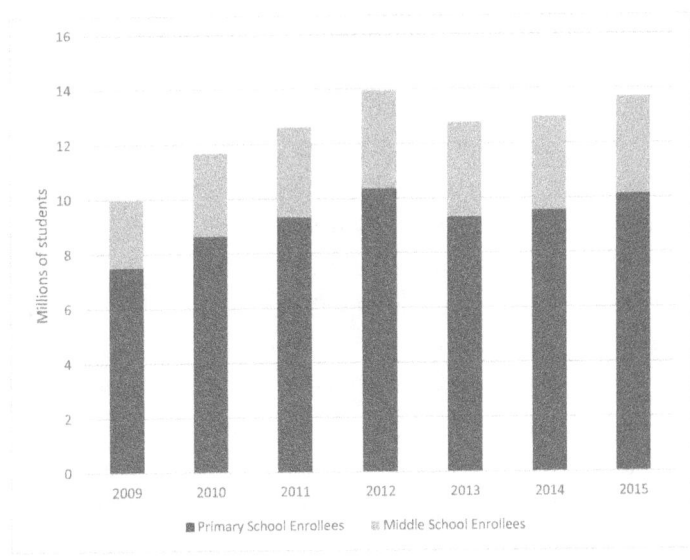

FIGURE 3.1 Migrant children's enrollment in compulsory education.

Source: Dongping Yang, Hongyu Qin, and Jiayu Wei, eds., *Zhongguo Liudong Ertong Jiaoyu Fazhan Baogao (2016)* (Beijing: Shehui kexue wenxian chubanshe, 2016), 14.

schools also reemerged.[3] In urban areas, primary schooling had largely been administered and financed by work units (*danwei* 单位) in the Mao era, but that responsibility was increasingly shifted to district governments.[4] While schools were given greater autonomy to diversify their revenue streams, including charging various fees, reform often forced local governments and school administrators to find creative ways to fund education.[5] Fiscal decentralization in the 1980s was followed by a degree of recentralization in 1994. But local governments' mandates to provide compulsory education did not come with increased ability to levy taxes, and central government redistribution has remained minimal for most localities. With this fiscal backdrop, it should be of little surprise that local governments in receiving areas were unenthusiastic about footing the bill for migrant children, a group to which they had no legal obligation to provide education. And yet, cities certainly wanted migrant parents to continue to provide low-cost labor.

Just as rural-urban migration was really taking off in the 1990s, the central government created a seeming escape from this dilemma: fully privatized schooling. So-called community-operated (*minban* 民办) schools received official backing in the State Council's 1993 Program for China's Educational Reform and Development and further specification in the *Minban* Education Promotion Law of 2002. Within the context of a general increase in private school enrollments in the 1990s and 2000s,[6] the approach of leaving migrants' educational needs to the market had received the center's stamp of approval. Thus the migrant school was born, a privatized institution to serve those who had been excluded from public education in the cities. These schools quickly gained notoriety for being poorly managed, severely underresourced, and generally unable to provide decent education.[7] Given that migrant schools have been shown to have a significant negative effect on educational outcomes, with students generally faring even worse than in underresourced public rural schools, many scholars have suggested that they would likely enhance social and economic inequality.[8] At a period of time that saw increasing educational inequality in general, indicators abounded that children of working-class migrants were falling further behind.[9]

It is, however, worth noting that migrant children are not categorically excluded from public schools in receiving areas; rather, they are not *guaranteed* access. As detailed in the previous chapter, official central policy since 2001 has been to place a majority of migrant children in public schools, with receiving areas shouldering the majority of the associated costs. After more than a decade of central government exhortations to increase migrant access to urban public schools, the Minister of Education announced in 2014 that more than 80 percent of migrant children nationwide were enrolled in public schools.[10] This number is highly suspect for a number of reasons, notably that the most marginalized individuals and schools (including unregistered ones) are the least likely to be counted. Even assuming this estimate is wildly off the mark, it is probable that a majority of migrant children are indeed enrolled in public schools. But as we have already seen, the category of "nonlocal" is highly heterogenous—enrollment numbers in the aggregate say nothing about variation based on class, place of residence, or any other of a number of factors that I have already demonstrated to be of critical importance.

Students in migrant schools by no means represent the modal experience. The perspective presented here—that of the excluded—reveals critical insights into the methods of population management more broadly, depicting how deprivation is concentrated in the space of Beijing's migrant schools and the devasting social and educational implications of this arrangement.

SCARCE RESOURCES

Migrant schools are privatized institutions that are largely or entirely dependent on tuition to fund their operations. There is significant variation, even within Beijing, since some schools are unlicensed and completely tuition dependent whereas others receive some subsidies from the state or foundations. But even Zhifan School, the high-end case in my study, was significantly underresourced when compared to its public counterparts.

The issue of tuition dependence was particularly pressing at Yinghong, the low-end school I studied. The associate principal of the school talked about how their inability to register precluded it from receiving any state subsidies: "[aside from tuition] we don't have anything. . . . As far as the government is concerned, there's never been any [support]. . . . Since 2001, none of the migrant schools here have been licensed. . . . If they're licensed they might get some small subsidies, the government might give some portion of the student's tuition, including heating fees. But in our school, we completely depend on ourselves."[11] In fact, Yinghong had received a contribution from the government, but it was so minimal as to only further incense one teacher: "[Yinghong] has been here for nine years, and we haven't received one penny of government subsidy. The only thing we've gotten from the government was three fire extinguishers."[12] Although many other cities, notably Shanghai, have mobilized public resources to support private migrant schools, that has not been the case in Beijing.[13]

This market orientation is highly problematic, for as we saw in the previous chapter, the children who end up in migrant schools are likely to come from households with the least economic and cultural capital. Teacher Xu from Yinghong explained it thus: "[Parents] of our students rarely have regular jobs. Usually they're doing some kind of business, like selling vegetables, running a breakfast stand, selling things in the morning market, or selling other things in market stalls. There are very few with 9–5 jobs."[14] The consequence is that tuition was quite low, with schools in Beijing typically charging from 500 to 1,000 yuan per semester during the early to mid-2010s.[15] This was not an inconsiderable sum for many informal and poorly paid workers, but it was still far less than they would have to pay to get into public school, if that option even existed.

The majority of schools in Beijing often face intense market pressures, and owners tend to prioritize profit over pedagogy (the foundation-supported schools are somewhat different, an issue to which I will return). Teacher Guo from Yinghong opened up about a school where she had previously worked: "I feel like they just saw the school as a business. If you obey him [the boss] then you're fine, it doesn't matter if you're good or bad at teaching, you just need to obey."[16] And market competition between schools had often been quite fierce, resulting in a variety of unsavory business practices, a zero-sum struggle in which one school's loss could be another's gain. Teacher Lin explained how Yinghong had attracted more students (and their tuition) when neighboring schools encountered difficulties: "Last year we didn't have as many people. But then a few schools in this area went out of business, they were poorly run. When the school goes under, the students need to find somewhere to continue their studies."[17] Given migrant schools' position in the education market, they were generally not in a position to make major investments in their workers or facilities.

A final issue that restricted schools' access to resources, certainly more pressing in Beijing than in other megacities, had to do with their position of legal uncertainty. Many dozens of unlicensed schools in Beijing had no legal right to operate. In addition to shutting them out of credit markets, it also meant that the government could close their operations with no legal proceedings and without having to pay the owners any compensation. An NGO officer in Beijing compared local conditions with the somewhat more regulated education market in Guangzhou: "In Guangzhou, people are willing to invest and they can charge higher tuition. In Beijing, people think it's too risky to invest much, they don't care if the [school's] conditions are poor."[18]

Decrepit Physical Plant

This extreme dearth of financial resources manifested in the poor state of many migrant schools' physical plant. This was the thing that immediately struck me when I first walked into Shusheng School back in 2011: in the midst of the fabulous wealth of Beijing, children were going to school in deplorable conditions. Neither Yinghong nor Shusheng had indoor plumbing or central heat. Physical education and playground facilities were similarly degraded. Teacher Xu from Yinghong couldn't help but hide her discomfort as she detailed her school's poor conditions: "My son goes to school here, every day he comes in with clean clothes. But after one day at school, you can see the environment here, by evening when we go home it's completely dirty. There isn't a playground worth the name [see figure 3.2],

FIGURE 3.2 The playground at Yinghong School.
Photo by the author.

their so-called playing is just running around in this space."[19] Shusheng's facilities were only marginally better, with a somewhat more even, albeit smaller, concrete slab, a ping-pong table, and a small play structure. The massive pile of coal heaped in the schoolyard (see figure 3.3) that I saw children playing in captured two aspects of the school's deprivation: lack of central heat and lack of adequate play facilities.

The poor conditions, particularly in Yinghong and Shusheng, were not just a nuisance but also had a direct impact on teachers' work and student learning. Teacher Zhou from Yinghong depicted a tragic scene of students fighting the elements during exams: "Public schools get subsidies every year from the government for their facilities. . . . In our school, when it rains a lot outside, it also rains a lot in the classroom. The roof is full

FIGURE 3.3 Children in the yard at Shusheng.

Photo by the author.

of holes. . . . Two days ago was the final exam, and the floor was covered with water. All of their exams got soaked . . . some even took an umbrella and used books to block the water, this is how they took their exams. Our facilities cannot compare with public schools."[20]

Even when it was not raining, the elements could present a major challenge. My field notes from a December visit to Yinghong reflected on the health concerns of teaching in extremely cold classrooms: "I taught Zhang Xin's English class, which was 40 minutes. In a class of about 30–35 students, there was almost continuous coughing for the entire class."[21] At the beginning and end of the school year, heat presented yet another obstacle to teachers and students. Teacher Xu complained, "We have asbestos tiles, if it's 35, 36 degrees [95–98° F] in the summer, when we come in the morning it's pretty cool. But by afternoon, you just can't stand it. After baking in the sun, this room is like a steamer, it's extremely hot."[22] It is also noteworthy that the tiles' being made of asbestos was not part of her complaint.[23]

Narrow Pedagogy

A common refrain among teachers, more so even than for parents, was that their school was unable to provide adequate classes or other experiences in nonacademic subjects. Teacher Wang from Yinghong exemplified this concern:

> Our school doesn't even have a sports field. What are we supposed to tell these kids who love to play? At least they should be able to have a happy and enriching childhood, there are just too many things they lack. And we don't have enough teachers, there is only math, Chinese, and foreign languages, there's no arts. Some children are really good at singing and dancing, but [their talents] can't be discovered. Their parents don't have the resources to send them to art school. A lot of them have natural talents in the arts, but they've been buried. A lot of schools are like this.[24]

Teacher Xu, also from Yinghong, similarly worried about how the school's lack of resources would impact student development: "[Public schools] frequently organize free field trips for students. When they come back, they do journal entries, they turn their observations into new knowledge. But this kind of school like ours has never had a field trip. The only things in our students' brains are Chinese, math, and English. Their perspective is extremely narrow."[25]

Conditions at Zhifan were somewhat better, and it had hired one music teacher and one art teacher. But with more than nine hundred students in the school,[26] the music teacher still felt overburdened and believed that she could not adequately address the students' needs: "Actually, I think that the reason teachers in migrant schools are [overworked] like this, at the end of the day, it's because of money. If there were more money, they could hire. . . . I wouldn't have to teach music to the entire school. If there were two people, I could do a thorough job preparing for class. With just one person, sometimes they are in a bad state and they still have to persist. Of course it has to do with money."[27] The meager arts offerings at Zhifan, the high-end migrant school in my study, however, paled in comparison to the public Xingfu School in central-western Beijing. The principal described the school as "one of the top ten" in the district, and she ticked off the many available activities: "The students have a wind instrument band, one of your American jazz bands, a Latin band. We also have dance troupes. Our chorus is quite excellent. There are the photography and painting associations. We also have a drumming troupe, and a Western wind instrument band."[28]

MOBILITY AMONG TEACHERS AND STUDENTS

The concentrated deprivation in migrant schools was clearly reflected in their exploitative labor practices. Not all school employees were as biting in their critique as Teacher Lin from Yinghong, but his complaints about overwork were nearly universal among Beijing's migrant schoolteachers:

> To put it crudely, the boss of a private school is a capitalist, they're in it for the money. They think that in the education industry, they employ teachers and they absolutely won't let you be too

relaxed. . . . The workload is quite heavy; it's like this everywhere in China. Of course, some bosses are concerned with education, but the overwhelming majority of private schools are there to earn money. Public schoolteachers' workload is at least half [of ours], because public school managers won't be too strict. Private school bosses are savage.[29]

I will extensively detail teachers' perspectives on work in chapter 6. But this highly exploitative work environment is relevant here in that it made it extremely difficult for schools to maintain a qualified workforce. This is by no means to question the persistence and creativity of many teachers who labored under seemingly impossible conditions. Nonetheless, deep structural problems prevented migrant schools from stabilizing a quality workforce.

Lack of preparation was endemic among migrant schoolteachers. On my first visit to Shusheng, the principal presented an overview of the school in which she said that her teachers "don't get as much training as in public schools."[30] At Yinghong, Teacher Wang confirmed that he had received no formal training before starting the job:

EF: Did you have any training when you arrived?
WANG: No. I had worked [in a school] before, a relative of mine is a school principal, sometimes I would go and help out by substituting. I did that for about a month, back in my hometown. . . . You just learn gradually, nobody teaches you. Other teachers are quite busy, they don't have any time to teach you. So you see if you can adapt to the environment.[31]

The first time I taught a class myself, I witnessed this lack of preparation in a visceral manner. When the principal of Shusheng asked if I would teach an English class, I enthusiastically agreed, eager to witness in-class dynamics from the teacher's perspective. Just before the class, I met with the instructor, a reserved woman in her early twenties from remote western China. After first engaging her in English, it quickly became apparent she did not actually speak the language, and I awkwardly switched back to Chinese. My efforts to question her on the course materials and students' level of preparedness elicited no response—she eventually handed me a tattered English textbook and told me I could use it. When I asked how much of the textbook they had already covered, she told me to do "whatever" (*suibian* 随便). I was then thrust in front of a classroom of more than forty unruly six-year-olds. Suffice it to say that I was badly humbled in my effort to impart any English language skills. I was a bit taken aback by the encounter, but it was a reasonably good indicator of most migrant schools' ability to deliver decent English language instruction.[32]

Since migrant schools in Beijing were so chronically under-resourced, teachers who had the ability to leave generally would do so. This could mean moving on to a more lucrative position in a different industry, as frequently happened with college-educated teachers who came to migrant schools motivated by altruism. Teacher Wang from Yinghong was just such a case. He grew up as a "left-behind" child, raised by his grandparents in the countryside while his parents bounced around the country working a series of jobs. I met him in 2012 shortly after he started working at the school. Despite his sincere commitment to the social mission, he left after two years for a job designing an app. I reconnected with him three months after he had started his new job, and his explanation of his decision was simple: "Well, [I switched jobs] because at the time, I had been there for two years, and I was getting older. So I started to have more pressure in life. Because in migrant schools, the salary is very, very low. It is maybe just enough to support myself. So I looked for something with a higher salary."[33] It was so common as to be expected that teachers who had more lucrative options working in other industries would stay in the schools for only a short stint.

A similarly damaging dynamic was public schools pilfering the best teachers from migrant schools. For totally understandable reasons, teachers who had the opportunity would want to move to public schools, where they would enjoy higher salaries and status, better job security and benefits, and lower workloads.[34] Indeed, there were quite a few teachers in migrant schools with college degrees and official licensing (even if they were proportionally small), and with a good enough track record of improving student test scores, they could be snapped up. Teacher Guo, an accredited graduate from a teacher training college, talked about her wish to leave Yinghong: "Those of us teachers who are licensed, usually we want to go to public schools, but it's pretty difficult. Getting a job is hard now, the industry is saturated. So our only choice is to come to this kind of school."[35] The implications of this were profound, since migrant schools had immense difficulty retaining their most promising young teachers. As Mr. Li from a local education NGO put it, "Young people generally think of [working in a migrant school] as a springboard, it's quite dangerous. As soon as they find another job, they'll leave."[36]

The pull of the public system was not limited to teachers. Those students with the best test scores could also be recruited away from migrant schools.[37] Although in the previous chapter I detailed the seemingly impartial bureaucratic procedures by which admission to public school was governed, the reality is that there have always been informal channels for certain people. Student test scores are a key metric by which public schools are assessed, which then creates an incentive to admit students with a proven track record. Principle Ma from Yinghong explained how this dynamic created immense difficulties for migrant schools in retaining high performing students: "The kind of students we get in this kind of school, there are very few good ones. Basically, it's just those who can't get into public schools. As long as the student is good in school, and the parents have the [financial] ability, or they know someone, they'll transfer right away. So we work hard at educating this child, and if their scores go up one day, then they'll go to a public school."[38] Here we see how migrant children with high scores gain access to the public, while migrant schools are there to absorb everyone else.

For high-achieving migrant children from families that could not pay the requisite bribes to get into urban public schools, returning home was also an option. If students had any ambition of one day attending university in China (going abroad was beyond the consideration of any families I encountered in my fieldwork), going to the village before the end of middle school was almost a necessity.[39] The high school entrance exam (*zhongkao* 中考) differs by locality, which means that students would need to attend at least some portion of middle school in their *hukou*-designated hometown in order to have a chance of one day going on to university. Students who do poorly on the *zhongkao* are put on the nonacademic track, and their chances for upward social mobility dim accordingly.[40] Principal Ma recalled how one of their students chose to return home: "One of the best children we've had was here from first until fifth grade. After returning to her hometown in Shaanxi, she had the top scores for all eight classes in her grade."[41] While the principal clearly took some pride in the student's subsequent success, it also was an indicator that the best students were looking for exit options. Certainly, very few students who stayed in migrant schools went on to a university education. Song Yingquan tracked 1,866 students in fifty different migrant schools in Beijing from their second year in middle school and made a startling finding: only 6 percent of students were admitted to a university, 34 percent lower than the general population.[42] In a social environment were educational advancement and self-worth are closely linked, those trapped in the migrant school would seem likely to internalize a sense of inferiority.[43]

NONPROFIT SCHOOLS, NGOS, AND FOUNDATIONS

China's civil society has always operated within tightly regulated constraints. Nonetheless, migrant-focused NGOs have been able to survive and even prosper if they can secure support from local government.[44] In a few cases in Beijing, migrant schools' deprivation was somewhat ameliorated by support from foundations or NGOs. School administrators and teachers referred to these kinds of schools as "public interest" (*gongyixing* 公益性) or "nonprofit" (*feiyingli* 非盈利) to differentiate them from the profit-oriented outfits described earlier. Although such schools still charged tuition, they were generally able to provide much better conditions for their students than was the case at Shusheng or Yinghong. Among the schools I studied, Zhifan School (the high-end case) was considered "public interest."

Zhifan was established in 2001, after which it faced frequent government harassment, demolition and relocation orders, and severe financial difficulty. However, it was officially licensed in 2004, and within a few years the school's fortunes had improved dramatically. In 2007 Zhifan received major gifts from a corporation and local foundation, totaling more than 2.7 million yuan that year alone. By 2011, the school claimed to have raised a total of 7 million yuan via donations.[45]

These donations were critical in allowing Zhifan to provide a better learning environment than was possible at Shusheng or Yinghong and to be less tuition-dependent. School administrators said that the 700 yuan semester tuition covered only a third of the school's expenses, with the remaining two-thirds coming from external support. Teacher Gu suggested that the school maintained a major advantage over the more commercially oriented schools: "Before I was at a private school. It was started by a boss. It was quite different in a number of ways. Because it was started by an individual, so everything was done in consideration of his personal interests. This school [Zhifan], as far as the students or pedagogy is concerned, it's not that different from a public school."[46] Teacher Li noted, "We lose a lot of money every year, we're a public interest school, so we need to think of various ways to get investment. . . . The government contributes only 70 yuan per student per semester. It's far too little."[47]

Whether Zhifan was indeed up to the standards of an average public school in Beijing is debatable, but it was certainly an outlier among migrant schools. External financial support allowed the school to provide facilities that Shusheng and Yinghong lacked, including a computer lab, indoor plumbing, and a large outdoor playground and track. As noted before, the school had hired one music teacher and one art teacher, and even though these teachers were overburdened, they were able to provide students with regular nonacademic forms of learning and expression. These features were widely understood to be quite exceptional, and Zhifan received a steady stream of official awards, positive evaluations in the media, and visits from domestic and foreign scholars.

While few if any migrant schools in Beijing could match Zhifan's fundraising prowess, many schools had received some civil society support. Shusheng had received an initial donation from a local NGO, which was critical in covering their startup costs. Although they had not succeeded in getting additional large grants, the school would occasionally have recent college graduates placed there as teachers through Teach Future China (*wei zhongguo er jiao* 为中国而教), a program similar to Teach for America. Yinghong received support from an NGO that occasionally dispatched young people, typically local college students, to conduct music, arts, or athletics programs. Principal Ma talked about the role that these volunteers played at Yinghong: "These [sports and arts] activities really allow children to increase their knowledge and to enrich their extracurricular activities. These are things that our school can't do. Each day we're busy teaching the core subjects, in dealing with parents we need to think about test scores. So we overlook these [extracurricular activities]. These volunteers help to make up for this shortcoming."[48] There is nothing objectionable about these programs, and indeed, they were quite popular among students, teachers, and parents. But they also served to highlight the structural deprivation of migrant schools: programs that were provided regularly and as a matter of course in the public system were occasional affairs in these schools. Given the fickleness of foundations, not to mention the political vagaries of China's civil society, migrant schools could not depend on this kind of support in long-term planning.

CONCLUSION

As the option of last resort for those deemed surplus by the state, migrant schools exhibit *concentrated deprivation*, providing almost fully marketized education to those with the fewest resources. The results are predictably bad, with students subjected to decrepit physical plants, underprepared teachers, and a pedagogy narrowly focused on test scores. Teachers and students who have the opportunity to move to public schools inevitably do so, leaving behind the least well-prepared and least well-resourced. Government subsidies and support from civil society play a negligible role in ameliorating these conditions for most migrant schools. There is therefore a grain of truth in the Beijing municipal government's claim during the 2011 mass demolitions that these schools are "not up to standard." But these woefully underresourced schools are in fact a problem of the state's own creation.

How do families cope with such challenging conditions? As we have seen, exit from the school is one common approach. And yet, many families would simply not be able to survive if they returned home, since they could not forgo the opportunities of the urban labor market. In the next chapter we will approach the problem of education directly from the perspective of these parents, and in so doing elucidate the deleterious consequences of their inclusion and indeed *tethering* to the city as workers paired with ongoing repulsion in the realm of social reproduction.

4

RENDERED SURPLUS

Parents Navigate "Population Control Via Education"

Last year I heard that all workers without a formal labor contract would be cleared from Beijing. This is what I heard, I don't know if it's true or not.

—Migrant from Sichuan

The wage-labor relation suffuses the spaces of nonwaged everyday life.

—Tithi Bhattacharya

By 2014, "population control via education" was a central element in urban China's population management regime. In concert with other forms of expulsionary pressure directed at the workplace and housing, this series of measures appeared to have produced the desired effect. As can be seen in figure 4.1, an already falling population growth rate fell further still after 2014. In 2015, Beijing Party Secretary Guo Jinlong bragged about the accomplishment, revealing the city's quota-driven approach: "[in 2014] Beijing was able to clear out a section of the population, reaching our annual population control target."[1] Certainly the general trajectory of population

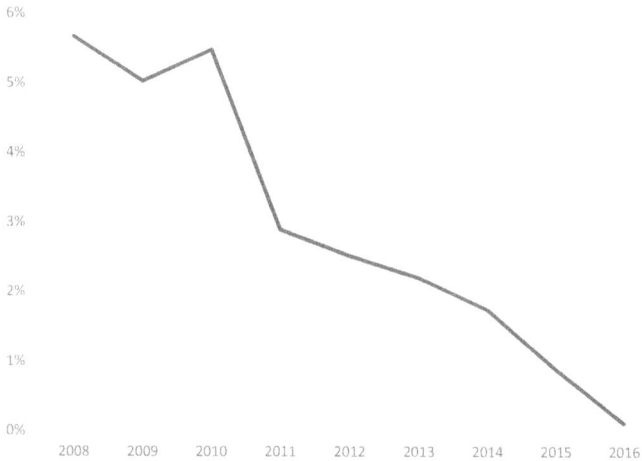

FIGURE 4.1 Population growth rate, Beijing.

Source: Beijing Tongji Nianjian, 2017.

growth was already declining, given the extremely low birth rate among locals, rapidly increasing cost of living, and expanded economic opportunities in interior cities over the course of the 2000s and 2010s. Nonetheless, by the end of 2017, Beijing's total population was falling in absolute terms, down 22,000 from a year earlier.[2] Then, in 2017–18, the city lost an astonishing 165,000 residents.[3] The number of nonlocal children who were able to enroll in first grade dropped by 18,000 between 2013 and 2014. The decline among children enrolled in migrant schools was similarly precipitous; one study estimated that the city's total dropped from 100,000 to 50,000 between 2014 and 2018.[4] While I am unable to tease out how much of the population decline was due to shifts in education policy, it certainly played a significant role.

What were the concrete mechanisms of "population control via education," and how did migrant families experience this intensification of expulsionary pressure? Institutionalization of degraded education for those children enrolled in migrant schools derives not simply from parents' status as nonlocal *hukou* holders but also from their class position, broadly conceived. As parents attempted to enroll their children in public schools, these efforts were confounded by their labor market position and access to housing, increasingly so from 2014. A related but distinct issue is the question of enrolling children born in violation of birth control policies. Parents were forced to weigh various options between trying to stay in Beijing, sending their children to the countryside, or potentially sending them further into the urban periphery in neighboring Hebei. The emotional costs that this byzantine and deeply unequal system produced for migrant families were severe.

The empirical evidence here shows that the urban state is pushing out groups of people that are making critical contributions to the economy, either via waged or informal labor. Migrant families are *rendered* surplus as a result of concrete decisions taken by state actors, which then undermines their ability to secure social reproduction in the location where they work. The problem is not that these migrants are of no utility to capital *in general*, but rather that they do not provide a kind of labor that comports with the state's vision for economic upgrading.

Given that I contacted parents via migrant schools, the data presented here are largely from the perspective of those who have been shut out of the public system. This is by no means the only valid perspective from which to study education, social services, or the urbanization process more broadly. It does, however, give clear insight into who is excluded from subsidized social reproduction and why, as well as the social consequences of this particular approach to managing human movement. Most of the interview data here come specifically from parents with children enrolled at Shusheng School, the mid-tier primary school I studied in eastern Beijing's Liwanzhuang. Some of these parents had older children who had graduated from Shusheng and been accepted to public middle school, a trajectory that was not unusual prior to 2014. In what follows, I detail the devastating consequences of the intensifying rupture between the spaces of work and life, as manifested in parents' attempts to navigate the constantly shifting and highly unequal bureaucratic terrain.

ACCESSING SCHOOLING OUT OF PLAN

I have already detailed the arcane bureaucratic procedures by which urban governments determine which children without local *hukou* will be admitted to public schools. As that account of the formal process made apparent, there is no categorical ban on migrants accessing these schools. Rather, the state has established an array of metrics, oriented largely but not exclusively to parents' perceived labor market value, which determines their children's ability to gain admission. Working-class and precarious migrants in Beijing encounter obstacles, both formal and informal, that systematically exclude their children from public education.

Informal Work, Informal Schooling

While conducting fieldwork in the summer of 2014, the significance of parents' labor market position for their children's education opportunities arose as one of the most widespread and intractable problems. Even those migrants who had enjoyed relative economic success in the informal labor market faced increasingly insurmountable obstacles. This was made apparent one June afternoon when Wu Ping, an NGO researcher, and I met with a family from Shandong Province at their home, about a ten-minute walk from Shusheng School. Once inside the large gate guarding their house, we passed through a small outdoor area and then into a large, bright living room with high ceilings. The house was clean, with new-looking tile floors, a decent sized kitchen off to the side, and a large bedroom in the back. This was the nicest accommodation I had seen in Liwan-zhuang. The parents of three were very engaging and offered us tea, lychee, and cigarettes throughout the interview. Although housing conditions are just one indicator of a family's class position, I anticipated that this family was in a "best case" scenario.

Mr. Fan and Ms. Xu had been in Beijing for twenty years, having moved to the capital as teenagers. They came from the same town in Shandong but were first introduced by former classmates after they moved to the city. Although they came from a poor village where their families had little land, they had encountered modest economic success in Beijing. After spending years in factories and on construction sites doing metalwork, Mr. Fan eventually opened a home renovation business, while Ms. Xu had engaged in various small-scale entrepreneurial activities such as running a small supermarket.[5] Although they had moved around the city some in their youth, they had been in Liwanzhuang for nine years. This was a family that had contributed to and seemingly benefited from Beijing's economic transformation, and they were committed to staying in the city they had called home for more than half their lives.

Despite their relative material comfort, the parents' informal work would likely prove a decisive shortcoming in the increasingly restrictive school admissions environment. As noted in the previous chapter, one of the "five permits" required for nonlocal admission to public school is a Beijing labor contract. Indeed, local labor contracts are a requirement nationwide. In 2014, education departments in Beijing increasingly began demanding proof of payment into local social insurance plans, despite the fact that this was not stipulated as a "five permits" requirement. But as Ms. Xu revealed, these demands essentially excluded their children from public schools:

> We've been self-employed [*getihu* 个体户] all along, we've never had a [formal] job [*shangban* 上班]. And we don't want to have a job, because we're used to doing our own business. With a job, you can't earn enough money. So without a job, there's no company to provide us with social insurance, so we've never had social insurance. . . . They [the Education Department] require a labor contract, and we don't have a contract. So these permits are the hardest to get.[6]

Dong Huanli, a mother of two from Hebei Province, related a similar challenge. Her family was not as well off as Mr. Fan and Ms. Xu, with her husband able to secure only very part-time informal work. Their primary source of income was from running a small convenience store in Liwanzhuang. With her daughter about to graduate from Shusheng, and almost certainly to be excluded from public middle school, their informality would likely force them out of the city:

> DH: The two of us . . . neither of us can get a labor contract! Where can we go to get one? We also don't have that . . .

what's it called? A business license [for their convenience store]. People from the factory won't issue a labor contract. If you don't have a job here . . . so we can't overcome this.

EF: What does your husband do for work?

DH: He just does odd jobs [*da linggong* 打零工]. For instance, today he'll do this, then someone will call and tell him there's a job and he'll go do it . . . if there's no work, he'll stay here and look after the store.

EF: So the reason you're going back [to your hometown] is because it'll be hard to get your daughter into middle school?

DH: Yeah, there's no hope. We're workers [*dagong* 打工], if someone had a labor permit then there would be a possibility. But we don't have a labor permit, and nobody is going to just give us one![7]

Here we see Ms. Dong implying that "people from the factory" won't issue a fake labor contract. Indeed, parents often considered finding fake forms of documentation as a means of overcoming administrative obstacles. While forged papers have long allowed migrants greater possibilities to stay in the cities, there was evidence that the government had begun making greater efforts to regulate such practices. One indicator of increasing enforcement in Beijing came with the widely covered case of the "fake documents mother," Cao Haili.[8] After failing to secure some of the required "five permits," Cao attempted to use fake documents, at the time a widespread practice among migrants. Presumably in an effort to make an example of her, the authorities arrested Cao, who then delivered a tearful confession in court, photos of which were prominently displayed in media reports. While informal workers in Beijing have continued to try to utilize fake documents to gain access to services, this event suggested a tightening of control.

Of course, many migrant parents do work in the formal sector, which allows them to produce legitimate labor contracts and increases the likelihood of accessing social insurance (while certainly not guaranteeing it). But as has been widely reported in the literature, migrants are likely to be employed in the most unstable forms of employment, including temporary and dispatch positions.[9] And by all indicators, the proportion of migrant workers in informal settings has been increasing. Nationwide, the number of migrants with labor contracts fell over the course of the early 2010s, decreasing from 42.8 percent in 2009 to just 35.1 percent in 2016.[10]

Furthermore, the economic geography of the city tends to funnel poor migrants into informal labor. Upon arrival in Beijing, most people cannot afford to pay market price for rentals in the urban core, and they are excluded from all publicly subsidized housing, be it centrally located or otherwise. With economic upgrading, the city has sought to move labor-intensive industries further out of the urban core. As a result, both the housing and labor markets tend to drive migrants toward the periphery, into the informality of the urban villages (*chengzhongcun* 城中村). Feng Huai, a mother from Henan living in Liwanzhuang, explained: "When I came to Liwanzhuang [five years prior], there was nothing, it was a farming village, totally decrepit. There was nothing, in this place you felt like there was no work, no factories."[11] She had previously had a formal job working as a meeting attendant, serving drinks and cleaning up for a foreign company in Wangjing, a prosperous neighborhood in northeastern Beijing. But when her husband's company was relocated to Liwanzhuang, she had to leave her job. With no other formal labor market opportunities available, she decided instead to open a small store.

Bribes

In addition to formalized methods of exclusion, nonlocals widely understood that they would need social connections or the ability to pay large bribes in order to get their children into public schools. As mentioned in chapter 2, parents I interviewed believed they would need to pay bribes of 20,000–100,000 yuan in order to access public schools. It should be noted that my sample is biased in that nearly all of my informants had their children enrolled in migrant schools. Nonetheless, the understanding among my informants was so uniform as to suggest practical validity—even if the bribes were not absolutely necessary, the universal belief that they would be required excluded those who could not afford to pay.

Teacher Xu Huina from Yinghong confided in me about her desire to register her child, currently enrolled in Yinghong's preschool, in public school. Between having her husband living in a different province and her incredibly busy work schedule, she felt helpless to supplement the basic education he would receive in a migrant school. Still, the required bribes posed a potentially insurmountable obstacle:

XH: Sometimes I feel depressed. I'm really busy and I live apart from my husband. He's in Inner Mongolia, and I'm taking care of our child alone. I'm trying various methods, but I don't think I can help him develop his language, math, and English. For him to develop comprehensively he should go to a public school. He's still young, he's enrolled in preschool here, but when he starts first grade I want him to go to a public school.

EF: Is that possible?

xʜ: You need to spend money and find some personal connection. There's a one-time payment of at least 20,000. According to government regulations, they shouldn't take this money.

With a monthly wage of just 1,400 yuan at the time, 20,000 yuan was equivalent to the entirety of more than fourteen months of wages for her.

Teacher Xu was correct in her assessment that these bribes were illegal, but they nonetheless remained widespread. Urban public schools had long charged migrants an educational surcharge (*jie du fei* 借读费) in order to pad their budgets. According to a January 1, 2009, notification from the State Council, these fees were to be canceled—a step that received official legal backing with a decision from the Ministry of Education at the end of 2010. Nonetheless, public schools continued to find ways to extract fees from nonlocals through other means, as revealed in an interview with a principal from a public school in Beijing:

ᴘʀɪɴᴄɪᴘᴀʟ: China doesn't have [educational inequality] anymore. We use catchment-based enrollment now; we're no longer divided into rich people districts and poor people districts. This kind of school is free for both locals and those from outside Beijing.

ᴇғ: So there are no fees?

ᴘʀɪɴᴄɪᴘᴀʟ: That's right. But they can voluntarily make an educational donation [*juanzi zhuxue kuan* 捐资助学款] to the state.[12]

She did not explain what would happen if parents refused to make such voluntary donations, nor how large these donations were.

The persistence of under the table payments was likely due to school officials' desire for self-enrichment, but also to the reality that nonlocals are not adequately accounted for in education budgeting. In some regions of the country, education officials recognized that "education donations" were simply a vehicle for corruption, and took some steps to curb the practice.[13] Nonetheless, the practice remained widespread in Beijing, and the effect was to provide yet another obstacle to working-class migrants securing quality public education in the city.

Exclusion of Surplus Children

In my visits to migrant schools, I quickly found them to have a preponderance of "surplus children" (*chaoshengzi* 超生子), or those born in violation of China's notorious birth control policies. If parents are unable to pay the fines levied for unauthorized births, which vary widely by region, their children will be left with no *hukou* of *any* kind, either in their hometown or the receiving area.[14] Even in cities where public school access is relatively unrestricted, students will have to produce *hukou* (even of the nonlocal variety) in order to enroll. These children are "surplus" because they are, by dint of the conditions of their birth, excluded from state-subsidized public schooling, condemned to a shadow system of informal life. It is then of little surprise that they are severely overrepresented in migrant schools.

This overrepresentation of surplus children enrolled in informal schools is a general phenomenon, appearing not just in Beijing but around the country. Nor is it a marginal issue: according to the 2010 census, China had 13 million people without *hukou*.[15] A migrant school principal in Guangzhou, a city that admits a smaller percentage of migrants to public schools than does Beijing, discussed the problem: "China has a lot of illegal births, [and] these surplus children don't have *hukou*. China is a household registration country; the first thing all public schools require is household registration. . . . Because we private schools are unregulated, we can accept students without household registration. . . . In private schools, there might be twenty or thirty students out of fifty who don't have household registration."[16] It is impossible to verify his estimate, since there are no official statistics or representative survey data. Nonetheless, there is no question that surplus children are significantly overrepresented in migrant schools in Beijing, as in Guangzhou.

One important detail to note is that surplus children are not necessarily second or third children, but also those born out of wedlock. A migrant mother related why she would be unable to get her child into public schools: "My oldest child was born before marriage. It was an illegal birth. I wasn't old enough [to get married], we couldn't get a marriage license, but I still had the child. . . . He was born when I was eighteen."[17] As noted with respect to point-based enrollment in chapter 2, parental violation of the heteronormative order of the state has grave consequences for the educational opportunities for children.

The difficulties faced by surplus children are not restricted to the migrant population, even if they are more prevalent. Surplus children born to families living within their place of *hukou* registration can face similar obstacles to educational advancement. This problem was clearly illustrated by the nine-person Zhang family from Tongzhou District in Beijing.[18] The mother and father, both local Beijing residents, had a total of seven children, the eldest thirty-one and the youngest nine years old. Although both the parents and the eldest child had always maintained Beijing *hukou*, the family found great difficulty in paying the fines associated with registering *hukou* for the remaining six children. As of 2015 there were still four children who did not have any *hukou*. Without documentation, the second, third, and fourth children had been prevented from educational advancement, leaving them with no choice but to accept menial wage employment.[19] The authorities demanded 700,000 yuan in fines before they would be willing to issue *hukou* for the remaining children, but despite their strong desire to avoid the difficulties of their elder siblings, this was likely an insurmountable sum for the family.[20] This example demonstrates that in exceptional cases, the children of the poor can be rendered surplus by birth control policies, regardless of whether they are migrants.[21]

Nonetheless, on average rural migrants face a much greater likelihood of having surplus children. This is due to a combination of higher rural birth rates, less financial capacity to pay associated fines, and distance from their officially designated hometown. Mr. Fan and Ms. Xu, the small-scale entrepreneurs from Shandong who had been in Beijing for twenty years, illustrated the difficult position of migrants, even though they likely had resources to pay the fines to register their children (while many other families did not). When we met, they had three children, ages twelve, six, and four. The family was of mixed status, since only the eldest child had a fully legal *hukou*.[22] The six-year-old was supposed to begin primary school that fall. But in order to avoid fines in their hometown, they had registered his *hukou* (illegally) under a friend's name who lived elsewhere. The parents knew that without Beijing *hukou*, they would be unable to get him into public school locally. But without a *hukou* from their hometown, the child was caught in bureaucratic limbo. Mr. Fan complained, "We could only register his *hukou*

there [in the friends' hometown]. Without a *hukou* in our hometown, he can't go to school there. So we're going to push things
back and have him start next year." Their plan was to return to
their hometown to try to register him that summer. They were
confident that there would be no repercussions other than a
fine, but they did not know how much the fine would be.
Mr. Fan estimated that it would be between 50,000 and 80,000
yuan. Ms. Xu remarked, "If you want more [kids] you can go
ahead and have them, but they won't give you *hukou*. If you
can't pay the fine they won't give you *hukou*. And if you don't
have *hukou* you definitely can't enroll in school. In our hometown they won't let you attend even one day of school. Our
hometown is extremely strict now."[23] Even though the couple
believed they would be able to pay the fine, it meant pushing
back their son's enrollment by one year and then returning
home unsure of how much they would have to pay in fines.
Unless there were relatives back in the village able to care for
the children, it would also mean one or both of the parents' for-
going the higher income they could earn in Beijing. Escaping
surplus status required returning to their officially designated
location in the sociospatial hierarchy.

The condition of being surplus follows these children into
adulthood, and even across the generations. When one of the
Zhang children, Zhang Jinxin, attempted to get married, her
surplus status engendered tragic results. After she and her fian-
cée held a wedding ceremony, they discovered that her lack of
hukou prevented them from getting a marriage license. The situation became direr one year later when their first child was
born, since the baby could not receive *hukou*, having been born
out of wedlock. Ms. Zhang became severely depressed, and
the child's father left her and took the baby with him. Given the
dim prospects for surplus children, parents sometimes resort to

extreme measures, in some cases abandoning or killing their newborn children. Such incidents became so widespread in migrant-magnet Shenzhen that in 2013 the city announced it would be opening a "baby hatch" where parents could drop off unwanted children in a safe place, hit an alarm, and then have several minutes to leave before a staff member would come to the child's aid.[24]

Again, surplus children can be urban or rural, local or migrant. But the conditions necessary to absolve oneself of state-determined superfluity and secure *hukou* clearly work against working-class migrants: most important, to register requires having money and being in one's officially designated location. For many migrants, meeting the latter condition comes at the expense of meeting the former condition. Once again, we see the nefarious synthesis of status-based exclusion and market-based inequalities relegating migrants and their children to a life of informality, denied access to state-subsidized social reproduction. It follows logically that surplus children would appear in disproportionately high numbers in migrant schools, a last resort for a population rendered surplus by the state.

USING EDUCATION TO CONTROL THE POPULATION

Beijing and other large cities have continuously negotiated the vicissitudes of the urban growth dilemma for decades, alternatively allowing more rural people in as a source of exploitable labor and then expelling or applying expulsionary pressures when they feared overpopulation and political chaos. Nonetheless, the largest cities grew continuously, particularly so in the era of market reforms when *hukou* restrictions were somewhat loosened. But in 2014 something changed in Beijing, and the government made a clear decision to resolve this tension in favor of expulsion. As has been mentioned, population growth had already been slowing for several years, due not only to expulsion-oriented policies, but also to broader economic and demographic conditions. But a downturn in growth happened in 2014, and by the end of 2017 the total population began to shrink. The urban government did not directly expel people but rather took numerous measures to realize the interrelated goals of upgrading the structures of the economy and the population while strictly limiting the number of people residing in the city. In addition to relocating labor-intensive, low-value-added industry and evicting people from informal housing, "population control via education" became one of the primary means for the state to apply pressure on the most precarious migrants.

From the perspective of migrant parents, this shift was felt immediately. For many years earlier, parents with their children in Shusheng had a high degree of success in enrolling their children in the local public middle school. A conversation with mother of three Hu Qianxin, her eldest daughter, and their friend Zhu Wen revealed how things had changed with middle school enrollment:

ZHU WEN: Wasn't your middle child directly accepted into Yuhuang School because her grades were so good?

HU QIANXIN: No. With the older two, they could directly enroll.

DAUGHTER: Right, before you could directly enroll.

HU QIANXIN: Of our three kids, the two older ones went to Yuhuang, but the youngest can't go. Before it was easier to take care of the procedures, you could do it and directly enroll, but now that's not possible. . . . With this youngest one, I've run all over town, but he won't be able to get in.[25]

Zhang Huixu, a mother of three from Shaanxi, confirmed how the requirements for documentation had recently become much more stringent: "In the beginning they just wanted your *hukou* booklet, and that birth control permit for the parents to have a kid, and a birth certificate. And then, then you could just enroll . . . but later, now, they want . . . there are new requirements, they want social insurance, they want your education registration . . . they add one demand after another. They added, what's it called? They told me but I forgot."[26] Enrolling children in public middle schools had always been a stop-gap method, as students would have to go back to their place of *hukou* registration to take the high school entrance exam. Nonetheless, based on previous experience, many parents counted on having these few extra years.

As indicated earlier, one of the most insurmountable obstacles that was added in 2014 was the demand for parents to have paid into local social insurance plans. Parents reported different sorts of demands across and within Beijing's districts, with uneven requirements for length of time paying into insurance. Some education departments required parents to have paid into social insurance within the district where they live, and some required both the mother and father to have social insurance. As indicated in the chapter's epigraph, rumor and misinformation were widespread—an understandable outcome, given the government's strategic lack of transparency with regard to enrollment requirements.

The new demand for social insurance was a way for the state to build on and intensify the demands for parents' labor market

value. Workers without a labor contract have essentially no possibility of enrolling in social insurance, since the system is mediated by employers. And a small minority of rural migrants enjoy
social insurance coverage: in 2017 migrant worker participation
was only 22 percent in urban pensions and health insurance,
27 percent in workplace injury insurance, and 17 percent in
unemployment insurance.[27] But many migrant workers who *do*
have a formal contract do not receive social insurance, since
employers frequently flout their legally required payments.
Indeed, employer failure to pay their employees' social insurance
has been a growing source of grievances for workers, in some
cases leading to major strike actions as with 2014's Yue Yuen
mobilization.[28] Another authoritative survey of service-sector
migrant workers with secondary education or less in Beijing,
Shanghai, Guangzhou, and Shenzhen found nonpayment of
pensions of 60–70 percent over many years, thus suggesting that
even those workers who have insurance on paper cannot enjoy
the full benefits.[29]

Even relatively economically successful migrants could find
themselves excluded by the new requirements. This was the case
for Mr. Fan, the Shandong native, who had alternated between
formal employment and running his own business. By no fault
of his own, he lost his insurance when his employer went under:

MR. FAN: At the time I was working for a renovation company.

MS. XU [MR. FAN'S WIFE]: Back then he had just gotten social
insurance.

MR. FAN: I had a labor contract and insurance.

MS. XU: But then the company went out of business.

MR. FAN: The business was disbanded.

MS. XU: The company disbanded, so even if he wanted social
insurance there was no place to go. He wanted to continue

paying into social insurance, but if you aren't employed where can you go? It's impossible.

MR. FAN: I paid into the insurance for two years, and then it was discontinued.

EF: So now you aren't paying insurance?

MR. FAN: There's nowhere to pay it.

MS. XU: He wants to pay!

MR. FAN: I went to the Shunyi [District, in northeast Beijing] Social Insurance Department. I went to pay by myself, but they don't accept payments from individuals, only from work units. Our work unit doesn't exist, so how can I pay in? Those payments I made before were wasted.[30]

Bear in mind that Mr. Fan was relatively well off—most workers would not be in a position to make insurance payments in the absence of formal employment. But across the board, migrant children's access to public schools is mediated by the vagaries of the urban labor market.

Education Registration: *Xueji*

I have already made reference to the education registration, or *xueji* (学籍), which has not been extensively studied but is of increasing relevance for all students in China. *Xueji* is a form of official documentation that some have likened to a *hukou* for education. It is managed under the auspices of the Ministry of Education and contains basic information about a student's identity and educational history. Although *xueji* has nominally existed for years, it was not until 2009 that the central government decided to establish a unified nationwide system. Every student from primary to university level was to be assigned a *xueji* number that would stay with them for life. From that point on, students would have to secure *xueji* as a requirement for enrolling in schools anywhere in the country.

As the nationwide system was rolled out in 2013–2014, parents—regardless of *hukou* status—found that attaining a *xueji* ID was necessary to enroll in schools. As is the case for much education policy, urban districts maintained a relatively high degree of autonomy in implementing *xueji* procedures. One consequence of this was highly uneven procedures and demands for *xueji* registration, nationally and even within Beijing. In general, attaining *xueji* in Beijing entailed meeting the requirements for public school enrollment. There were different requirements with regard to the location of the school vis-à-vis the parents' housing and employment location, with some places requiring that all three be located in the same district. And the location of the parents' *hukou* could also have a decisive impact on where they could register for *xueji*.

The rollout of *xueji* gave city officials yet another mechanism for denying nonlocals access to education. In some cases, these bureaucratic rules frustrated even extremely privileged nonlocal residents. This came to national attention in 2018 when the CEO of a tech company, Zhang Xiaolong, posted a diatribe on Weibo about his difficulties enrolling his child in a local private school (which, as with public schools, began requiring *xueji*). Zhang complained that in his four years working in Beijing, he had personally paid 4 million yuan in taxes, while his company had paid upward of 80 million.[31] Owing to the different locations of his home, work, and the school, Zhang's child was unable to secure local *xueji*, and their admission application was thus denied. Although Chinese citizens have become rather inured to class-based forms of exclusion, Zhang's case dramatized the persistence of insurmountable status-based exclusion.

Unsurprisingly, and in line with the broader political trends I have extensively mapped out, working-class migrant parents faced the greatest challenge in securing *xueji* for their children. For many of the parents I got to know, attaining Beijing *xueji* was as unlikely as enrolling in public school. Initially, this might not have had much impact on their lives, inasmuch as their children were not going to make it into public schools anyway. As Zhang Huixu, the mother of three from Shaanxi, put it, "Registering *xueji*, well anyway, here it's impossible. It can't be done. We can register back home. Our children must go home to go to school."[32]

Confusion and lack of information about *xueji* was widespread at the time. It is not apparent that adequate information would have made a difference for most, but it nonetheless fed a sense of helplessness:

> DONG HUANLI: We haven't gotten the "five permits" [for enrolling in public schools], but we need to get *xueji*. We need *xueji*.
>
> EF: Have you tried to get *xueji*?
>
> DH: When my child was in first grade, we were back home, and we registered her *xueji*. But nobody's been back home for the past few years, I'm guessing nobody kept it for us. Maybe they got rid of it a while ago. We'll have to register again!
>
> EF: So what will you do?
>
> DH: I'm not sure. Maybe we'll have to give them . . . well, if they want money, we'll have to give them money. If they're going to make you run all over the place, then you'll just have to run![33]

But even in the midst of parents' widespread confusion about how to secure *xueji*, those migrants in Liwanzhuang understood that they would likely be shut out:

ZHANG HUIXU: [after requiring the "five permits"] they want something more, what's it called?. . . They also want social insurance and *xueji*. They want those, what's it called? It's something or another. They said they want something else. Well, I can't remember . . . anyway, I heard from my fellow villager [*laoxiang* 老乡], she ran all over the place, had gotten all the right documents, but she couldn't get *xueji*. If you get this completed, they'll give you something else, they want this thing. And then you deal with this and they give you something else. Anyway, they're just trying to trap you.[34]

It seemed as though the new *xueji* requirements, while likely not intended as a tool for managing flows of people when devised by the Ministry of Education, were being employed in just such a manner. Indeed, with hundreds of thousands of migrants in Beijing unlikely to secure local *xueji*, returning to the village was going to be a necessary step to ensure educational opportunities down the line. And the window for returning to the city would be small. A mother in Liwanzhuang explained it thus:

EF: Have you considered returning home to register *xueji*?
MOTHER: I have. But if we return home to register *xueji*, then our child can only go to school there.
EF: Is that right?
MOTHER: Yes, I've inquired about this. If you register *xueji* back home, then it's impossible for the child to enroll elsewhere. Yeah, if you register it back home, they have to go to school there.[35]

Many parents were put in the impossible position of choosing between the earning possibilities of the city and their children's educational future back in the village.

Given the general lack of information and hasty rollout of the program, some families were left in administrative limbo, able neither to register in the city nor to return to the village. While visiting Zhenhua School in northern Beijing's Changping District, I met a father who was desperately trying to get his nine-year-old son admitted, even though the registration date had already passed. The previous year, his child had been enrolled in an unlicensed school right next to the family residence. As a totally informal institution, this school would have been unable to issue *xueji*. When I asked whether he had considered going back to Hunan, the family's place of *hukou* registration, he explained that the date for school enrollment had already passed, so there would be no way to get his son in. Furthermore, "I work here, there's no way I can go back. The old folks [grandparents] are in their seventies and eighties. . . . There's nothing to be done [sighs]."[36] Zhenhua was by no means a high-end private school, but it was registered and could therefore theoretically provide students with a *xueji* ID. As the father revealed shortly thereafter, there was no guarantee that even if his son were allowed to enroll at Zhenhua they would be able to get *xueji*. Still, he believed it was better than the alternative: "We'll have to see if we'll be able to get *xueji* in the future. At least this place [Zhenhua School] is licensed. Just in case a new policy comes out. If you're always in an unlicensed place, and a policy comes out that will allow us to get [*xueji*], you won't be able to get it. If [the school] is licensed, you can do it immediately. At the least, it will be somewhat better [than in an unlicensed school]."[37] Tragically, this father did not know that the school he was pleading with to enroll his child was slated for imminent demolition. Even in the best-case scenario, his son would have to move schools again after just one semester.

Housing and School Enrollment

As is the case in school districts around the world, some proof of local housing has long been a requirement for migrants wishing to enroll their children in urban public schools. For the overwhelming majority of migrant workers this has meant producing a rental contract, since migrants—particularly those working in the informal sector—are largely shut out of homeownership.[38] As has been widely shown in the literature, informal apartments in "urban villages" play a crucial role in providing affordable housing to migrants in Beijing and other large cities.[39] A 2010 survey found that a mere 27.8 percent of residents in Beijing's urban villages had a written rental contract.[40] While China's urbanization is often characterized as being distinguished by a relative dearth of slums—and there is some validity to this when considering state regulation of space and general living conditions—millions of migrant workers nonetheless reside in informal housing. Without a formal rental contract, parents are categorically shut out of the city's public school system.

In addition to social insurance and *xueji*, in 2014 authorities in Beijing began to demand property tax receipts as a condition for enrolling in public schools. This new demand represented a major roadblock for migrant residents, even for those who had a rental contract. Feng Huai, a mother of one from Henan in Liwanzhuang, depicted an absurd series of events that migrant parents had to endure:

> Then there's the landlord's property tax receipts. This housing is self-built, so the landlord doesn't pay taxes at all. But they [the Education Department] say that you're not qualified if you don't pay taxes, it's illegal, the house is illegal . . . these are all

self-built, it's village-style, so there's no need to pay taxes. How
can we deal with this? A lot of parents have gone with their
landlords to the tax bureau to try to get a tax receipt and have
offered to help the landlord pay the taxes. They're helping them
to pay taxes that don't need to be paid, just to get this receipt.[41]

In order to understand why attaining property tax receipts
would be so difficult, particularly for the least well-resourced
tenants, it is necessary to understand something about land tenure in the urban villages that house so many migrants. Land in
China is designated as either urban or rural, with the former
owned by the state whereas the latter is, nominally at least, collectively held. The urban village refers to a space officially designated as rural, but which has been incorporated into urban
space as a consequence of the city's outward expansion. While
the rural designation certainly does not prevent the flourishing
of urban processes within this space, the persistence of formally
collective land is significant. Although there is great diversity
even within a single urban area, this land tenure arrangement
generally results in the village seeking to generate market-based
profit by leasing out collectively held land.[42] Rent derived from
use of collectively held land, such as that leased to a factory, is
supposed to be divided up among villagers—this is one of the
benefits of maintaining rural residency on the periphery of
wealthy cities.[43] But many villagers have also decided to maxi-
mize profits from land designated for housing, often construct-
ing small and poorly regulated informal apartments. While city
governments have frequently sought to redevelop urban villages, both to encourage more profitable land use and to expel
what they see as socially and politically undesirable communities, cities would not be able to secure a low-cost migrant labor
force were it not for the village's low-cost informal housing.[44]

Because the land is collectively held and the housing is informal in nature, this also means that it is a near certainty that the landlords do not pay taxes and therefore could not secure the paperwork that became a requirement for school enrollments in 2014.

Many well-off migrants have sought housing in the formal rental market. And to some extent, urban governments in China have been moving toward a system of school enrollments that more closely hews to the pattern of class-based sorting that is common in other national settings. In the United States and countless other countries, quality of education is heavily mediated by the real estate market. The clearest indicator of this trend in China has been the movement toward proximity-based enrollment (*jiujin ruxue* 就近入学). With the dissolution of the Mao-era work unit and the upward relocation of responsibility for social service provision to the level of the city, the old status-based system of enrollment has been gradually supplanted by proximity-based enrollment. For many years, elite schools continued to reserve a significant share of their enrollment slots for students outside their catchment area—including some whose parents were employed by an associated work unit, some students with particularly high test scores (a key evaluation metric for schools), or simply for those who could afford to pay a hefty bribe. Following an order from the Ministry of Education in April 2014, schools in Beijing and nineteen other key cities were required to conduct *all* enrollments based on proximity. This meant that Beijing *hukou* holders from anywhere in the city could purchase a home with the promise of being able to enroll their children in the neighborhood school.[45]

While the shift to catchment-based enrollments by no means ended educational inequality, it did begin to reorganize the basis of that inequality. In the months that followed the ministry's order, lurid if anecdotal reports emerged of parents paying astonishingly high prices for housing within the catchment area of top public schools. One report told of a woman named Li Xin, who purchased a run-down five square-meter-apartment without central heat or its own bathroom for an astonishing 1.35 million yuan (approximately USD $220,000). Li and her husband already owned a much larger apartment elsewhere in the city and had no intention of moving, noting, "we will absolutely not really live here."[46] Rather, they bought the home because it was in the catchment area of the elite Shijia Elementary School.

This suggested another shift in China's capitalist transition, from education resources' being distributed based on access to political capital to distribution based on economic capital. The Ministry of Education touted proximity-based enrollment as a fairer, more transparent method for managing school access. But while this real estate–mediated form of sorting certainly enhanced market-based forms of inequality, it hardly did so at the expense of status hierarchies: Beijing *hukou* was still required as a condition of proximity-based enrollment. School districts even set up residency term requirements for Beijing *hukou*-holders moving from other parts of the city. As just one example, the Jingshan school not only demanded Beijing *hukou* for proximity-based enrollment but also required that the family had been living within the catchment area for at least three years. Here we see another instance in which capitalist and state-socialist forms of inequality, far from being mutually exclusive, are deeply intertwined and even mutually reinforcing. Finally, it should come as little surprise that the movement toward proximity-based enrollment barely even registered for my migrant worker informants. It did, however, suggest that even those unbelievably well-resourced migrants who managed to secure Beijing *hukou* would now face further market-based forms of education inequality.

In sum, this period of time saw Beijing continually increasing demands for nonlocal enrollment in public schools. Teacher Pan from Shusheng eloquently summarized how migrant families were administratively squeezed out of the city: "[After the five permits] they then demanded *xueji*, and this wiped away a group of children because they can't get *xueji*. Then they wanted social insurance; they said you need Beijing insurance and Chaoyang District insurance, so these children basically can't get into school. But even if you get all of these together, the [Education Department] will say you need housing paperwork. It's like a sifter, they're gradually sifting people away."[47]

RETURNING "HOME"

Given the myriad challenges migrants face in securing decent education for their children in the city, all of which were severely intensified in Beijing from 2014, parents often reflected on the prospects and problems of leaving the city. I employ scare quotes in the subheading to emphasize that the place to which migrants are returning often does not evoke a sense of belonging for them. In some cases, particularly for migrant children, they are going to a place where they have never lived, and perhaps have only visited on holidays if at all. Although migrants themselves often referred to a "return home" (*hui laojia* 回老家) in conversation, from an analytical perspective it is more precise to refer to this place as the officially designated position in the sociospatial hierarchy. Whether this is a place that evokes the kinds of sentiments and security associated with a "home" should be left as an open question.[48]

This disjuncture between officially designated home and migrants' lived experience could not have been starker for Mao

Ding, a father from Sichuan living in Liwanzhuang. Facing the strong likelihood that his child would not be able to enroll in school the following year, he kept repeating throughout our interview that he had lived in Beijing for twenty years, and he was clearly having great difficulty coming to terms with this new reality:

> If we suddenly take our child back home to study, we feel like it's too quick. We've worked here for twenty years, and to just suddenly go back, just leave and not come back, because we think it's best to be there with our child. . . . Just think, if we suddenly go back, we won't be able to survive. We've only been back once every three or four years. Back home there's no work, we're used to things here, we're not used to things back home. At the end of the day, it's already been so long, we aren't used to things back there. If we go back, I don't even know how to farm, which crops to plant in which seasons. I've learned technical work, there isn't this kind of work back home.[49]

Ms. Xu similarly complicated the question of where "home" is, as she mulled the possibility of having to return to Shandong: "Although we aren't Beijingers, our [three] children were all born here. And we've been here for more than twenty years. To be honest, we are more familiar with Beijing than we are with our own home."[50]

As already alluded to, leaving Beijing could mean returning to a life of poverty. A multiprovince study by the Chinese Academy of Social Sciences of two thousand rural households found that 40 percent of migrants who return home are unable to find work, with most leaving the village again.[51] As Hu Qianxin, hailing from an impoverished part of Sichuan, put it succinctly: "What will I do if I go back? Back in our hometown you can't even earn more than 1,000 yuan."[52] This prospect of subsistence crisis led nearly every parent I spoke with to express emotional anguish in trying to figure out how to balance their desire to live in the same place as their children with the need to earn a decent living. Dong Huanli talked about the difficulty she faced in deciding to send her daughter to Hebei while she stayed in Beijing:

> DONG HUANLI: If we go back home, I think getting settled will take six months. Because if you go home, you don't know what you're going to do, and there's no work. Then you have to gradually look for something to do. And then . . . it's just not easy, moving a family and getting them settled, it's not easy.
>
> EF: Do you think [your children] can adjust [to living at home]?
>
> DH: Of course they can't. . . . My daughter doesn't want to leave . . . she says, "I want to be wherever you are." But we have to have her in school![53]

Given the conflicting interests to have their children enrolled in school while also earning enough to live, family life was often thrown into disarray. Zhang Huixu discussed the complexity of this challenge. She had counted on the fact that her eldest daughter would be able to go to local middle school after graduating from Shusheng:

> ZHANG HUIXU: [The new education policy] just started this year. . . . Getting into middle school, if it's like this now, even if you want to go you can't get in.
>
> EF: So are you considering returning home?
>
> ZH: I will have to endure going home.
>
> EF: What are your plans?

ZH: Well there's nobody to look after the kids back home . . . let's see if we can go home and they can go to school there. If we can't . . . well, we also have a small child, going home isn't convenient, so we'd have to bring the young and older ones together. And I'd have to look after them by myself.

EF: So you haven't finalized your plans?

ZH: No, not yet. Originally, I wanted to think of a way to send them home, but there's nobody there to look after them. And our three kids have always been with me. I've never given them to someone else to look after.

WU PING: What about their grandparents? Are they not in good health?

ZH: They don't have [paternal] grandparents.

WP: They've passed away?

ZH: They already passed away before we even got married. So I've always looked after my children myself.

As she considered the prospect of having to send her eldest child back to the village for middle school, she couldn't help but reveal her frustration and indecision: "Maybe after she finishes sixth grade we'll send her home for middle school. We'll see what she says, we'll discuss the issue of returning home. None of my family members know what to do. I can't decide either what to do with our children."[54]

Much has been made in China's media about the more than 60 million left-behind children, those who remain in rural areas and small towns for schooling while their parents go to the city for work.[55] But while the *hukou* system and China's geographically uneven development are generally cited as the origin of this phenomenon, it is important to also note that the urban state has continually and actively *produced* left-behind children. Kam Wing Chan and Yuan Ren have shown that Beijing is responsible for producing more left-behind children, in relative terms, than any other province-level unit in China.[56] By depriving migrant children of access to education, rendering them surplus, particularly when they had the expectation that they would be able to enroll in school, parents are faced with no choice but to return their children to their designated place in the sociospatial hierarchy. If, as in the case of Hu Qianxin, the village did not offer enough economic opportunities to support a family, the inevitable result would be the production of a left-behind child: "If I send my youngest home this year, next year we'll still, well, this year we'll send one home and then next year send another one home, this would just cause me too much worry. Since they've never left me, I just don't know what to do, they've never left me so I'm so worried." Despite her worry about sending her middle school–aged child home alone, she indicated that she would not have any other choice. When asked if she would consider going home with her children, she responded:

> If I go back, we'll just have to rely on their father's income, it won't even be enough to eat [calculates approximate living expenses]. . . . His father has said the same thing. And my eldest daughter [an adult] doesn't want me to go back. [She says,] "It's useless for you to go back, he [the son] can live at school." If I'm back at home, I can't earn any money, whatever small amount you can earn won't cover expenses. [My eldest daughter] says, "We can take care of ourselves." It's really pitiful.[57]

The situation was made even more tragic by Hu's acknowledgment that there were no extended kin in the family to take care of the children: "At home there is nobody at all to take care of them. . . . His grandparents passed away long ago, and there are no other relatives to do it. His aunt won't do it, she says she's afraid she'll do a bad job." The existent population management regime has shredded the very family form being extolled by the increasingly Confucian-oriented Chinese state. For tens of millions of people, living in the same place as their children has been constructed as a privilege to be earned.

Sending Noncapital People to Hebei

With education access in Beijing becoming increasingly restricted during the 2010s, many parents who were unwilling or unable to send their children to the village began enrolling their children in schools in neighboring Hebei Province. The satellite cities surrounding the capital have continued to maintain lower requirements for nonlocals to enroll in public schools. And from 2013, the province announced a new plan relaxing the requirements for taking the university entrance exam. Migrants without Hebei *hukou* could register their children for the exam if they could provide proof of local employment and residence and demonstrate that the student had been enrolled in a local high school for at least two years.[58]

Many cities in Hebei such as Langfang, a prefecture just to the east and south of Beijing, saw a major influx of students. The number of students enrolled in primary schools in Sanhe, a city within Langfang's jurisdiction, increased by 9.8 percent between 2013 and 2014. One middle school principal in Langfang reported that fully 50 percent of new enrollees in 2015 were nonlocals, including many who had been forced out of Beijing.[59] This option was particularly attractive for families who wanted to stay relatively close to their children but did not want to forgo the economic opportunities of remaining within the orbit of the capital. But enrolling children in these neighboring cities still required relocating residences and likely their employment, since a local lease and labor contract were generally required for admission. And it was likely that parents would have to still pay bribes: one teacher from Shusheng School reported that her former students had to pay 20,000–30,000 yuan to enroll in middle school in Sanhe.[60]

Parents unable to leave Beijing proper could instead consider sending their children to private boarding schools in Hebei. As private entities, these schools did not require the parents to live and work within their district. One private school in Hengshui, a city 270 kilometers from Beijing, seized on this market opportunity. The boarding school gave children a few days off each month so they could return to Beijing to see their parents, and the school even arranged their transportation.[61] The fees associated with such a program likely made this option out of reach for most informal workers. But given that many relatively well-off migrants were caught up in the 2014 expulsion, these private schools appeared to have a hit on a growth industry.[62]

The expulsion of people from Beijing to Hebei should be seen in the context of the *Jingjinji* (京津冀, Beijing-Tianjin-Hebei) planning efforts. Launched in 2014, this was a pet project of Xi Jinping to advance regional integration, and, crucially, to relocate "noncapital functions" (*fei shoudu gongneng* 非首都功能) from Beijing's urban core to more peripheral surrounding areas. In the official language, this is talked about as a process of *clearing* (*shujie* 疏解) the city in order to make space for more capital-appropriate functions.[63] This has involved a wide array of expulsions, but low-value-added manufacturing, warehousing, and wholesale markets have been high priorities for relocation to Hebei. Similarly, the migrants being forced out into the Hebei exurbs had been deemed "noncapital" in nature and were thus being subjected to a process of dispersal in parallel with the clearing of undesirable industries.[64]

EMOTIONAL STRAIN

Amid the capricious population management of the urban state, migrant families were managing a great deal of stress. Although I was always cautious in bringing up the topic, given the traumatic circumstances many had been subjected to, parents were often quite forthcoming with me in discussing the costs of triaging financial, emotional, and reproductive needs. While the precise experience of having a child ejected from Beijing was structured by parents' type of employment, economic capacity, and the location and level of development of their hometown, as well as family arrangements, anxiety about the future was a universal sentiment among parents in Liwanzhuang. Xu Zheng, a mother from Shaanxi, related her fears about being forced out of the city. This situation was worsened by the fact that there was nobody back in the village to look after her child, which meant she was faced with the prospect of sending her child alone: "There's nothing to be done . . . no matter how worried and anxious, and worried once more I am, there's nothing to be done, we just don't have . . . it's not like there are grandparents who can help to watch the kid for a while, who can worry for you for a while. I'm out of luck, I don't have even one person. It doesn't matter how much I worry, this is the reality!"[65] Hu Qianxin, facing separation from her two middle school–aged children, was similarly wracked with anxiety, confessing, "I'm often so worried about the kids' education that I can't sleep at night. I stay up until the morning just thinking about it."[66] This stress was likely heightened by the pervasive lack of transparency and uncertainty in the process of expulsion. As Teacher Ma from Shusheng put it, "It's always hope, disappointment, hope, disappointment, this kind of back and forth. It's a real attack on your emotions."[67]

Migrant parents who had brought their children with them to the city had done so understanding that it could affect their children's education. Nonetheless, for many, the value of being there while their children grew up outweighed the potential downsides for socioeconomic advancement. Huang Zhijun, a father from Henan, reflected on his decision to bring his son and his possible expulsion from the city:

> [Our son has been enrolled here] from first grade on. . . . As migrants, our child can more or less make do. If he's smart and is willing to study, he can become talented in the future. If he's not smart and doesn't want to study, well he can still go to high school and learn a few characters then go get a job or something. But at least you're in one place. Most migrant parents have this attitude. If they get into university that's great; if they don't it's ok. But we're a family, the parents and the children are together.[68]

From 2014, even the low end of Mr. Huang's aspirations appeared increasingly unattainable.

For many migrant children, the experience of sociospatial dislocation was not new. Relocation and changing schools have been a regular occurrence for migrant children and their families in Beijing for many years, and I found in my study that most migrants schools experience 25–30 percent student turnover every year. But migrants' familiarity with a peripatetic existence did not inure them to the trauma. As noted in the introduction, I did not directly question children about their responses to dislocation, since I could not figure out how to do so in a way that did not raise ethical concerns. Teacher Pan from Shusheng discussed her students' emotional well-being in the midst of great uncertainty: "At this time, students are really anxious. They want to find someone who can tell them what will come next, but there isn't anyone who can tell them."[69]

Children's emotional strain of course impacted their parents as well. Dong Huanli compared her thirteen-year-old child's likely imminent departure to an earlier move they had made within Beijing after her workplace was demolished:

> Back then [during our previous move] she was young. She didn't have much attachment, a young child won't be so nostalgic after moving around. But not anymore, now she's already thirteen, she's got opinions. If she's forced to transfer schools again, she'll long for the past and won't want to leave. . . . She understands everything now, she'll have a really hard time if she has to transfer again. A lot of her classmates have to go back to their hometowns because they can't get into middle school. All the kids are having a hard time. They'll exchange QQ [an instant messaging app] and phone numbers to keep in touch, they're afraid they won't be able to find each other in the future.

She then expressed a simple, powerful longing that had been repeated by countless others: "If my child could go to school here . . . then I would definitely stay here. I'm trying to figure it out, how to stay here. We're used to being here, and we just want to keep staying here. We don't want to go back."[70]

CONCLUSION

When migrant workers are pulled into the city as workers but expelled as full social beings, included in production but excluded from social reproduction, the results are dehumanizing. For

many years, the consequence of this system was not to eliminate migrants altogether, but to concentrate deprivation in the
informal school system. Then in 2014 the Beijing government
made a clear and decisive turn toward expulsion. Among the
many levers the urban state has at its disposal for applying pressure on migrants, "population control via education" appeared
as one of the cruelest but also most effective. This deprivation
of access to the means of social reproduction resulted in tens of
thousands of families' being rendered surplus, denied access to
social reproduction, even as they had quite literally built the
city. Once these people were deemed "noncapital" and therefore
superfluous to the imagined future of the city, nearly any and
all means of expulsion were politically legitimated. In addition
to denial of school admissions, the state retained yet crueler
tactics: school closures and demolitions.

5

POPULATION MANAGEMENT'S "HARD EDGE"

School Closures and Demolitions

[The demolition] will happen sooner or later. We just don't know when . . . but we're definitely going to lose out. We'll have to go to a strange place and start over once more. Us outsiders, our survival skills are quite strong. We are continuously starting over.

—Ms. Xu, migrant from Shandong

Surplus populations are produced. In chapters 2 and 4 I traced the various administrative arrangements that aim to admit certain types of migrants, while others maintain provisional access to social reproduction or are rendered fully surplus, left to their own devices for social survival. I now turn to a much more active form of rendering populations surplus, an immediate and subjective rather than impersonal relationship of denial: school demolitions and closures. In doing so, we should keep in mind the administrative arrangements operating quietly in the background—in tandem with the bulldozer, these represent the consent-coercion dialectic of the population management regime in contemporary China.[1] If the sifter was an apt metaphor for the administrative processes dispersing migrants from the capital, it is the bulldozer that *pushes* them into a state of superfluity.

In turning to the coercive ejection of migrant children, we will need to be attentive to the complex interplay of political and economic dynamics, or more specifically the control and accumulation imperatives of local government. This is particularly important as the urban state may be interested in eliminating informal schools because of increasing land values, desire to reduce the low-end population, or both. While there is no smoking gun accounting for why the municipal government has repeatedly subjected migrant schools to seemingly arbitrary and vindictive demolitions and closures (that would require a level of access that is extremely rare), it is possible to delineate the kinds of pressures and political relations that give rise to these physical expulsions. Crucially, once the administrative process has relegated migrants to a space of informal social reproduction (i.e., forced them into migrant schools), they are left vulnerable to removal, thus smoothing the way for evictions in general, be they primarily motivated by a demand for land or for population reduction. In this sense, the control and accumulation imperatives push in the same direction toward rendering a segment of the population *potentially* surplus. This is, however, not a simple story of coincidental interests of state and capital—each eviction has the potential to undercut the city's labor reserves, putting pressure on employers in labor-intensive industries. Particularly in the capital city, the political imperative to control overpopulation can easily override demands from employers for a cheap and expansive workforce. While this urban growth dilemma will continue to pull city officials in different directions, empirically speaking the period of 2011–2017 saw increased expulsionary tendencies in Beijing that coincidentally or not advantaged land-intensive forms of economic activity while enhancing political control over a migrant subpopulation presumed to be unruly.

While there is significant literature on the impact of housing demolitions in the course of urban development, I highlight the analytical advantages of focusing on schools, a related but distinct site of reproduction. Demolitions can result from a variety of political and economic pressures, and they have effects on the spatial organization of reproduction, student resettlement, and families' emotional state. I draw on data from my core field sites of Yinghong, Shusheng, and Zhifan Schools, but I was also interested in investigating schools that had more recently been subject to closure or relocation. I therefore include significant data collected in Dongxiaokou, an area of Changping District that was in the midst of significant redevelopment during my fieldwork. I also rely on media reports and other digital documentation in my account of Huangzhuang School and other closures.[2]

URBAN DEVELOPMENTALISM AND DISPLACEMENT

As has been widely discussed in the scholarly literature, Chinese capitalism has become increasingly urbanized since the 1990s.[3] The separation of land use rights from land ownership rights combined with fiscal decentralization led local governments to turn to the private sector to advance urban redevelopment projects.[4] A strong pro-growth alliance emerged in which the interests of local governments and private developers were tightly aligned.[5] Given state ownership of urban land, the government has played a central role in redevelopment of the urban core as well as outward expansion into suburban and rural areas.[6] In short, from the 1990s onward, the urbanization of capital proceeded rapidly, as real estate and associated industries came to play a foundational role in catalyzing growth in China—even sparking a boom in commodity markets around the world.[7]

Serious questions began to arise about the social consequences of this massive transformation of urban China's built environment. A large body of scholarly literature has emerged over the past generation documenting the impact of displacement and dispossession on residents. We now have studies that assess the consequences of development-related displacement in the urban core, "urban villages" and the urban periphery and rural areas.[8] These studies demonstrate that the state plays a major and often coercive role in removing residents and pushing development projects though, while residents are given little meaningful voice.[9] One consequence of this is that even redevelopment projects that explicitly valorize social inclusivity produce less than desirable outcomes for displaced residents although there are indications that rural residents in advantageously located peri-urban areas can stand to benefit.[10] Another general feature that is of particular relevance here is that migrants residing outside their place of *hukou* registration fare the worst in terms of influencing the course of urban redevelopment or receiving compensation for their displacement.[11] Indeed, Xuefei Ren interprets increased compensation as evidence of a political wedge between urban villagers and migrant workers.[12] Even though policy changes have led to urban residents often having a greater say in redevelopment, migrants remain institutionally excluded.[13]

My intervention here is not to refute these insights about the consequences of urban development and redevelopment.

Rather, it is to expand the scope of inquiry and insert displacement within an analysis of the broader population management regime. By focusing on school demolitions, relocations, and closures, I bring a somewhat different social dynamic to light than is the case for existing literature that focuses on the effects of urban residents losing their housing or peasants losing their land. While schools and housing are the core spaces of social reproduction and therefore intimately linked socially and spatially, zeroing in on the school holds some distinct analytical advantages in understanding the politics of urbanization. First, and most important, it highlights how intergenerational social reproduction is managed more precisely than is possible by looking at housing. Cities can and have arranged to house workers while denying their children the right to schooling, but the reverse situation is uncommon.[14] In this sense, it is a more appropriate location for assessing the impact of development on the durability of the urbanization of people. Second, the question of compensation has been central to analyses of urbanization-driven housing displacement.[15] But the compensation issue for schools is distinct in that it is not primarily a financial question; rather, the issue is whether students will be resettled, in what kind of school, and where. While rural migrants are excluded from compensation for redevelopment of urban land, in theory the state should make arrangements for displaced students, regardless of their *hukou* status. Finally, I also focus on the issue of school closures rather than just demolitions. In contrast to looking at housing, the former perspective highlights the rising significance of population control in motivating state action. In order for this distinction to be meaningful, we will need to address some definitional issues.

DISTINCT PATHWAYS OF
SCHOOL ELIMINATION

While the bulldozing of a school is a powerful dramatization of the state's callousness toward migrants, in fact not all demolitions are created equal. The critical difference is between "demolition and relocation" (*chaiqian* 拆迁) and "closure" (*guanbi* 关闭). The former has been a regular feature of China's urban landscape for decades, as cities' built environments have undergone a dramatic transformation in the reform era. As noted earlier, the process of demolition and relocation is by no means benign. It is typically dominated by developers and their revenue-hungry allies in the state, while affected residents are given few meaningful avenues for exercising political voice. Nonetheless, from a legal standpoint demolition and relocation implies a responsibility on the part of the government to indeed *relocate* residents affected by the redevelopment.[16] Affected populations may not have a say in the matter, but the government is obligated to provide compensatory space elsewhere within their jurisdiction.[17] Many migrant schools in Beijing and elsewhere have been impacted by demolition and relocation as massive new infrastructure projects are rolled out, land values in the core rise, and the city seeks more profitable uses for the land. In these cases, schools are not specifically targeted *because* they are migrant schools; rather, they are simply caught up in the maelstrom of China's urban revolution, as are countless other occupants of the city.

Closure, on the other hand, represents an entirely different politics. A closure is final, and the state has no obligation to provide compensation to the school. While there is some ambiguity as to the legal obligations with regard to placing affected students in other schools, in practice the government has not been proactive. Migrant schools operating without official licensing—a significant majority in Beijing—are particularly susceptible to closure since the government need not provide any legal justification. Unlicensed schools operate at the discretion of local officials, thus leaving them in a precarious position. While demolition and relocation are associated with a process of spatial peripheralization (with its own attendant social and economic costs), closure is more directly expulsionary in nature. As Mr. Li, an experienced NGO activist in Beijing, said, "[Schools] aren't afraid of demolition and relocation . . . because people in one district can move to another district and rent another space, and they'll be ok. What they fear is closure."[18]

From 2010 a huge number of Beijing's migrant schools were closed or demolished and relocated, impacting tens of thousands of children, a summary of which appears in table 5.1 at the close of this chapter.[19] Data were collected by collating publicly available reports, both from traditional and social media, and thus should be seen as underreporting the extent of demolitions. I have verified that at least 76 schools were closed and/or demolished in Beijing between 2010 and 2018, affecting at least 46,965 students. However, this latter number excludes observations for which I could not find specific information on the number of students affected. By including estimates from these additional nineteen observations, that number increases to more than 62,000.[20] This should be taken as a baseline. As just one indicator of the shortcomings of these data, I only have twenty observations for the entirety of the year 2011, whereas numerous media reports claimed that between twenty-four and thirty schools were demolished that summer alone. I could not include observations without adequate verifiable information (e.g., school name, location). Even if the number of affected students

TABLE 5.1

Year	School Name	District	Most precise location
2010	Rongqian School (荣乾学校)	Daxing	Daxing District, Jiugong Township, Wu Dian Er Dui (大兴区旧宫镇庑店二队)
2010	Xinyuan School (新苑学校)	Daxing	Daxing District, Jiugong Township, Shu Qiao Village (大兴区旧宫镇树桥村)
2010	Xiangshang School (向上学校)	Changping	Changping District, Huilongguan Village (昌平区回龙观村)
2010	Tenglong School (腾龙学校)	Chaoyang	Chaoyang District, Dongba Xiang (朝阳区东坝乡) —> Chaoyang District, Shibalidian Xiang (朝阳区十八里店乡)
2010	Yingjie School (英杰学校)	Chaoyang	Chaoyang District, Dongba Xiang, Qikeshu Village (朝阳区东坝乡七棵树村)
2010	Yingjie School (英杰学校)	Chaoyang	Chaoyang District, Shibali Dian (朝阳区十八里店)
2010	Xinli School (新利学校)	Chaoyang	Chaoyang District, Shibali Dian (朝阳区十八里店)
2010	Beigao Shiyan School (北皋实验学校)	Chaoyang	Chaoyang District, Cuigezhuang Xiang (朝阳区崔各庄乡)
2010	Yuying School (育英学校)	Chaoyang	Chaoyang District, Cuigezhuang Xiang (朝阳区崔各庄乡)

(continued)

TABLE 5.1 *(continued)*

Year	School Name	District	Most precise location
2010	Cuigezhuang Shiyan School (崔各庄实验学校)	Chaoyang	Chaoyang District, Cuigezhuang Xiang (朝阳区崔各庄乡)
2010	Nangao Jinghua School (南皋京华学校)	Chaoyang	Chaoyang District, Cuigezhuang Xiang (朝阳区崔各庄乡)
2010	Taoyuan School (桃园学校)	Chaoyang	Chaoyang District, Cuigezhuang Xiang (朝阳区崔各庄乡)
2010	Qinglian School (青莲学校)	Chaoyang	Chaoyang District, Cuigezhuang Xiang (朝阳区崔各庄乡)
2010	Xingxing School (星星学校)	Chaoyang	Chaoyang District, Cuigezhuang Xiang (朝阳区崔各庄乡)
2010	Wende School (文德学校)	Chaoyang	Chaoyang District, Cuigezhuang Xiang (朝阳区崔各庄乡)
2010	Nangao Shiyan School (南皋实验学校)	Chaoyang	Chaoyang District, Cuigezhuang Xiang (朝阳区崔各庄乡)
2010	Hongjunying Xiwang School (红军营希望小学)	Chaoyang	Chaoyang District, Guangying Xiang, Beiyuan Village (朝阳区广营乡北苑村)
2011	Yingcai School (英才学校)	Chaoyang	Chaoyang District, Jinzhan Xiang, 114 Leizhuang (朝阳区金盏乡雷庄114号)

(continued)

TABLE 5.1 *(continued)*

Year	School Name	District	Most precise location
2011	Tianyuan School (田园学校)	Daxing	Daxing District, Xihongmen Township (大兴区西红门镇)
2011	Yuhong School (育红小学)	Daxing	Daxing District, Xihongmen Township, 24 North Tonghua Street (大兴区西红门镇同华北大街24号)
2011	Tuanhe Shiyan School (团河实验小学)	Daxing	Daxing District, Xihongmen Township, Tuanhebei Village (大兴区西红门镇团河北村)
2011	Jianxinzhuang Shiyan School (建新庄实验学校)	Daxing	Daxing District, Xihongmen Township, 52 Jianxinzhuang Industrial Park (大兴区西红门镇建新庄工业区52号)
2011	Lantian Shiyan School (蓝天实验学校)	Chaoyang	Chaoyang District, Dongba Xiang (朝阳区东坝乡)
2011	Dongba Shiyan School (东坝实验学校)	Chaoyang	Chaoyang District, Dongba Xiang (朝阳区东坝乡)
2011	Yuying School (育英学校)	Chaoyang	Chaoyang District, Dongba Xiang (朝阳区东坝乡)
2011	Dongba Peixin School (东坝培新学校)	Chaoyang	Chaoyang District, Dongba Xiang (朝阳区东坝乡)

(continued)

TABLE 5.1 *(continued)*

Year	School Name	District	Most precise location
2011	Yucai School (育才学校)	Chaoyang	Chaoyang District, Jiangtai Xiang (朝阳区将台乡)
2011	Xiwang Zhi Xing School (希望之星学校)	Chaoyang	Chaoyang District, Jiangtai Xiang, Dongbajianfang Village (朝阳区将台乡东八间房村)
2011	Dong Beiya School (东北亚学校)	Chaoyang	Chaoyang District, Jiangtai Xiang, Yongjia Village (朝阳区将台乡雍家村)
2011	Miaomiao School 苗苗小学	Haidian	Haidian District, Sijiqing Township, Beiwu Village Street, Zhongwu Village (海淀区四季青镇北坞村路中坞村)
2011	Lǜyuan School (绿园小学)	Haidian	Haidian District, Haidian Xiang, Shucun Xiaoqinghe Street, north side (海淀区海淀乡树村小清河路北侧)
2011	Xin Xiwang School (新希望小学)	Haidian	Haidian District, Xisanqi, Dongsheng Xiang (海淀区西三旗东升乡)
2011	Hongxing School (红星小学)*	Haidian	Haidian District, Xisan Qi, Dongsheng Xiang, Xiaoying Dadui, North Panzhuang Village (海淀区西三旗东升乡小营大队潘庄村北)
2011	Chunlei School (春蕾小学)	Shijingshan	Shijingshan District, Liuniang Fu, Yinliao Chang (石景山区刘娘府饮料厂)

(continued)

TABLE 5.1 *(continued)*

Year	School Name	District	Most precise location
2011	Taihe School (太和小学)	Shijingshan	Shijingshan Village, Yongwangfu Village (石景山区雍王府村)
2011	Hongxing School (红星小学)	Shijingshan	Shijingshan Village, Yongwangfu Village (石景山区雍王府村)
2011	Xianfeng School (先锋小学)	Shijingshan	Shijingshan Village, Yongwangfu Village (石景山区雍王府村)
2012	Tongxin Shiyan School (同心实验学校)	Chaoyang	Chaoyang District, Jinzhan Xiang, Pi Village (朝阳区金盏乡皮村)
2012	Xinli School (新利学校)	Chaoyang	Chaoyang District, Jinzhan Xiang, Pi Village (朝阳区金盏乡皮村)
2012	Diyi Xingong-mian School (Xiwang School) （第一新公民学校(希望学校))	Chaoyang	Chaoyang District, Jinzhan Xiang, Magezhuang Village (朝阳区金盏乡马各庄村)
2012	Ma Ge Zhuang Shi Yan School (马各庄实验学校)	Chaoyang	Chaoyang District, Jinzhan Xiang, Magezhuang Village (朝阳区金盏乡马各庄村)
2014	Shiji School (世纪学校)	Fengtai	Fengtai District, Wangzuo Township, Dianqi Village (丰台区王佐镇佃起村)
2014–2016	Chengxin School (诚信学校)	Daxing	Daxing District, Xihong-men Township, Si Village (大兴区西红门镇肆村)

(continued)

TABLE 5.1 *(continued)*

Year	School Name	District	Most precise location
2014	Zhenhua School (振华学校)	Daxing	Daxing District, Xihongmen Township, Xingguangming Juweihui (大兴区西红门镇星光明居委会)
2014	Zhiquan School (智泉学校)	Changping	Changping District, Dongxiaokou Township, Zhongtan Village (昌平区东小口镇中滩村)
2014	Mingxin School (明欣学校)	Changping	Changping District, Huilongguan Township, 319 Qiliqu North Village (昌平区回龙观镇七里渠南村319号)
2014	Zhenhua School (振华学校)	Changping	Changping District, Dongxiaokou Township (昌平区东小口镇)
2014	Jingwei School (经纬学校)	Changping	Changping District, Dongxiaokou Township, Dingfu Huangzhuang (昌平区东小口镇定福黄庄)
2015	Yuxing School (育星园学校)	Chaoyang	Chaoyang District, Sunhe Xiang, Xiaxinbao Village (朝阳区孙河乡下辛堡村)
2015	Shaziying Shiyan School (沙子营实验学校)	Chaoyang	Chaoyang District, Sunhe Xiang, Shaziying Village (朝阳区孙河乡沙子营村)
2015	Huacheng School (华成学校)	Chaoyang	Chaoyang District, Sunhe Xiang, Shaziying Village (朝阳区孙河乡沙子营村)

(continued)

TABLE 5.1 *(continued)*

Year	School Name	District	Most precise location
2014–2016	Peiyan School (培彦学校)	Tongzhou	Tongzhou District, Taihu Township, Dongshi Village, North Dongshi Street (通州区台湖镇东石村东石北路)
2014–2016	Shahe Shiyan School (沙河实验学校)	Changping	Changping District, Shahe Township, 73 Gongwanhua (昌平区沙河镇工丸华73号)
2014–2016	Cuigezhuang Weilai Bilingual School (崔各庄未来双语学校)	Chaoyang	Chaoyang District, Cuigezhuang Xiang, Dongxindian Village (朝阳区崔各庄乡东辛店村)
2014–2016	Chunlei School (春蕾学校)	Chaoyang	Chaoyang District, Gaobeidian Xiang, 315 Banbicdian Village (朝阳区高碑店乡半壁店村315号)
2014–2016	Qinghua Ao Xiao (青华奥小)	Chaoyang	Chaoyang District, Gaobeidian Xiang, Baijialou Village (朝阳区高碑店乡白家楼村)
2014–2016	Qi Cai School (七彩学校)	Tongzhou	Tongzhou District, Taihu Township, Tianfu Village (通州区台湖镇田府村)
2014–2016	Li Hua School, Gao Lou Jin Campus (立华学校高楼金分校)	Tongzhou	Tongzhou District, Liyuan Township, Gaoloujin Village (通州区梨园镇高楼金村)
2014–2016	Mingyuan School (明圆学校)	Chaoyang	Chaoyang District, Xiaohongmen Xiang, Long Zhua Shu Nan Li (朝阳区小红门乡龙爪数南里)

(continued)

TABLE 5.1 *(continued)*

Year	School Name	District	Most precise location
2014–2016	Xinghe Bilingual School (星河双语学校)	Chaoyang	Chaoyang District, Jinzhan Xiang, Changdian Village (朝阳区金盏乡长店村)
2014–2016	Hongxiang School (宏翔学校)	Chaoyang	Chaoyang District, Sanjianfang Xiang, 263 Xinfang Village (朝阳区三间房乡新房村263号)
2014–2016	Anmin School, Chenguang Campus (安民学校, 晨光校区)	Chaoyang	
2017	Haidi School (海迪小学 (3rd relocation))	Daxing	Daxing District, Jiugong Township, Xi San Street, Nan Xiao Jie, No.2 Village (大兴区旧宫镇西三路南小街二村)
2017	Jianxinzhuang Shiyan School (建新庄实验学校)	Daxing	Daxing District, Xihongmen Township, No. 52 Jianxin Zhuang Industrial Park (大兴区西红门镇建新庄工业区52号)
2017	Mingyuan School (明圆学校)	Daxing	Daxing District, Demao Zhuang, 18 De Yu Jia Street (大兴区德茂庄德裕街甲18号)
2017	Tuanhe Shiyan School (团河实验小学)	Daxing	Daxing District, Xihongmen Township, Tuanhe South Village (大兴区西红门镇团河南村)

(continued)

TABLE 5.1 *(continued)*

Year	School Name	District	Most precise location
2017	Jingwei School, Dingfu Primary (经纬学校, 定福小学)	Daxing	Daxing District, Ding Fu Huang Zhuang (大兴区定福黄庄)
2017	Jingrui School (京瑞学校)	Changping	near Zhenhua School (near 振华学校)
2017	Chunfeng School (春风学校)	Changping	Changping District, Xiaotangshan Township, Jiang Li village, north of Zhiquan School (昌平区小汤山镇讲礼村, north of 智泉学校)
2017	Limin School (利民学校)	Changping	Changping District, Dongxiaokou Township, Ban Jie Ta Village, West of Zhiquan School (昌平区东小口镇半截塔村, west of 智泉学校)
2017	Zhiquan School (智泉学校)	Changping	Changping District, Beiqijia Township, South of Dong San Qi Village (昌平区北七家镇东三旗村南部)
2017	Zhenxin School (振兴学校)	Changping	Changping District, Beiqi Jia Township, Yandan Village (昌平区北七家镇燕丹村)
2017	Haiqing School (海清学校)	Changping	Changping District, Longguan Township, Sanhe Zhuang, 10 Ma Jia Di (昌平区龙观镇三合庄马家地10号)

(continued)

TABLE 5.1 *(continued)*

Year	School Name	District	Most precise location
2017	Shuren School (树仁学校)	Shijingshan	Shijingshan District, Lugu Shequ, Yamenkou Village, South Street (石景山区鲁谷社区衙门口村南街)
2018	Taijing School (台京学校)	Shijingshan	Shijingshan District, Lugu Shequ, Yamenkou Village, 100 Southwestern Street (石景山区鲁谷社区衙门口村西南后街100号)
2018	Huangzhuang School (黄庄学校)	Shijingshan	Shijingshan District, East Lianshi Street, 43 Southwestern Miaopu (石景山区莲石东路西南郊苗圃43号)

is just 62,000, this represents a massive amount of social disloca-tion targeted at a specific group. How then, did migrant schools come to be specifically targeted for elimination?

The Regulatory Context in Beijing

As informal schooling in Beijing expanded rapidly in the early 2000s, the municipal government became wary about this large swath of the education sector exceeding their control. Announced in October 2005, the "Beijing Department of Edu-cation Notification on Strengthening Management of Migrant Population Self-Run Schools" aimed to assert greater regulatory power under the guiding principle of "supporting some, approv-ing some, and eliminating some."[21] A specific breakdown of what share of schools were to be eliminated was not provided, nor were details about financial support. In 2006, the Department of Education accepted licensing applications from migrant schools, but few were approved.[22] By 2011, school principals and civil society actors were unanimous in their assessment that it was nearly impossible for migrant schools to become licensed. If schools could not expect financial support or licensing, that left them with but one option: elimination.

The principles established in the 2005 notification were haltingly put into practice. Following the 2006 invitation for license applications, only sixty-two out of approximately three hundred migrant schools in the city had official recognition.[23] According to most accounts, no migrant schools were licensed after this, while the state began taking measures to gradually winnow away the unlicensed schools. Despite ongoing pressures, there were still 112 schools as of 2016.[24] In part this was due to the relative autonomy of the districts in implementing directives from the municipal government, and indeed there were important differences within Beijing. Although it could never be publicly acknowledged, the persistence of wholly informal schools is at least partly explained by the fact that they provide an important service—albeit one of poor quality—while costing the government nothing or almost nothing. Nonetheless, the general trend of eliminating wholly unregulated schools had been clearly established in 2006.

Regularized Relocation

Within this regulatory context, migrant schools have become accustomed to continually facing the dual threats of relocation and closure. Zhifan School, which by 2008 was regularly winning praise from the government and associated institutions, had suffered repeated attacks in its early days. An official history of the school recounted these difficulties in a forthright manner:

As a start, [Zhifan] School used the 2,000 RMB loan from its founders as the school's building fund. The school was built from scratch and opened its doors on the 6th of August [2001]. However it was closed shortly after on August 25th, as it did not have an operation permit. After August 25th, the newly established [Zhifan] School fought to survive despite the extremely difficult conditions. During this period, the school was made to move five times. In addition, it was also penalized and forced to close down four times. The path to provide a well-rounded education for migrant children proved to be exceptionally arduous.

Stormy Days: There were various reasons behind [Zhifan] School's frequent moves in the beginning of its establishment. For the first two times, it was because the school was forced by the government to close its doors. For the following three times, it was because the school buildings had to be demolished in order to make way for the expansion of the city of Beijing. This explains why Zhifan School slowly made its way from the Fourth Ring Road to the Fifth Ring Road and eventually to its current position within the Sixth Ring Road. As for the four closures, the school was forced to close by the government for the first two times; for the following two times, the school was unable to pay rent due to financial difficulties, hence resulting in the landlord cutting water and electricity supply, and eventually reclaiming the school's facilities.[25]

The report does not provide a specific timeframe within which these closures and relocations took place. Although I did not verify this, it would seem likely that the school was not forced to close or relocate after 2008, at which point they had substantial foundation support and official recognition. At most, these numerous closures and relocations happened over a ten-year period, since this document was produced in 2011.

Having secured significant external fiscal resources, Zhifan escaped the threat of imminent closure that so pervades Beijing's migrant schools. But as depicted in previous chapters, Zhifan is quite exceptional in many regards, notably its official registration and relatively abundant foundation support. Other schools that occupied a legal gray zone could be summarily closed down, with the government free of legal responsibility to resettle the displaced students or provide financial compensation. Rapidly increasing land values and an increasingly nativist political sentiment over the course of the 2010s provided plenty of motivation for local officials to remove migrant schools, for based on official metrics of valuation, the schools provided almost nothing. As a result, many schools in this period of time were forced to regularly fight for their survival, which often involved relocating further into Beijing's periphery.

Demolition and Relocation

Demolitions due to urban redevelopment are a fact of life for many people and institutions in Chinese cities, but migrant schools are particularly vulnerable. Even migrant schools in the enviable position of having official licensing can be subject to highly coercive pressures, a tendency that was made patently clear in the case of Jingwei and Huangzhuang schools.

Jingwei School, located in Dongxiaokou township in the southeastern corner of Changping District since 2003, was living on borrowed time when I first visited in 2014. This area has better connections to transportation infrastructure than most parts of Changping, located as it is just to the north of the Olympic park and a short bus ride away from three different subway lines. Dongxiaokou had a high concentration of migrants from Henan Province who lived in ramshackle informal housing set amid piles of waste (see figure 5.1). Most of the residents were involved in waste recycling—an essential function for the city, but less desirable from the perspective of village officials than the rapidly encroaching high-rise apartments developments.[26] Jingwei was one of three migrant schools in the community (the other two, Zhenhua and Mingxin, will be discussed later). It received official licensing from Changping District in 2006 and enrolled more than seven hundred students in 2013.

These schools, and indeed the entire community, had known since 2010 that Dongxiaokou was included in a major citywide

FIGURE 5.1 Dongxiaokou neighborhood.

Photo by the author.

redevelopment plan. The plan aimed to redevelop fifty urban villages dispersed across Beijing, covering a total land area of 85.3 square kilometers, which housed 214,000 locals and more than one million migrants.[27] Five of these villages were within Dongxiaokou. Seemingly attentive to earlier rounds of land requisition, which had resulted in conflicts and complaints about social equity, the government planned to emphasize villagers' interests during this redevelopment push. Indeed, Dongxiaokou Township Party Secretary Li Zhijie said, "Before demolition and redevelopment, first we convene a village representative congress to allow villagers to discuss the compensation plan and design for their resettlement housing. . . . We ensure that villagers take care of villager business, and nothing will be demolished unless approved by the village representative congress."

As extensively documented in the literature, however, nonlocal residents are not considered part of the village, and the state has no obligation to consult with them or consider their interests. The Dongxiaokou village committee, without prior notice to school administrators, cut Jingwei's electricity on December 22, 2013, in an effort to push the school out. This coercive action came despite a lease on the property that lasted through 2017. The principal of the school, who I would later discover was perfectly amenable to relocation in principle, was furious, since the school was left with no lighting and no heat, at one of the coldest times of year: "Cutting the electricity was not okay. We still hadn't gone on break, and the Education Department didn't consider this. They said it was maintenance. . . . They didn't inform the school, they just cut [the power]."[28] The story gained significant media attention as the image of hundreds of children braving the Beijing winter to attend classes underlined the inequities of the city's education system. But the deputy secretary of the village committee suggested he was not to blame.

He noted that the school's landlord had been informed on December 2, twenty days prior to cutting the power, and therefore "we already gave them enough time [to vacate]."[29]

The school's official licensing was apparently of no use in averting such coercive steps on the part of the government. Following the electricity shutoff, the principal visited various government offices more than ten times, but to no avail: "The village committee wants [us] to negotiate with the landlord, the township wants us to negotiate with the village committee."[30] The principal was dismissive of the school's official status, suggesting that it could not prevent the forced relocation: "The Education Department changes lots of names, they say you are illegal, or you're self-run [ziban 自办], or you're a migrant school. . . . There is no distinction between having a license or not when they are demolishing and relocating."[31] As soon as the semester ended, Jingwei abandoned its Dongxiaokou location amid a sea of rubble (see figure 5.2).[32]

FIGURE 5.2 Jingwei School and demolition.

Photo by the author.

I went to visit Jingwei in its new location in June 2014. The school had been relocated fifteen kilometers to the northwest of the original location, or more than an hour by bus depending on traffic. Although I had not been able to get into the previous location before it was closed, the new facilities appeared to be an improvement.[33] While still a far cry from most public schools in the city, the new location was relatively tidy and spacious and in a decent state of upkeep. About half a year after the school had been unceremoniously dispatched from Dongxiaokou, the principal seemed to be relatively satisfied with the outcome: "[At the old location] there were demolished bricks everywhere around the school, if one of the children fell on their way to class, that would cause difficulty for the school. . . . At the time, I thought they just wanted to shut us down, and when they froze our assets my heart was full of resentment. Later I thought about it; actually, it was the right thing."[34] As I learned in interviews with numerous school administrators and parents, many could not imagine a city in which coercive redevelopment was not the norm. For most, the relevant question was not whether they would be forced to move or not, but the kinds of resettlement conditions they could secure.

While Jingwei eventually received decent accommodation deeper in the periphery, the move was not without costs. The clearest indicator of social stress resulting from the relocation was the precipitous drop in student enrollment, from more than seven hundred to some three hundred. I was not able to interview parents of children who did not move to the new location, but one may speculate that the new more peripheral location would have made it impossible for many children to remain enrolled. In fact, a majority of the three hundred or so remaining students lived in on-site dorms, traveling to other parts of the city to see their parents on weekends.[35] It seems plausible that this demolition and relocation introduced new sets of social and possibly economic stresses into the lives of hundreds of migrant families. As a licensed school, Jingwei certainly received better treatment than its totally informal counterparts. But as the Huangzhuang School case reveals, by 2018 official recognition was no longer an adequate prophylactic against the finality of *closure*.

Closure

Whereas many migrant school demolitions in Beijing had historically resulted from a combination of rising land values and state indifference to these communities' well-being, by 2011 school demolitions were increasingly justified or motivated by population control. Beijing officials had likely come under greater pressure to be proactive, and a population "redline" established in 2005 to cap the city's population at 18 million was surpassed in 2010, ten years ahead of schedule. Over the next several years, the city employed a number of strategies to limit the population, most important among them the increased restrictions on accessing public schools that have already been discussed. Squeezing children out of the public system worked in tandem with elimination of informal options. Given that these schools generally had no operating license to revoke, the state resorted to direct and coercive demolitions.

This change in tack was marked decisively in August 2011 when an unprecedented campaign was launched across multiple districts in the city to crack down on unlicensed schools. With little forewarning, and only a few weeks before the fall semester was to start, at least twenty-four schools were shuttered, leaving up to thirty thousand students with nowhere to go.[36] The

Education Department claimed these closures were in response to schools' failure to meet safety standards. Furthermore, it promised that "most" students would be resettled in licensed public or private schools, with Chaoyang District claiming fully 90 percent would be resettled within its boundaries (these goals were almost certainly not met).[37] Suspicions about the willingness of the state to resettle students was seemingly confirmed when one official made their intentions quite explicit in an interview with *Caixin*: "An official at Beijing's education department said it's difficult to properly arrange for educating a student who's been dismissed from an unauthorized school. One reason is that the municipal government must consider population control when designing and implementing educational policies."[38] Clearly, these demolitions were not simply about enforcing safety regulations.

The concentrated spate of demolitions in 2011 received significant domestic and international media attention and generated something of a public backlash, as well as disruptive protests from parents. In light of this, the government made efforts to space out the demolitions somewhat over time. By all outward appearances, officials were under immense pressure to succeed in population reduction where they had failed previously. Indeed, the national-level urbanization plan from 2014 specifically called for extra-large cities such as Beijing to "strictly control" their population. Within Beijing and Shanghai, street-level officials were given population reduction targets, with wide latitude in method of implementation. Informal schools continued to be a popular target, both because of their immediate effect and also because of the presumed knock-on effect within migrant communities.

As might be expected, families, teachers, and school administrators were often vigorously opposed to seemingly arbitrary demolitions. One consequence of this is that the state often deployed contingents of police and/or thugs in order to enforce eviction notices. A former teacher from a school in Shaziying, a village in the northeastern district of Shunyi, related how his school's eviction was both unexpected and violent:

> A lot of security just showed up. I was so terrified I didn't want to come out [of the school grounds]. I said, "What is this all about?" They said we were being shut down, there were more than a hundred of them. They weren't actual security, they were just a bunch of thugs . . . more than a hundred of them blocking the gate, like the mafia. They dragged the parents inside and beat them. . . . I said, "I'm calling the police." The police came, but it was useless, the government had already made a decision.[39]

As already indicated, it is not always possible to fully untangle whether a school is being closed in order for an official to reach his or her population expulsion quota or to secure land for more valuable uses. When we turn to the case of the Huangzhuang School, however, it is apparent that the two pressures, political and economic, are linked. Regardless of original intent, we see that the increasingly nativist political environment provides further rationale for urban land dispossession, even when the school in question is fully licensed and highly reputed.

Shuttering an Award-Winning School

Huangzhuang School was first established in 1998 in response to the growing demand for education from those shut out of the public system.[40] The school grew rapidly in the relatively laissez-faire environment that existed at the time, and quickly grew to include a number of branch schools. In 2003 the main school moved to what would be its final location in western Beijing's Shijingshan District, renting a large space from a subsidiary company of the Beijing Urban Construction Group.[41] While the move had been precipitated by their previous site being demolished, this new larger space was only two hundred meters away. Subsequently, Huangzhuang was able to secure an official operating license. The school began to attract widespread media attention for its high standards, and significant domestic and international foundation support followed (including from Save the Children and the NBA). In 2017, the school's total enrollment was 1975, making it the largest and perhaps best-known migrant school in the city.

The school's relative success was not enough to prevent their landlord from taking steps to remove them. In August 2017, the company told the school it was canceling its lease to clear the area. Anti-migrant policies in the capital had been ratcheted up yet further in 2017, when the government announced the new population redline of 23 million. In this context, the company framed its eviction efforts as helping to relocate non-capital functions out of the city. Students, parents, and teachers mobilized in response, writing a widely circulated open letter and pleading with the Education Department to intervene. Implicitly accepting the terms of the population management regime, the open letter argued for leniency based on the parents' presumed contributions to the economy: "Basically all of the parents of our school's 1975 children have formal employment. 90 percent of these parents are not targets for clearing [*shujie* 疏解]. 80 percent of these students were born in Beijing. If the school is demolished, 95 percent of these children will become left-behind children or will drop out."[42] In response to pressure from the community and media attention, the

Education Department sided with the school, and Huang-zhuang was able to keep its doors open.

But things did not work out so well in 2018. Taking a different tack this time, on August 9 the company once again sent a notification to the school announcing it was canceling the school's lease, despite its being set to expire in 2025. On the night of August 10, the company sealed the entrance to the school. A crucial difference this time was that the company had the support of the Education Department—indeed, the latter had as of that summer failed to renew Huangzhuang's license. The lack of license was in turn part of the company's justification for eviction. In the month leading up to the eviction notice, school principal Chen Enshi had been in negotiations with the authorities. But no satisfactory relocation plan emerged, at least in part because there were no adequate spaces for rent in the area that were within the school's budget. Principal Chen was eventually resigned to closing down after twenty years in operation, and the school's gates shut for good in August.

Although the Education Department was unable or unwilling to relocate the school, it had still promised to resettle the students. The previous few years had seen more and more migrant schools shuttered, and Shijingshan District was no exception. Three other schools in the area had been recently closed, and there was only one remaining in the entire district. Since most displaced children had little hope of getting into public schools, the majority of Huangzhuang's students were to be placed several kilometers away in this remaining school, or somewhere still further afield. Although it is unclear whether Huangzhuang's earlier assessment that 95 percent of its students would drop out or become left-behind children was accurate, there was anecdotal evidence that many parents would have to send their children to the village. As the parent of one displaced child said, "[the remaining] private schools are so expensive, and we can't get into a public school."[43]

The proximate cause of the demolitions of both Jingwei and Huangzhuang was developers pushing to make more profitable use of land in a context of rapidly increasing real estate values. The Dongxiaokou government had demarcated the community of recyclers and migrant slums for redevelopment, a process that had already laid waste to half the village when I visited in 2014. In Shijingshan, the lease Huangzhuang signed thirteen years before had locked in rent that was far below what the market was fetching by 2017. In this case, the eviction was spearheaded by the landlord rather than the state. The broader context of the municipal government's growing hostility toward migrants is critical; in both cases, a more sympathetic district or municipal government most certainly could have intervened to avert the demolitions or to secure better relocation conditions. Over the course of the 2010s, the economic *and* political impetuses for evicting migrants grew, leaving increasingly dim prospects for migrant schools, even those that were licensed. As principal Chen Enshi trenchantly remarked, "the fate of migrant schools is tightly linked with urban development and population policy."[44]

Demolitions at Home, Work

While the focus here is on schools, evictions and demolitions of the home or the workplace have an immediate impact on children's education, even if the school itself remains unscathed. Working-class migrants generally occupy a position of informality and precarity in both labor and housing markets, which means that, as with the schools, they are frequently subject to eviction and demolition. When a residence or parents' workplace is demolished, families often face lengthened commutes or the prospect of switching schools, putting further pressure on the social and educational life of the children. In Beijing and other cities, a large portion of migrants are engaged in small-scale entrepreneurial activity, and opening small shops is a popular choice for those who have escaped the lowest rung of informality. Regardless of the market viability of such operations, such businesses are rarely a priority for government officials, since they cannot generate the kind of returns associated with high-rise apartments or high-end consumption. As a result, many of these small business owners found themselves subject to the centrifugal force that structured so much of migrant life in Beijing. Ms. Xu, the Shandong native living in Liwanzhuang, talked about the difficulty of managing a small business in the context of rising rents: "The main problem with doing business is that rent is extremely expensive. If you go to a more remote place, then there's a real possibility that as soon as your business is running well, as soon as you've established a base, then you'll immediately get demolished again."[45] As Ms. Xu's husband, Mr. Fan, notes below, these workplace demolitions had an immediate impact on their children's education.

Workplace or housing demolitions can also undermine parents' ability to enroll in public schools. As was detailed extensively in chapters 2 and 4, parents' labor market position is the single most important factor in gaining admission to public schools. If parents lose their employment as a result of their workplace's being demolished or relocated, their child may not be able to enroll in public school the following year. Mr. Fan talked about how continual demolitions prevented him from maintaining the business license necessary to get his children into public schools: "I'm an individual (*geti* 个体) contractor.

After setting up my business for a short time we were demolished once again, so I couldn't get a business license. With a business license you can get those permits or whatever they're called. But we didn't have [the license] because we were demolished, so it became invalid."[46] Since migrant children are seen as an appendage of their gainfully employed parents, their social reproduction is provisionally linked to the value of parental labor. When that labor is rendered invaluable, the child's access to education is similarly thrown into question.

Home demolitions do not always result in students being forced to change schools, but they can result in other kinds of disruptions. Mr. Lu, the grandfather of a student in Dongxiaokou's Zhenhua School, detailed the hardships his family had endured in the face of repeated home demolitions:

> We've moved several times. They demolish and we move. Last month, we still lived quite close [to the school], I'd get him to school on my tricycle in just five minutes. Now from [where we live] it takes thirty minutes. Getting to school every day is just exhausting. You need to watch the clock carefully. After this semester, they're going to demolish things again. We'll have to move, we can't let the kid miss school before then. If we move to a different school in the area, we'll have to pay more money. What a pain.[47]

In this case, the family was fortunate to have a grandparent who was able to take on a share of the reproductive labor. Even so, it came at the expense of less time at home, and it was physically taxing for Mr. Lu. These kinds of continual commuting fixes were a common feature of migrant life.

Finally, it would be remiss to fail to mention the exclamation mark at the end of the 2011–2017 expulsionary hard turn. On

November 18, 2017, a fire broke out in a migrant housing complex in southern Beijing's Daxing District, resulting in nineteen deaths. The fire was likely caused by shoddy construction and poor implementation of safety measures, features that are common in the city's informal housing sector. The municipal government used the pretext of ensuring fire safety to launch a campaign of mass eviction, affecting perhaps more than 100,000 migrants.[48] The evictions targeted migrant communities in general rather than schools in particular. Nonetheless, schools were subject to this orgy of destruction, either directly or indirectly via housing demolition. In addition to helping the government secure its population control aims, it was also a clear indication that they were siding with real estate interests against labor-intensive industries. Indeed, Alibaba and JD.com, companies highly dependent on a poorly compensated migrant workforce, had to scramble to arrange housing for their displaced couriers.[49] These and tens of thousands of other workers were being pushed from the city, often over the protests of their employers. As one warehousing company executive commented in the wake of the evictions, "Many delivery companies have stopped receiving Beijing-bound packages because they don't have the capacity to deal with them. . . . Delivery companies face hundreds of millions of renminbi in losses."[50] While certain segments of capital were suffering from the expulsion of viable laborers, Beijing's political class would soon learn the happy news that city's population was already falling.

IMPACTS OF SCHOOL DEMOLITIONS

As would be expected, school demolitions leave a path of destruction—physical, social, and psychological—in their wake.

Even in the best-case scenario of adequate relocation of students, such events are deeply disruptive to daily life.

Sociospatial Reorganization

Perhaps the clearest consequence of school demolitions is the increased spatial peripheralization of the spaces of migrant social reproduction. Given economic and political pressures for migrants to move further from the urban core or out of the city altogether, school demolitions simply thrust migrant families into an already intensifying centrifugal current. In 2013, an interactive map compiled by the New Citizen Program (a Beijing-based NGO) revealed only four of eighty migrant schools in Beijing within the Fourth Ring Road.[51] As can be seen in a 2016 map (figure 5.3), a large majority of the city's migrant schools are outside of the Fifth Ring Road (which runs along a roughly twenty-kilometer radius from Tiananmen Square). As an expert from the New Citizen Program put it, "There will always be more suburbs, there will always be a place where the city meets the country. Now it's the Fifth, Sixth Ring road, soon it will be the Sixth, Seventh ring road. These people will once again be squeezed out to where the city meets the country."[52]

When one leg of the school-work-home commuting triangle is subjected to centrifugal pressures, it can result in severe disruption for families. If children either need to find a new school following closure or move with their relocated school, it will generally lengthen commuting time, either for one parent, the child, or both. For those parents who need to work in the urban core, the peripheralization of available school options adds time demands by further separating the spaces of production and

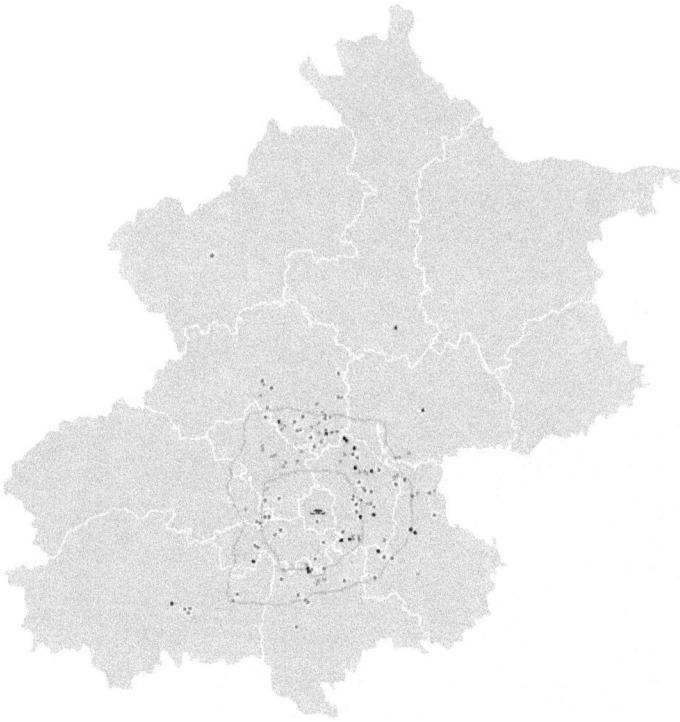

FIGURE 5.3 Location of migrant schools in Beijing, 2016.

Note: The dark black dots represent schools that were closed down or demolished between 2014 and 2016; other dots represent both licensed and unlicensed migrant schools. The two roughly circular lines represent the Fifth and Sixth Ring Roads.

Source: http://thegroundbreaking.com/archives/38007 (permission to use the image explicitly granted).

reproduction within the city. As the boundaries of the school-work-home triangle push up against the limits of social and/or economic feasibility, parents then must consider a range of unpalatable options including searching for new work, moving homes, or sending their child to boarding school or to their home village.

As the periphery of the city has extended outward, migrant communities have been subject to waves of rapid growth followed by the threat or reality of redevelopment and demolition. Liwanzhuang was just such an example, located as it was in the eastern reaches of Chaoyang, far beyond the Fifth Ring Road. The principal of Shusheng School estimated that the surrounding village's population grew from one to two thousand people in 2005 to more than ten thousand by the end of 2011. Many parents I encountered in the community had relocated to the village in response to evictions closer to the urban core. For example, Feng Huai, a mother from Henan living in Liwanzhuang, explained how she had to relocate from Wangjing, a section of Beijing that had been dramatically remade in recent years amid rapidly increasing real estate values: "We moved to [Liwanzhuang] because my husband's company was demolished and relocated here. So I came along with him, and I left my job."[53] The relocation of her husband's work also meant that their son had to change schools. While not specific to schools, the social ephemerality generated by ongoing waves of demolition was directly reflected in the peripatetic nature of the student body.

Student Resettlement

As might be expected, much parental and public attention is focused on the question of student resettlement in the wake of school demolitions. The Beijing government is keenly aware of the optics of evicting children from their schools and has been at pains to publicly state that appropriate accommodations will be made. An official notification on migrant children's education from the Beijing municipal government affirms that "various tasks must be properly addressed before eliminating [the school]. Appropriate arrangements must be made for current students to continue their studies elsewhere, ensuring that their studies are not impacted, and upholding social stability."[54] Following the mass closures of 2011, the Chaoyang District Education Department stated that it was fully prepared and that the authorities would "absolutely not allow even one child from a closed school to be deprived of an education."[55]

Nonetheless, thousands of children *have* in fact been deprived of their education as a result of school closures and demolitions. Although it might be reasonable to make an a priori assumption that this would be the case based on the general anti-migrant politics of the 2010s, in fact there is clear empirical evidence as well. The New Citizen Program conducted a survey of families displaced when Xin Gong Min School, which the NGO operated, was shut down in July 2012.[56] Located in Chaoyang District, the school of more than eight hundred students had included not only a primary school but also a preschool and middle school. Prior to the demolition, the Education Department produced a resettlement plan for the affected students, promising to make arrangements for students in grades 1–5 and 7–8. Because preschool students about to begin grade 1 and recently graduated primary school students about to enter middle school were excluded from the plan, only 650 out of 854 were included. Since the NGO operated the school, it used parents' contact information to follow up with them in late August 2012 to inquire about their children's resettlement after the closure, and it was able to collect information on 746 out of 854 students.

The results of the survey are unmistakable: a significant portion of students were forced out of Beijing following the closure, and most of those who stayed behind faced new inconveniences or stresses on daily life. Among all students, 71.85 percent stayed in Beijing, 18.63 went to their village, .54 percent (four in total) dropped out, and 8.98 percent were still unsure—a precarious position, given that registration for the new school year had passed when the survey was conducted. Even among those students included in the resettlement plan, 18.82 percent reported sending their children back to the village. Of those not included in the plan, only 61.22 percent were staying in Beijing. Finally, of those who were resettled and stayed in Beijing, only 16.51 percent were settled in public schools, indicating nonenforcement of the national "two primaries" policy (in which migrants are to be primarily enrolled in public schools).

Aside from remaining shut out of the public system, migrant families who stayed in Beijing encountered new hardships after Xin Gong Min was closed. The report found that in the less than two months between the announcement of the closure and the survey, fifteen families had to move homes because their children were resettled in a distant location, with most reporting significant increases in rent. A majority of students experienced lengthened commuting times, with an average increase of 20 percent. One of the students who was forced to drop out did so for tragic reasons. As explained in the report:

> One student who suffered from hemophilia had lived [near Xin Gong Min School], and the school was able to accept students with special illnesses. His mother was also a teacher at the school, and so it was convenient for her to care for him. But with the school closure, he was to be resettled in a school that was unwilling to accept him [because of his illness]. . . . Although this person really loved studies and strongly desired to return to school, he was left with no choice but to drop out.

Indeed, demolitions and closures are themselves a kind of bio-political sorting process, since families and individuals have uneven capacity to respond to the shock of displacement.

This survey only covered one school, and the objection may be raised that it would be unfair to assume that it is representative of the experience of displaced students in general. Certainly that is the case, but if anything, students from Xin Gong Min were likely to receive *better* treatment than most. The New Citizen Program is perhaps the country's largest and best-known NGO focusing on migrant education issues. Given the organization's ability to corral and disseminate information in civil society, both domestically and internationally, there is every reason to believe the government would take extra steps to ensure a positive outcome for the displaced students. Furthermore, the school was located in Chaoyang, the district that had publicly promised that it would "not allow even one child" to be deprived of education because of a closure. In contrast, Haidian District in northwestern Beijing stated that following a closure, students who could gather the "five permits" (discussed in previous chapters) could apply to public schools. Since that had been the policy in place all along, and the parents presumably had their children enrolled in a migrant school because they could not get into public schools, this approach was tantamount to telling families that they were on their own.[57] While the survey data reveal that Chaoyang was far from perfect, the Education Department there was making more of an effort than in other districts.

Other anecdotal evidence hints at a variety of problems in resettling displaced migrant children, and even in the best-case scenario of resettlement in public schools, migrant children have been saddled with challenges and indignities. A public school in Haidian District that was forced to admit students displaced in the 2011 mass demolitions had to quickly erect temporary steel buildings to accommodate the new arrivals. But rather than integrate the migrant children into the existing student body, it kept them segregated in the temporary buildings, which were located on the far side of the playground. One parent, Ms. Liu, was pleased to have left behind the badly underresourced school from which her child had been removed. But the separate classrooms were a cause of concern: "I think it seems like two different worlds. I'm worried the children will suffer psychologically."[58]

Hasty construction of new buildings to accommodate displaced students presented schools with safety challenges as well. Following the 2011 demolitions, one private school in Chaoyang with a student body of six hundred was ordered to accept hundreds of displaced students, pushing the school to use teachers' offices and meeting rooms as classrooms. In an interview just two days before the start of the semester, the principal was worried about their preparedness: "When the new buildings are finished, I estimate that at max the school could hold nine hundred people. . . . Whether or not these rush-job buildings are safe [is a question], it might become another illegal migrant school."[59] Such ill-planned construction called into question the government's primary justification for the initial school demolitions, namely, that the targeted migrant schools were not up to standard and were therefore unsafe.

As these examples suggest, migrant school demolitions produce ripple effects in neighboring schools. Even if a large share of displaced students leaves the city for rural areas, a single demolition is still likely to produce several hundred students who will enroll within the city (be it with the assistance of the government or not). As would be expected, parents typically try to enroll their children in proximate locations. Following the

2011 demolitions, a number of principals in schools accepting displaced students confirmed that they had received a notification from the Education Department informing them that they must "unconditionally accept [the students], admit everyone who registers, and that accounting will happen after the students are admitted."[60] When schools are forced to admit large numbers of students with extremely short lead times and without promises for commensurate financial support, even sympathetic public schools are likely to be resistant.

Nonetheless, the schools that are most deeply impacted by resettlement following demolitions are inevitably other migrant schools where huge numbers of children are sometimes absorbed with little notice. One teacher from Yinghong related how students from a sister school were managed:

> The boss [i.e., owner of the school] has another school [elsewhere in the city]. Why was it shut down? The city was expanding and that area was a village. According to the Beijing urban plan, that area was all single-story buildings, they wanted to consolidate the land, so they demolished. Last year there were five hundred to six hundred people at the school, and after it was demolished they were displaced. A neighboring school originally had five hundred students, but now it's eight hundred.[61]

It is important to point out that most migrant schools are profit-oriented organizations, and there is very little state oversight in terms of ensuring student-teacher ratios or other pedagogical standards. Such an influx of students might be seen as a boon from the owner's perspective, but could engender massive disruptions for students and teachers.

Finally, many parents found that enrolling their children anew at *any* school proved to be a challenge, particularly given that they often received little advance notice of the demolition. A migrant domestic worker I interviewed recounted the hardship her family experienced after her child's school was demolished in 2011 to make way for a major infrastructure project:

> The place where we were living was going to be demolished, and the school was also demolished. As soon as it was demolished, our school's kids had nowhere to go to school. So we moved elsewhere [in Beijing] and tried to get our child into the school there, but it was too hard to get in, so we registered at a private school. . . . After we registered, that school's land was assessed for something, for planting trees, so the school couldn't accept any more students, and we were kicked out. And it was already the end of August and school started on September 1, and our child still didn't have a place to enroll. There was nowhere to enroll, and there wasn't anyone back in the village to look after him.[62]

While there are clearly heterogenous experiences in post-demolition resettlement, migrant families inevitably encounter severe disruptions to established patterns of social reproduction.

Radical Uncertainty

Ongoing demolitions within an increasingly nativist political environment left migrants with a general sense of unease and resignation to their eventual relocation.[63] Most migrants could not imagine a city in which they were not frequently uprooted by the development imperative, but they were still concerned with how the process of demolition and relocation would play out.[64] This meant that children, parents, teachers, and school administrators had to contend with a state of radical uncertainty about the future. In 2014, Principal Ma from Yinghong described it thus:

> At the moment I'm not worried [about demolition]. But it's impossible to say whether we'll be demolished in the future. . . . In 2002 there was a plan to eliminate all of the single-story buildings in Changping District by 2007, before the 2008 Olympics, but they still haven't followed through. This is just an idea the government has, but if they're really going to demolish us. . . . It probably won't happen in the next year or two, but after that I don't know.[65]

This uncertainty was experienced differently by parents, many of whom had extensive experience with scrambling to find new schools for their children. When asked about the village government's widely acknowledged designs on the land under her child's school, one mother in Liwanzhuang responded, "If they demolish us, our child will once again have to face choosing a new school, we'll once again have to run around to various schools, right?"[66] The threat of the bulldozer was a constant presence in Beijing's migrant schools, with all sorts of attendant issues for pedagogy and social time horizons, for student and teacher recruitment and retention, and for the general affective state of the community.

Even for those schools whose fate was sealed, the precise date of their demolition could remain a mystery. This was very much the case for Mingxin and Zhenhua, two schools just to the west of the former site of the defunct Jingwei campus in Dongxiaokou. When I visited Dongxiaokou in 2014, the village was divided by an enormous mountain of earth that had been removed from the construction site of a massive neighboring housing development.

To the east of this mound (visible in the background of figure 5.4) was the sea of rubble surrounding the former Jingwei site and the aforementioned in-process housing project. There were no active human settlements, only destruction and construction. The remaining portion of the village was to the west of the mound, and hundreds of migrant families did their best to go about their lives with this visible manifestation of their impending destruction literally looming over them.

In addition to the environmental hazards of living in the shadow of this project—sand and vehicle exhaust frequently blew through the settlement—it produced a great sense of uncertainty on the part of the remaining inhabitants. None of the administrators, teachers, or parents from Mingxin or Zhenhua knew exactly when the schools would be demolished, but they all knew it was coming. A father who worked as a recycler in Dongxiaokou expressed this sense of powerlessness: "The demolition will happen whenever they say so. They let the school

FIGURE 5.4 Dongxiaokou neighborhood.
Photo by the author.

operate for one year at a time. If they just get one year, then they just get one year."[67]

This pervasive sense of uncertainty I witnessed among migrant parents was rooted in the process, noted above, of continual sociospatial marginalization. Migrants have often found that just as they establish a toehold in the city, as intimations of community and predictable reproduction emerged in the institutional interstices, they would again be uprooted—if not by impersonal bureaucratic rules, then by the much more immediate violence of demolition. Mr. Lu, grandfather of a student in Zhenhua, discussed the experience of recurrent relocations and his anticipated departure from Dongxiaokou with political acuity:

EF: Are you thinking of moving?

LU: [sighs] Since our child's school is not secure, we'll have to move again. Now the demolitions are really severe, we can't say for sure when they'll demolish the place where we live, but we'll have to move. These little houses, our government says that they're "chaotic." Wherever there are lots of people it's chaotic. If they demolish and we move somewhere else, it'll be the same. As soon as there are lots of people, it's chaotic, the environment and hygiene are no good. Do you think anything will be different in the future? If they want you to live in high-rises, can you afford it? Some people can, but the large majority cannot. So if we move again, we'll move to some distant suburb, some place with a migrant school . . . we're just afraid of demolitions.[68]

As is clear from Mr. Lu's comments, the experience of being subjected to round after round of radical uncertainty and social service denial via sociospatial marginalization was exhausting and demoralizing, even if it had become normalized as a feature of migrant life in the capital.

CONCLUSION

Mass demolitions in 2011 were followed by a series of migrant school closings that then proceeded at a steady rate up through at least 2017, when the city's population began to shrink. These events furthered the sociospatial marginality of migrant communities and added new stresses on family life. There is strong evidence that migrant school closures and relocations forced many families to send their children out of the city, thus contributing to the ongoing production of left-behind children, while those who remained in Beijing faced longer commutes and the challenge of integrating into a new school. The generally unsettled landscape left migrant families with a pervasive sense of uncertainty about the future.

A focus on school closures, relocations, and demolitions provides further insight into the politics shaping the urbanization of people in China. Impersonal, transparent administrative arrangements relegate tens of thousands of people in Beijing (and millions nationwide) to a sphere of informal education. Exclusion from the formal system of education is problematic not only because it enhances educational inequality, but also because it leaves migrant children and their families subject to the whims of an urban government that is at turns anxious about overpopulation and interested in cashing in on rising land values. While demolitions are a spectacular display of callousness by the state, they are not an aberration but a direct extension of a political logic that is objectified in official regulations.

We can think of physical elimination of migrant schools as an elemental tool—a blunt one, certainly—in the urban state's population management regime. As state officials navigate the vicissitudes of the urban growth dilemma, informal schools are an easy target when demands for population control and/or access to land override the desire for abundant labor. Whereas housing demolitions in migrant neighborhoods target current workers, zeroing in on the schools is both practically and symbolically a powerful intervention to short-circuit intergenerational renewal for a particular segment of the population. Those impacted are denied access to social reproduction by the bulldozer, irrespective of the family's contributions to the city as workers. The demolitions render them surplus.

The state's efforts at treating people as depersonalized bearers of labor powers in the governance of urban space engenders massive affective strain within migrant schools. While families of course bear much of this burden, teachers play a critical role in responding to rolling crises of social reproduction. The content of their labor both reflects the broader social crisis and serves to ameliorate some of its cruelest effects.

6

REPRODUCTIVE SHOCK ABSORBERS

Teachers in Migrant Schools

Their parents are migrant workers, they don't have any time . . . some parents don't have any schooling, and they say they can't tutor their children, they themselves don't understand the homework. So the entire burden is put on the bodies of us teachers.

—Teacher Zhang, Shusheng School

T he urban state's efforts to pursue a just-in-time approach to the urbanization of people is a utopia—human movement simply will not adhere to the plan. But to work *and live* outside of one's officially designated position in the sociospatial hierarchy is to accept a whole series of indignities and social frictions, up to and including the possibility of physical expulsion. The necessity of generating a wage keeps migrants from poor rural areas pinned to prosperous cities, even as the institutions of social reproduction, be they public or private, are continually foreclosed or subject to malignant neglect.

Teachers play an essential role in mitigating some of the cruelest effects of the urban population management regime. While families of course bear the lion's share of the burden, teachers and schools are for many migrants the only point of institutional support in an otherwise grim biopolitical landscape. Teachers accept wages far below the city average and toil exceedingly long hours while taking on a series of reproductive responsibilities that ought to be dispersed across a wider array of institutional settings (and *are* for those considered part of the urban population). In addition to formal pedagogical responsibilities, teachers loan money to students and provide them with basic medical care, and, crucially, emotional support. All of these demands from students and families are intensified by their provisional position within the city. Teachers interpret and justify these difficult conditions though a gendered lens, often referring to themselves as "mothers" to their students. While their affection is often reciprocated in profoundly moving ways, working in migrant schools remains a highly exploitative and stressful profession. I conceive of these teachers as "reproductive shock absorbers," for they are on the frontlines of responding to the ongoing crisis of social reproduction generated by the failed urbanization of people.

I mostly present empirical material from Beijing, but my research in other parts of the country revealed qualitatively similar conditions (with some quantitative differences, e.g., wages and hours worked). Approaching the urbanization of people from the perspective of teachers provides another window onto the myriad dislocations experienced by migrants and migrant schools. Crucially, we will see how teachers' greatest challenge at work is managing generalized social entropy as refracted into the classroom. But the story is not entirely bleak: we will also see that teachers play a critical role in sustaining and nurturing their students, intellectually, emotionally, and physically. These individualized coping methods are certainly insufficient to overcoming the profound structural inequalities that pervade urban society, but they are nonetheless crucial in making life bearable for children in the present. In this sense, teachers are yet another example of a feminized, underpaid, and overworked segment of the working class whose labor is critical to the maintenance of life.

THE MIGRANTS, THE IDEALISTIC GRADUATES, AND THE RETIREES

The "migrant" is certainly the most common type of teacher in Beijing (and likely in other cities throughout China).[1] As with the communities they serve, these teachers are from rural areas and of modest means. They generally have somewhat more education than the parents of their students, with most of them having graduated from junior colleges or lower-tier universities. Typically, they are young: most of my interviewees were younger than thirty. Many of these teachers do not hold official teaching credentials. While the situation may have improved somewhat in recent years, a 2004 survey in Guangzhou found that only 55 percent of migrant schoolteachers were licensed, and it is almost certain that Beijing fares even worse.[2]

This is not to suggest that teachers do not have important ethical and emotional attachments to their work—indeed, this is the norm. Rather, it suggests that they do not envision a lifetime in the profession, either because they do not have the vocational orientation or simply because of the poor wages and working conditions. Teacher Zhang from Shusheng exemplified the rather casual relationship many migrant schoolteachers had to the profession:

At first, because my child was young, I didn't dare leave home to work, so I stayed back at home and ran a fruit stand. I came [to Beijing] in 2007, and I spent a year at the furniture company where my husband worked. . . . After a day of work I was so tired, since it was factory work, and it was really filthy, I felt like I couldn't handle it physically. After that I saw there was a school hiring, so I started doing this, even though the wages were half of what I was making before.[3]

Teacher Gu from Zhifan had a similarly uneven career path. After working as a teacher in the public school in her home village in Henan, she came to the city to work in a factory producing construction-grade sealing strips for more than a year: "But then the factory was going to relocate and my contract was ending. It was moving too far away, and I thought the work was too tiring and didn't suit me. After all, I was used to [teaching] so I looked for a job in a school."[4]

In addition to the possibility of a sense of social affiliation, there are structural reasons why migrant schools end up with a disproportionate number of migrant teachers. Teacher Lin from Yinghong detailed the link between superior social welfare for Beijing residents and the existence of an overwhelmingly migrant workforce in the schools: "People who were born and raised in Beijing rarely do this kind of job, the wages are so low. Beijing's education system is highly developed, there are a lot of universities, and it's easy for Beijingers to get into university. . . . If they get into a good university, of course they won't [take this job]. All of us are migrant teachers."[5]

As discussed in chapter 3, teachers who had an opportunity to land jobs in public schools invariably would do so. The migrant teachers generally found themselves excluded from the public system and working in a migrant school was seen as a less desirable option. Without elaborating on why she couldn't get into a public school, Teacher Ma from Yinghong indicated that private schools were a clear second choice:

> After graduating in my hometown in Hebei I took the university entrance exam in 2000. After finishing I couldn't get a state job [*bianzhi* 编制]—for these jobs, the government pays your salary, it's an iron rice bowl, they can only move you to different positions within the school [rather than dismissal] indefinitely. That group of graduates that I was in couldn't get a state job, so we went out to Beijing to look for work. At that time in the city, I felt like it wasn't right for me to do other jobs, because I had studied this major, it was at an education college. I studied education at university for three years.[6]

Similarly, Teacher Su, also from Hebei, described the challenge of finding employment in her hometown: "In my hometown it's hard to get into public schools, and there are few private schools, I could only work in a nursery. I really do want to go back home, so I'm getting ready to be a nursery schoolteacher."[7]

A small number of locals and highly educated people *do* end up working in migrant schools, though usually not for very long: this is the "idealistic graduate." These teachers have a very different professional disposition and orientation to work. Having recently graduated from top universities, they view their work as a way of giving back to society. They recognize the injustice and inequality in China's education system and want to do something about it. Teacher Wang from Yinghong, himself the child of migrant workers, explained his logic in choosing the low-waged job: "[Yinghong] is special, it's not like a public school. The conditions are bad. We come here to help the children, they have little contact with [good] education, the conditions

196 REPRODUCTIVE SHOCK ABSORBERS

aren't good here, and they don't have much contact with teachers, [their education] is not comprehensive. So I'm primarily here to help the children."[8] Anecdotally, a number of these idealistic teachers referred to their firsthand experiences with the injustices of China's citizenship regime. Whether it was spending time as a left-behind child when their parents went to the city or trying to navigate the urban school system as a nonlocal, these adult migrants felt fortunate to have made it to university and wanted to do what they could to help others follow in their footsteps.

Teacher Zhou from Yinghong exemplified this tendency, having himself endured extreme hardship as a young person.[9] He grew up in a remote rural part of Yunnan Province in a village that did not even have a road. He dropped out of school after fifth grade, and at the age of twelve he moved to Chongqing to work. After bouncing around a variety of exploitative and dangerous jobs (including working on electrical infrastructure), he returned home at the age of fourteen because he wanted to continue his schooling. Zhou's parents refused, saying they needed the additional income, and he went to work in the local mine. He studied for the middle school entrance exam in secret and ended up getting the second highest score in the township. Eventually he was admitted to university in Beijing. Unable to speak Mandarin well, he continued to work construction and donate at underground blood banks in order to support his family. While Teacher Zhou left Yinghong for more lucrative employment shortly after we met, he spoke powerfully and emotionally—breaking down in tears several times during our interview—about how his own experience motivated his desire to try and do something for impoverished children.

Other college graduates expressed a more self-oriented motivation for taking up the work. When I asked Teacher Pan from Shusheng why she joined the Teacher Future China program, she said, "I also wanted to really experience those children that I hadn't encountered before. Since I grew up in the city, I haven't had contact with rural children. I've heard them, and seen them, but never come into direct contact, so I wanted to experience it myself."[10] Although there are isolated cases of this type of teacher's staying in the profession, the large majority leave within a year or two for better paying jobs. Their idealism notwithstanding, these teachers are often unprepared professionally, socially, and emotionally for the challenge of educating the urban underclass.

Finally, there are the retirees. Retirement age for female teachers in public schools is fifty-five, which means that retirees often have many good working years left. While they are no longer allowed to teach in public schools, private schools have no such restrictions. Although this is a numerically smaller group, these teachers are often highly valued by migrant school administrators, given their professional training and wealth of experience. Retirees take these jobs for a variety of reasons, both idealistic and practical.[11] This group of teachers included both locals as well as people from other cities and provinces. In at least a few cases, I found that they had followed their adult children to the city. Teacher Hu from Zhifan explained it thus: "My hometown is in Heilongjiang. My daughter got into university and got a Beijing *hukou*, and I have only one daughter. So after I retired there [Heilongjiang] I came here. I was bored just hanging around the house and felt lonely after leaving work and the children behind. So I got this job."[12] In sum, teachers ended up in migrant schools for a variety of reasons, and their social and professional trajectories had a significant impact on how they responded to the challenges of the workplace.

LABORING IN A SPACE OF CONCENTRATED DEPRIVATION

Teachers in migrant schools are, from nearly any perspective, engaged in socially necessary work. Migrant parents, excluded as they are from public schools and services more broadly, count on them to educate and care for their children. The teachers' role is all the more critical given that parents often have only completed primary or middle school education and are severely overworked, with little time to tutor their children. The state, too, relies on these teachers to shoulder the burden of delivering its curriculum and providing at least minimal social support to an excluded underclass that has at times been restive. Finally, even if urban governments in elite cities are single-mindedly focused on the production and retention of "elite talents," in reality capitalists still need a diverse pool of labor. Teachers in migrant schools are producing future laborers, helping to develop the capacities they will need in order to find employment.

And yet, as outlined in chapter 3, the workplace is a space of concentrated deprivation. The migrant school, particularly in Beijing, absorbs those students from families with the absolute *fewest* resources—cultural, economic, and social—at their disposal. The difficulty is compounded by the fact that it is precisely this deprivation that in turn prevents these families and their educators from accessing nominally public resources that might otherwise ameliorate the inequality-producing tendencies of the market. Migrant schoolteachers are faced with the monumental challenge of educating the worst-off students, and doing so with the fewest institutional and material resources.

This deprivation is most clearly indicated by teachers' poverty wages, which are often times below the legal minimum. One survey of 442 migrant schoolteachers in Beijing from 2009 found that nearly 30 percent were paid less than 800 yuan (the city's minimum wage at the time) and another 65 percent were paid between 800 and 1,200 yuan.[13] If anything, these numbers are likely to be misleadingly optimistic, since the minimum wage is based on a forty-hour workweek. It is exceptionally unusual if not unheard of for migrant schoolteachers to work so few hours. Teachers in Beijing were almost uniformly dissatisfied with their wages, and the highest monthly wage I found in my fieldwork was only 300 yuan above the legal minimum.[14]

Migrant schools were rife with violations of labor law beyond paying below the minimum wage. Many, though certainly not all, teachers worked without a labor contract, even several years after the implementation of the landmark Labor Contract Law in 2008. Teachers at Yinghong did not have contracts, and Teacher Lin explained his understanding: "We don't have labor contracts . . . why is this? Most important, it's because this way we don't have legal protection. Labor law is often tilted in favor of workers, so not signing a contract works to the boss's advantage."[15] Social insurance, a legal requirement for employees, was offered only at Zhifan. But even there, teachers had to forgo higher wages to have the security of social insurance: "In one month we earn 1,200 yuan. But there's something, that's the social insurance. I came here even though wages at this school are lower than some other places. But here we have insurance and other places don't have it. I wouldn't have peace of mind."[16]

Because teachers' *own* reproduction could not be guaranteed by their poverty wages, it was quite common for them to have second jobs on evenings and weekends during the school year as well as during summer breaks. Perhaps the most common moonlighting option was to work in private tutoring companies, helping mostly middle class and wealthy local students with their homework and exams. Teacher Zhou from Yinghong explained his reasoning in taking on a second job: "[Teaching at Yinghong] is purely a [social] contribution. . . . My monthly salary is around 1,200 RMB. When I go to an outside company to teach, I earn about 260 per hour. So if I teach one outside class, that's already more than one day of salary."[17] Most migrant schoolteachers were not university graduates and therefore could not get such highly compensated part-time work. One teacher in Beijing received media attention when her family's medical bills forced her to supplement the income from her teaching job by selling corn on the street.[18] And because migrant schoolteachers are generally not paid during school vacation, most of them must find work in the summers. Some found temporary work in factories, while others would go to their rural hometowns to help out on the farm.

In addition to the bad terms of employment, the generalized poverty of the community within which the schools were embedded was also directly reflected in teachers' work. I was somewhat surprised when Teacher Xu from Yinghong told me that not only is she a "nanny" and a "janitor" for the students, but "a lot of male students will raise their hand and say, 'you're our bank!'"[19] She continued to tell how me how she recently had a student who had forgotten his notebook, and she lent him money to go buy one. The next day he came to return the money, and she said, "I don't need it, you hold on to it to buy a popsicle or get a notebook for the next time you need one." Teacher Wang linked parents' absences with his spending money on the students: "Some children stay here at lunchtime and their parents don't come. We teachers will spend some money to get them something to eat, since we're afraid they'll be hungry otherwise. This happens quite a lot."[20] I encountered other instances where teachers provided basic medical care for their students, as the schools did not employ a nurse and children were generally without medical insurance. It is normal for teachers to care for their students—but paying for basic biological upkeep is by no means in their job description.

Uneven Abilities and Social Entropy

I was surprised to learn that one of teachers' biggest concerns about their work was unrelated to the poverty wages and grueling hours. In interview after interview, I found that teachers really struggled with the interconnected problems of high student turnover and *uneven abilities* of their students. We have already seen how the highest-performing students in migrant schools could be snatched up by public schools, thus leaving the students who required the most attention concentrated in migrant schools. But there were in fact myriad social and economic forces at play all of which conspired to produce astonishingly high student turnover. I could not find data on migrant student turnover for the entirety of Beijing, but the schools I studied lost upward of one quarter of the student body each year. A conversation I had with the principal of Jingwei is instructive:

EF: Is student turnover high here?

PRINCIPAL: Not too high.

EF: So how many people leave each semester?

PRINCIPAL: About seventy people. Our turnover rate is 30 percent.[21]

If 30 percent annual turnover was considered "not too high" in the context of Beijing's migrant schools, one begins to get a sense of just how ephemeral pedagogical and social encounters really were.

There were many structural conditions that furthered recurrent student loss, including families going to the village for public schooling, seeking better educational options within the city, and housing or school demolitions. But the greatest contributor to student turnover derived from parents' precarious position in the urban labor market. Recall that parents of children in migrant schools are those least likely to have formal employment, which means that they are generally engaged in marginal and informal types of work. Teachers were quite cognizant of the linkages between parents' work and student turnover. After Teacher Hu from Zhifan commented that student turnover is "very high here," I asked her why she thought that was the case. She responded, "Their home isn't here. Their work is fluid so their residence is fluid. Some of them are here because they find work here, but tomorrow they find a better job over there so they leave. For instance, in construction, today they're here, tomorrow they're there, then they have to move homes. It's really inconvenient. The fluidity of the work causes the high fluidity of the students."[22] Recall that the essence of just-in-time logistics is continual improvement in the precision of managing a "flow process."[23] Here we see that flow dynamics in the labor market are reflected into, and severely disrupt, processes of social reproduction.

The exceedingly high levels of student mobility in turn had a major impact on teachers' experience of work. In addition to the emotional challenges faced by both the children and teachers, it also resulted in a classroom of students with wildly uneven levels and kinds of preparation. Teacher Zhang's explanation of the situation helped to clarify the connection between high levels of student turnover and the added stress of teaching in a migrant school:

> This kind of school is different from public schools in Beijing. . . . Our students come from the four corners of the country. . . . and our turnover is quite high. This year we have these students, next year some parents will move or go back to the village, so a portion of students leave and new students come in. Real high turnover. And their [academic] foundations are not the same. They speak all kinds of different dialects, and their levels are all different. . . . If ten students [in a class of thirty] leave this year, and new ones come in, I'm under a lot of pressure because I have to once again learn about these students, learn their backgrounds. . . . Some come in the middle of the year. Some were enrolled elsewhere, others were out of school for half a year. Some of them have used totally different teaching materials, so where do we even start? This is a problem.[24]

Of course, all teachers, even those in elite settings, must carefully consider how to tailor their pedagogy to the abilities of their classroom. But the peripatetic student body of Beijing's migrant schools introduced dramatic uncertainty into classrooms already challenged by overcrowding and poor physical plant.

The difficulty of mediating students' uneven abilities was compounded by the fact that the faculty too were in a constant state of flux. In my research, I found that Beijing's migrant schools typically had teacher turnover rates of above

25 percent each year. A twelve-city survey found annual turnover rates of over 20 percent in licensed migrant schools and nearly 50 percent in unlicensed schools.[25] Teachers thus confronted a classroom that may have seen rotating cast of instructors shuffling in and out, even during the course of a semester. While the extreme disruption that Teacher Lin described in his math class at Yinghong was not the norm, the reasons he gives for regular teacher departures were a direct result of the structural position that all migrant schools face:

> When I started here it was already one month into the semester. A class I teach had already had three different teachers [that semester]. The first teacher was from a village in Zhangjiakou,[26] their house back in the village was about to collapse and the state gave them some materials to fix it, so they had to go back. The second teacher was a young girl, she had just graduated. She decided she wanted to quit after just seven days because the conditions were too bad. . . . The third one was our own Teacher Che, usually they do other things in the school . . . so they substituted in the class. After just a few days I arrived. So this semester they've already had four different teachers . . . in regular private schools, especially migrant schools, the turnover is extremely high.[27]

In a sense, the instability in the ranks of the students was mirrored by high levels of teacher turnover. The consequence was that students and teachers were in a perpetual state of pedagogical readjustment. It is therefore not surprising that the uneven abilities of students was one of teachers' primary work challenges.

Teachers and Parents

As is true for all primary school educators, the work of migrant schoolteachers was heavily structured by their students' family dynamics. Class inequalities and the citizenship regime conspire to funnel the least well-resourced families into the least well-resourced schools, as we have seen. By no fault of the parents, this institutional arrangement put massive pressure on teachers to pick up reproductive tasks that parents could not. This in turn produced a complex set of relationships between teachers and their students' families, with teachers' views of these families often vacillating between sympathy and condescension or even outright contempt.

An issue that often highlighted the delicate balance between sympathy and condescension was parents' ability to be active participants in their children's education. Principal Ma from Yinghong brought this up in the context of discussing problems the school had with their work environment: "A portion of our parents are completely illiterate. They aren't educated and have no schooling. Some of them, migrants, just have two or three years of primary schooling . . . so they can't tutor their children. . . . This means that they are putting the entire responsibility on the school. So our teachers really have a tough time, much more so than public schoolteachers."[28] Teacher Guo, also from Yinghong, confirmed her principal's assessment while expressing an understanding of parents' difficulties: "When we encounter some issue [with a student], a majority of parents are just like, 'Oh, we don't understand these things, we haven't been to school, you go ahead and figure it out, you take care of this child.' This is how they think about things. Maybe their life circumstances give them no choice, they're forced to scramble all day just to earn a living and they don't have any time."[29]

Even if teachers could understand and sympathize with parents' circumstances, the reality was that these limitations created significantly more work for them. In addition to class sizes that were generally in excess of legal limits, teachers felt that they had to pick up the slack that in better-resourced social and institutional environments parents would otherwise manage. A recurrent theme in my interviews was teachers' sense that they had to take *all* of the responsibility of educating the child, a situation that was universally seen as suboptimal: "A lot of parents are too busy with work to look after their kids. The kids are completely taught by the teachers. There are very few parents who will tutor their kids at home, so this is really strenuous for teachers. This is because the students are migrants, the parents have mostly come here to earn money and so they look after their children less."[30] Teacher Zhang, quoted in the epigraph to this chapter, repeatedly stressed in our interview the unique challenge of migrant schoolteachers: "Parents very rarely coordinate with teachers. If we give students a bit of homework, some parents cannot help them at all. Some parents are just too busy with work and don't have time. *The entire responsibility is put on the school and the bodies of teachers* [emphasis added]. I think that teachers like us are much more exhausted than public school teachers, and this is directly related to the type of parents."[31]

In some cases, parents' absence from the lives of their children was quite literal: parents were simply not at home or would fail to retrieve their children at the end of the school day. Teacher Wang from Yinghong could not contain his frustration with this sort of situation as he clearly laid out how reproductive tasks were shifted from overworked parents onto overworked teachers:

Sometimes these parents come at the end of the day, but sometimes they don't. So then we have to call them, it's really annoying. This is far too common and too normalized an event. Usually we call the parents and ask why they haven't come, and they'll say they've been held up by some issue, but they don't think to inform us ahead of time. . . . The industries they're working in are no good, their education level and *suzhi* isn't high, they don't even think about this issue [picking up their children], they only think about earning money. So this puts a lot of pressure on the teachers.[32]

Looking after children whose parents have failed to show up was a regular task at migrant schools. Some teachers complained that this amounted to unpaid overtime. But there was little other choice when children were left behind.

In an environment where both time and material resources are so constrained, conflict was bound to erupt, and indeed teachers sometimes clashed with parents. Perhaps the most poignant examples were struggles related to tuition collection. Although the practice is less common in Beijing than some other cities, teachers in some migrant schools were tasked with collecting tuition.[33] As the families were without exception nonlocal, and the overwhelming majority working in informal jobs, menial employment, or as small-scale entrepreneurs, this was a task that often proved quite difficult. Teacher Lin from Yinghong gave an unvarnished account of the possibility for conflict: "Some parents have bad habits. Even if they aren't divorced, they might not take responsibility. Some gamble, or drink, and don't take care of anything else. When we're asking for tuition, they can get really angry: 'My student is doing so poorly, you're lucky I haven't already come for you!' Sometimes they say crazy things like they'll destroy the school."[34] It should be noted that this is a category of problem that simply does not exist in public schools, as they do not charge tuition. Migrant schools and their employees bear all sorts of burdens that are either dispersed or mitigated in a public setting. Frequently the scope of this labor extended far beyond pedagogy to include a host of other socially reproductive tasks—and providing affective labor was one of the most salient.

MOTHER-TEACHERS AND RECIPROCATED AFFECT

The students in migrant schools had by and large experienced a highly transient childhood. Many had spent long periods of time apart from one or both of their parents, while enrolled in schools in which the student body was in constant flux. Thus, in addition to having minimal contact with their parents, peer friendships were often fleeting. As has been the case for migrant children throughout China, this meant that the schools I studied had a huge number of emotionally deprived students.[35] I found that many were incredibly emotionally engaged with and even demanding of their teachers. I came to see that children in these schools were not only demanding but also eagerly giving of emotion in a sometimes disarming manner.

As with reproductive work involving children in most societies, primary schoolteachers' work was highly feminized. A large majority of the teachers in migrant primary schools were female, while the handful of male teachers were likely to teach specialized classes in the upper years. When I asked teachers about the preponderance of women in the profession, their answers were quite uniform. Both male and female teachers referenced supposedly feminine character traits—most frequently affinity for children and *patience*—and low wages as the explanation. Principal Ma from Yinghong attempted to put a positive spin on the feminization of the profession: "Women are more likely to enjoy this job, because they like children. Second, as for the salary, women think that since they have a husband who can support the family, women can choose a profession that they enjoy, she doesn't need to chase something high-level, they don't need to earn money or what have you, they can pursue spiritual satisfaction."[36] It was not just male teachers or administrators who held such views—even if she did not actively *approve* of patriarchal gender relations, Teacher Zhang acknowledged that it accounted for the feminization of the job: "In our hometown, there are very few male teachers. First, I think this is because teachers' wages and benefits are quite low. And then, guys dealing with children usually, how to put it? It just seems like it's not the kind of thing a man should do."[37]

A recurring theme in my interviews in Beijing (and elsewhere) was teachers referring to themselves as a "mother" to their students. Susan Greenhalgh and Edwin Winckler have discussed the Deng-era emergence of the "good mother," one who is fully devoted to nurturing and educating a highly talented only child, one who is able to withstand the rigors of competition in the increasingly globalized capitalist economy.[38] This highly gendered form of social reproduction was certainly apparent in my own fieldwork, with one important twist: this fundamentally affective form of labor had been transferred from biological mother to teacher. While "mother-like" tasks are often expected of primary schoolteachers, the relative absence of many students' parents intensified these demands for teachers in migrant schools. Teacher Li from Zhifan explained, "One of our children, his mother does business outside of the house, and she can't come back until quite late.

Every night I take care of this child, so I have a lot more contact with him.[39] And Teacher Ma from Shusheng suggested that she had to fill the emotional gap left by overburdened parents: "Just yesterday the students were drawing in class, and one of the students wrote out, 'pursuing love.' Their families really are too busy with work, and they abandon the most basic things. Perhaps as the class director sometimes I'm like a mother. Sometimes we think we're a bit fussy and mother-like, if it's going to rain today I'll say, 'Don't forget your umbrella, keep your rain jacket on!'"[40]

The affection that teachers often displayed for their students was frequently reciprocated, and many teachers cited this as the most important reason for staying in the profession. I experienced this phenomenon firsthand at a graduation ceremony Yinghong held with three other migrant schools in the area. Approximately two hundred students were in attendance, and while I was informed that parents had been invited, there were hardly any there (I could not verify precisely, but I saw only two adults who were not teachers in the audience). Before the event began, I was standing in the large event hall when a boy I vaguely recognized from Yinghong came into the room. I recorded the interaction in my field notes thus:

> His eyes lit up and he ran over saying, "Teacher Eli! You came!" and then threw his arms around me. For some reason this really got to me, and I got a little choked up, it was an intensely emotional experience. Immediately thereafter, two successive students had a similar reaction, each of them enthusiastically referring to me as "Eli Laoshi" [Teacher Eli]. I couldn't believe they even remembered my name, and was certainly surprised by their enthusiasm.[41]

I was taken aback because our previous interactions had been quite limited, nothing more than exchanging a few words in the playground on perhaps two different occasions. The fact that I did not even know the boy's name juxtaposed to the obvious importance I held for him was unsettling, while at the same moving. The almost complete absence of parents at the graduation ceremony really drove home the impression that these children had to seek emotional support from diverse sources.

This experiential knowledge allowed me to see teachers' narratives about their work in a new light. And once I was paying attention, there was overwhelming evidence that this form of *reciprocated affect* between students and teachers—quite distinct from the alienated emotional labor of many service-sector jobs—was a distinguishing feature of the work.[42] Certainly, most teachers in any context will talk about the sense of satisfaction they derive from working with children and seeing their development as a primary motivation for staying in the profession. But in my research, teachers regularly talked about "loving" their students, and teachers often spoke of their affection for their students with visible emotion. This was not simply a platitudinous expression of *caring*. For instance, when I asked Teacher Hu from Zhifan about the best feature of the job, she responded, "I'm happy when I'm with the children. Every morning when I enter the school, the children greet me. When I leave at night, they say goodbye. They sincerely love their teacher, and you then have profound feelings toward them."[43]

Although this mutual affect was a regular feature of my interviews, none put it quite so poignantly as Li Yingxia, a teacher at a migrant school in Guangzhou.[44] Writing in a collection of blog posts from migrant schoolteachers around the country, Li focused on her relationship with a student named

Xiao Tan. She described this student as a difficult child who "refused to communicate with his parents."[45] Xiao Tan often caused disruptions in class and was difficult to manage, but Li believed he had potential. However, after struggling with him over the course of the semester, her confidence in her own abilities was badly undermined. When she saw that he had intentionally selected the wrong answers on a test and received a zero, she lost control and immediately called the principal to resign. However, the following weekend, she received a series of texts from Xiao Tan:

> Teacher, I know that you're so good to me, but I still oppose you. I'm so sorry, please forgive me!
>
> Teacher, please don't abandon us. Please give us one more chance to be your students.
>
> Teacher, I will work hard. Teacher, I love you!

Teacher Li was deeply affected by these messages:

> Each word of these texts touched my heart. And in reality, he did what he said. After I adjusted my mentality and started from the beginning, I once again threw myself into the work. I treated him just like a mother, I dearly loved him, and he was also like a child, and reciprocated in caring for me and helping me. . . . One year later, his English scores increased dramatically. He was proud of his hard work, and I too was proud of his efforts. After he took the high school entrance exam, I received another text message from him: "Teacher, I got a 114 on English! Thank you mother!" When I heard this word "mother," tears started streaming down my face because this "mother" contained so much bitterness, so much effort, so much struggle, and so much love!

Although the teacher-as-mother lens reflects important aspects of reality, male teachers were also deeply engaged in reproductive and specifically affective labor. While men are a small minority in migrant schools and indeed primary schools more generally, there were at least some in every school I visited. I could not definitively conclude whether men were doing an *equal* share of the work in migrant schools, but they similarly cited mutual affect as a or *the* primary motivation for staying in the job. Teacher Wang, with whom I had a closer relationship than just about any of my informants, opened up about his feelings for his class of fourth graders:

> One time, I was so mad, I gave them an English exam that required a parental signature. After three days, only three students had signatures. I was so mad, part way through class I walked out and went back to our office. They thought I wasn't going to teach them anymore. The whole class showed up in tears at my office and pulled me back [to the classroom]. They said, "Teacher, we're sorry, we'll always listen to you from now on." I was moved to tears. I thought that this group of kids is really great. They all apologized together saying, "Teacher, don't cry. We won't dare ignore you." Hearing this kind of thing from fourth graders, I was really moved.[46]

Just as with Teacher Li, Wang acknowledged his own frustration at the students' inabilities to follow basic instructions (and in both cases, there is a possibility that parents' lack of involvement played a role). The students' realization that they might lose their teacher—with whom, it seems safe to assume, they had a strong emotional attachment—brought forth an overt display of affection. And as with Teacher Li, Wang tearfully returned to the classroom. Thus, while men and women may have interpreted their relationship to their work differently, and men were certainly less likely to accept the poverty wages for extended periods of time, the basic relationship of intensified affective labor would appear to be similar.

This level of affective intensity was even personally transformative in some cases. Teacher Zhang was one of the most forthcoming people I encountered during my research and would be quite open about her emotional struggles in our conversations. The first time I did a formal interview with her, she repeatedly referred to herself as "trash" and detailed extensively how she didn't feel competent and was severely overworked. Despite this, her connection with her students was undeniable:

> I've felt that the children love me. And I've learned how to love other people. Nobody loved me while I was growing up, so I didn't know how to love other people, I didn't have this ability. But these children, they trust me, when they are bullied they come crying to me, they write me letters thanking me for teaching them to sing and they give me presents on holidays. Every time we're in class they give me little drawings, they'll tell me I look pretty when I dress up, and if I'm wearing a bandage they'll ask what happened. Every time they see me they'll say, "Hello teacher!" And they've said, "Teacher, we love you!" in unison. I think that everyone needs love to mature, and the love they've given me has allowed me to mature. So it's precisely because of this that I've gradually developed the ability to love other people, and I love these children.[47]

The conditions this highly feminized workforce confronted were challenging indeed—exploitative, exhausting, and lacking the social status typically afforded teachers in China. The mutual affect experienced by "mother-teachers" reflects a reciprocated striving for connection in an institutional context that militates strongly against durable sociality.

CONCLUSION

Nancy Fraser has powerfully expounded what she calls a "social-reproductive contradiction" within capitalism: Capital accumulation, on the one hand, requires a workforce that is continually reproduced, daily and intergenerationally. At the same time, however, "capitalism's orientation to unlimited accumulation tends to destabilize the very processes of social reproduction on which it relies."[48] While every individual capitalist requires workers who are competent at some given level of productivity, given the long time horizons and the unpredictability of a formally free labor market, there is little incentive for them to invest in transforming a child into such a worker. The formation of labor powers comes about as a result of noncommodified reproductive labor within the (patriarchal) family unit and broader community, as well as technocratic interventions of the state via a series of biopolitical interventions (chiefly health and education).

Chinese capitalism is of course dependent on the labor of migrant workers, but the urban state is not responsible for their upkeep or regeneration, and as a result their social reproduction is in a constant state of crisis or near crisis.[49] Whether it is due to job loss, changes in school admissions policy, or school/neighborhood demolition and redevelopment, the families who appear in migrant schools continually face the threat of expulsion and relegation to the surplus population. While the state plays some role in mitigating the social-reproductive crisis tendency for full members of the urban population, nonlocals have no such guarantee—the impacts of the crisis are unevenly distributed.

In the midst of the recurrent dislocation that characterizes urban life for China's migrants, families and teachers confront this reproductive crisis in raw form, unmediated by the cushion of public resources. Parents' subordinated position within urban labor markets and the population management regime more broadly is reflected in teachers' work. Laboring in a wholly privatized environment while serving a working-class community, teachers must first accept poverty wages. This situation is then justified with reference to patriarchal discourses that accept women's material subordination to their husbands. Teachers' employment is precarious and subject to the capriciousness of urban redevelopment and the business cycle, as is the case with the families they serve. Demands on teachers' affective labor are further intensified as their students are in constant flux and often grasping for some semblance of security. This is not a straightforwardly emotionally exploitative or alienating relationship, since teachers tend to cite their students' reciprocated affect as a key motivation for staying in the job. For better or worse, much reproductive labor, both material and affective, that typically occurs within the family is relocated *onto the bodies* of teachers. In this sense, teachers absorb the social shocks and displacement associated with urban China's perpetual crisis of reproduction.

Teachers' work is, from the perspective of state and capital, a necessary but unacknowledged and unsubsidized form of reproduction. But unlike the unpaid and feminized reproductive work that takes place within the family, teachers are engaged in a rather traditional, albeit barely regulated and highly exploited, form of wage labor. In this sense, migrant schoolteachers occupy a space that is simultaneously productive (for their employers) *and* reproductive.[50] A labor demand for better wages and reduced workload is simultaneously a demand for better services for the community. On the other hand, teachers' work conditions would also improve to the extent that parents' time and energy is freed from daily survival. As has proven to be the case in other national settings, this fusing of often distinct sites of struggle can be combustible.[51] Although teacher-community political solidarity has been rare in urban China's migrant community, it holds critical potential as a site of social resistance.

CONCLUSION

Global Extensions

The mental state of us migrant workers is very . . . well, if I go to a public school they want this or that: "How long have you lived here?" It's so humiliating, it's like they don't see us as human.

—Migrant father in Guiyang

In light of the state's increased emphasis on shifting to an urbanization-led model of growth in the 2010s, I began with the question: How does the state manage flows of people into cities? That is, how are people being urbanized? And what are the social consequences? My answer has been that the state has attempted to urbanize people—uniting spaces of work and social reproduction—according to a just-in-time logic in an effort to optimize the structure of the population. This political project aims to articulate distributions of labor and capital, in the right qualities and quantities, extending social protection to a worthy few while relegating social reproduction for those deemed unnecessary to the market. Accessing state-subsidized reproduction via *hukou* acquisition is dependent on an individual's successfully passing a host of evaluative criteria that are largely, but not exclusively, oriented to value in the labor market. The central state has expounded an imaginary in which an individual's qualities are quantified via a seemingly impartial bureaucratic apparatus, and then matched to the corollary position in the sociospatial hierarchy: elite cities for elite people, low-end places for low-end people. This technocratically determined distribution is imagined as the most appropriate for facilitating China's ascension to the ranks of rich countries.

JIT urbanization is, however, a stark utopia.[1] While such a smooth spatiotemporal articulation of labor and capital can never be realized in practice, the state's *pursuit* of this ideal has profound consequences. I argued in chapter 2 that the series of evaluative mechanisms, when situated within the context of China's highly uneven economic geography and concomitant fiscal capacities, results in an inversion of the logic of the welfare state. Briefly, nominally public resources are diverted to those *most* likely to succeed in the market based on given endowments of economic, cultural, and social capital. Everyone else has their social reproduction, and specifically access to education, left to the vagaries of the market. The consequence, as detailed in chapter 3, is *concentrated deprivation* in Beijing's migrant schools, in which those with the absolute fewest resources try to eke out reproductive existence without any social protection.

While bare survival can be possible in the city's administrative interstices, chapters 4 and 5 detailed the expulsionary pressures, administrative and physical, with which migrant families must contend. As Beijing's turn to expelling migrants hardened over the course of the 2010s, families who previously could have found their way into public schools were excluded. Ratcheting demands for school enrollment reflected the municipal government's increased emphasis on providing services only to migrants who fit with the city's plans for economic upgrading. These efforts came at precisely the same time that the government was eliminating informal schooling options, which resulted in dozens of coercive school closures and demolitions. This "hard edge" dovetailed with the desubjectified violence of administrative exclusion in *rendering surplus* a population that was, at least for some fraction of capital, a critically important source of labor. Finally, in chapter 6 I argued that the structure of urban China's population management regime results in a disproportionate amount of reproductive, and specifically affective, labor being pushed onto schools and teachers. Amid the chaos and social breakdown of the migrant school, teachers serve as affective shock absorbers as they endeavor to mitigate the worst effects of their students' social marginality. In short, the urbanization of people has proceeded unevenly, with tens of millions of proletarian migrants incorporated into the city as workers but subjected to expulsionary pressures as full humans. Massive implications follow for social and economic inequality.

In contrast to earlier emergent capitalist empires, China is developing at a moment of much greater geopolitical constraint. This in turn has resulted in a socially and spatially *intensive* form of dispossession and exploitation. In contrast to the racialized surplus populations associated with expansionist Euro-American capitalist empires, in China the state has inserted a racist break within the dominant Han race, thus producing a social group that is relatively disposable.

SITUATING BEIJING

The majority of empirical evidence presented here has been drawn from fieldwork in Beijing. As the capital, second largest city, and one of the wealthiest, Beijing is in and of itself an important case. But it is these conditions that also make it rather exceptional in a number of respects. How widely applicable are the insights generated from this case? Although a comprehensive response to that question is beyond the scope of this project, data drawn from fieldwork in Guangzhou and Guiyang can help in formulating a preliminary answer. However, these are not merely comparative cases; we need to understand these cities *relationally* as well, to further flesh out Beijing's position within the sociospatial hierarchy.

Guangzhou is a noteworthy point of comparison for Beijing in that it is also a wealthy megacity in the eastern part of the country that has attracted millions of migrants. But despite these superficial similarities, the urbanization of people, as viewed from the perspective of the education system, has proceeded in a significantly different manner than in Beijing. And by at least one measure, Beijing appears to be doing a better job at incorporating migrants: whereas official statistics maintain that 78 percent of nonlocals were enrolled in public schools in Beijing in 2015, in Guangzhou it was only 45 percent.[2] Guangzhou was an early adopter of point-based school admission for nonlocals, and each district has formulated their own set of policies. These policies assess applicants based largely on their potential to contribute to the city's economic upgrading, and therefore heavily favor the highly educated and wealthy. The city's low enrollment of nonlocals reveals that this formally equal and transparent system for assessing admissions has left a majority of migrants outside the public system.

The difference in the headline admissions rates between Beijing and Guangzhou, however, masks a more complex reality. While it is certainly true that it is exceptionally difficult for working-class migrants to get into public schools in Guangzhou, it is not apparent that the overall system is less equal. As in Beijing, migrants in Guangzhou who are excluded from public schools are restricted to private education. But whereas migrant schools in Beijing are subjected to ongoing threats of demolition while receiving almost no public oversight or support, private schools in Guangzhou are fully legal, licensed, regulated, and in many cases, financially supported in a charter school–like arrangement. In the mid-2010s, Guangzhou had roughly three hundred migrant schools[3]—twice as many as in Beijing, despite its smaller overall population. This privatized school system allowed more migrants to bring their children with them to the city: in Guangzhou, 46 percent of migrants were living in the same place as their school-aged children, whereas in Beijing it was a mere 22 percent.[4] While Guangzhou is more exclusionary with respect to public education, its private education system is more institutionalized and stable.

In my research I found that conditions in Guangzhou's migrant schools were certainly better than in Beijing. The physical plant and facilities were superior, since private capital could invest with confidence that the building would not be demolished at a moment's notice. Teachers' salaries in the four schools I visited in Guangzhou were significantly better (all received above minimum wage), and they worked fewer hours.[5] I do not have comparative data on student performance, but there is no question that Guangzhou's migrant schools provide a somewhat more settled environment than their Beijing counterparts.

Nonetheless, it also must be emphasized that Guangzhou's highly marketized approach suggests that class will become an increasingly prominent driver of educational inequality in the city. As I have argued throughout, the nonlocal population in coastal megacities is quite heterogenous and includes a significant number of well-off families. Since even many relatively wealthy families will be excluded from public education, an

224 Ȥ CONCLUSION: GLOBAL EXTENSIONS

entire ecosystem of private schools has emerged, some of which cater to this elite stratum of migrants. In other words, those excluded from public education in Guangzhou are not subject to the same aggressive administrative and physical expulsion as in Beijing, but the quality of private education they can access is highly contingent on their class position.

In my research, Guangfu School in the central Liwan District best exemplified the rapid stratification of migrant education in the city.[6] Started in 2004 by the Education Department's union, its aim was to "address the problem of school enrollment for the children of the floating population in Liwan District and surrounding areas."[7] Through a variety of subsidies from the government, the school was able to expand and upgrade its facilities and workforce. When I visited in 2012, I was taken aback by how well equipped the school was, from the koi pond at the entrance to the full ceramic studio and even a small museum stocked with a butterfly collection, wildlife taxidermy, and fine art. The school was adorned with plaques commemorating a series of awards from various levels of government, and an entire wall was covered with pictures from various dignitaries' visits. Administrators provided a highly professionalized overview of the curriculum, which was quite rigorous and comprehensive. This school was much more similar to the public schools I had visited, and it was clearly head and shoulders above Zhifan, the "high-end" migrant school in Beijing. But it came at a cost: tuition for one semester was 4,000 yuan, which at the time was more than three times the city's monthly minimum wage of 1,300 yuan. While the school was formally open to all nonlocals, it was now the market rather than formal citizenship distinctions that served to exclude working-class migrants from quality education.[8] And the school's financial support from the government represents yet another instance in which public resources are being diverted to those who need them least.[9]

This pattern of channeling the majority of nonlocal children into formalized private education appears to hold in other wealthy migrant-magnet cities in the region. In 2017, only 23 percent of nonlocal children in Dongguan and 46 percent in Shenzhen were enrolled in public schools.[10] It is not coincidental that these are among the cities with the highest proportion of migrants. Guangdong has been at the forefront of marketization for many decades, and the logic of privatization has had a greater impact in the education sector than in Beijing.

The Beijing-Guangzhou comparison is "horizontal" in that these two cities occupy a similar position in the national sociospatial hierarchy: they are both wealthy megacities that are highly selective in admitting migrants to the local population, albeit with their own specific strategies. When we shift to a "vertical" comparison with Guiyang, a new set of issues arise that are indicative of the inequalities built into the national population management regime.[11] As a provincial capital, Guiyang still occupies a relatively privileged position in comparison to the majority of cities and towns, and certainly the provincial authorities have done much to advance economic growth in the city. Nonetheless, we will see that things become even more dire for migrant children when we depart the rarefied spaces of the "tier one" cities.

Since the late 2000s, migration in China has become more localized, with a growing proportion of rural residents choosing to migrate within their province. This means that cities such as Beijing and Guangzhou are receiving a diminishing share of the nation's total migrants, while cities like Guiyang and other provincial capitals have seen more in-migration. Guiyang is, on paper at least, somewhat less exclusionary toward migrants than

Beijing or Guangzhou. Macro Polo's *"Hukou* Difficulty Index," which assesses the largest and most attractive cities based on the exclusivity of their *hukou* registration policies, ranks Guiyang twenty-first out of forty; Guangzhou is the second most difficult, whereas Beijing is eighth.[12] With an urban district population of just over 3 million, Guiyang is a "large" city according to the National New Urbanization Plan parlance, which means it should, "reasonably establish conditions for attaining local *hukou.*"[13]

Nonetheless, the nationwide pattern of favoring well-off migrants in the distribution of social services holds in Guiyang. In particular, home ownership is a critically important metric in securing local *hukou* in the city. The Macro Polo data show that property ownership is a much larger factor in Guiyang than is the case on average for the other forty cities included in the index, whereas educational attainment is less valued.[14] This property-centric *hukou* policy was reflected in my interview data as well. Mr. Liu, an NGO worker focusing on education issues in the area, said, "I've never heard of someone getting *hukou* without buying a house or having a [government] job."[15] As in other cities, *hukou* policy has been used as a means for supporting the real estate sector. Purchasing a house at market price in Guiyang is, however, far beyond the means of most migrant workers. This means that, as in the coastal cities, tens of thousands of migrant children do not have the guaranteed access to public education provided by local *hukou.*

With respect to public school admissions, Guiyang has been moving to incorporate more nonlocals into the public system. In 2010, less than half of migrant children were enrolled in public schools in Guiyang,[16] putting the city roughly on par with Guangzhou. In the midst of increasing migration,

Guiyang announced a plan to get at least 60 percent of migrant children in public schools by end of 2016.[17] Then in 2019 it set a target of enrolling 85 percent of migrant children in public schools by 2020.[18] These initiatives more closely resemble Beijing's efforts at public incorporation than the much more market-driven approach of Guangzhou.

I cannot verify if these targets were met, but based on official admissions policies it is evident that public schools maintained a high bar of entry for nonlocals. If we consider the two central districts of Yunyan and Nanming, as well as the somewhat more peripheral Guanshanhu, all had similar public school admission requirements for nonlocals in the late 2010s.[19] In addition to the normal requirements of *hukou*, proof of housing residence, and a labor contract or business license, all three districts require that parents have paid into local social insurance plans for three years. Roughly one-third of migrant workers nationwide have labor contracts, and there is no reason to believe that Guiyang would have a dramatically better ratio.[20] The formal requirements for admission are somewhat lower than in Beijing or Guangzhou, but the basic logic of excluding the lower tiers of the labor market from state-subsidized schooling clearly holds.

Without justifying such exclusionary policies, it is also apparent that Guiyang is in a much less favorable position to respond to the growing demand for public education among migrants than is the case for its wealthier coastal counterparts. An official with the Guiyang Department of Education described the lack of fiscal support thus:

> [Guiyang's] level of investment can resolve the educational needs of its *hukou* population. And we should take responsibility

for the influx of rural migrants, but the upper levels of government, the provincial and central governments, need to take responsibility too. But the provincial and central expenditures on private schools and city schools is very little . . . so of course Guiyang has an opinion on this: "You want us to deal with educating migrant children, but you don't give us any money."[21]

This official's assessment confirms the "inverted welfare state" argument developed in chapter 2, as do the data: in 2017, per capita spending on education in Beijing was nearly fifteen times that of Guiyang, whereas Guangzhou was more than nine times higher.[22] As migration has increased to interior cities, they are in an unenviable fiscal position to respond to such pressures.

Given the inability of the public system to incorporate many nonlocal residents, migrant schools have emerged throughout Guiyang, and they display the "concentrated deprivation" apparent in Beijing.[23] But perhaps the most remarkable difference between Guiyang and elite cities like Beijing and Guangzhou is the level of absolute material deprivation among the migrant workforce, a fact that is clearly reflected in the poor conditions in the schools. At one migrant school in the city, a teacher and vice principal described a level of poverty that I had not witnessed in Beijing or Guangzhou:

TEACHER: Some families don't have bathing facilities, so the principal built a shower here.

VICE PRINCIPAL: Some of the families pick garbage to make a living, and they don't have enough to eat or enough clothes to stay warm. They can't pay tuition. This situation is common in our school. Some of the families live nearby, so the school gives them rice and oil.[24]

Much as was the case in Beijing and Guangzhou, teachers and principals at Guiyang's migrant schools were worried about parents' inability to actively participate in their children's education. But the general level of education of migrant parents in Guiyang appeared to be significantly lower, with widespread illiteracy and inability to speak Mandarin. One mother was forthcoming about her frustration: "We are peasants, we can't even write our family name. We haven't been to school at all, so those like us, we can't even write our own name."[25]

We should view Guiyang, and Guizhou more broadly, not just as a comparative case but as providing a relational view from a different (and subordinate) position in the sociospatial hierarchy. One of the most remarkable features of these interviews was the extent to which the ideology that envisions a correspondence between human quality and location within the urban hierarchy had been firmly inscribed on people's consciousness. An intraprovincial migrant and the mother of a child enrolled in one of Guiyang's migrant schools expounded this logic with devastating simplicity:

cw: When you came to the city, did you consider going to another province?

MOTHER: Because people like us aren't educated, I can't read even one character. How could I go to some faraway place?[26]

Mr. Liu, the NGO worker, presented this view as a natural fact in explaining why people from Bijie, an impoverished area to the northwest of Guiyang, ended up in the provincial capital: "Bijie is one of the poorest parts of Guizhou. It's quite backward in terms of educational *suzhi*, economy, and various aspects. So a lot of these kinds of people come here to look for work, because their educational *suzhi* will only allow them to go as far as this place."[27] While this ideology doesn't map onto empirical reality—plenty of wealthy, highly educated people make their home in Guiyang, whereas lots of poor and under-educated people are in Beijing—it nonetheless reflects an underlying truth that elite cities try to selectively admit elite human capital. The view from Guiyang brought this sorting dynamic into sharp relief. And even the inferior public school system of Guiyang is guarded by a battery of assessments and evaluative criteria, certain to exclude those most in need of public goods.

These brief comparisons are helpful in situating the rather exceptional case of Beijing. The distinctive feature of the capital city is not how inaccessible public schools are to nonlocals; while there are indeed major obstacles, Guangzhou is even more restrictive, and even Guiyang has requirements that exclude large numbers of working-class migrants. Rather, Beijing is unusual in the coerciveness with which it has ejected migrants from the city, even those who are engaged in labor that is valued by capital. Guangzhou and Guiyang have been more comfort-able allowing informal and formal marketized education to develop alongside the public system, a pattern that would appear to hold in other cities. Places that are more dependent on labor-intensive industries than is Beijing have further incentive to allow migrants to occupy the space of the city, even if that does not mean extending access to social services. By adopting a rela-tional perspective, we see that Beijing's position at the apex of the sociospatial hierarchy allows it to siphon away those people deemed to be of sufficiently high quality from places like Gui-yang, as well as other cities and rural areas that constitute the vast majority of China's population. The upward funneling of fiscal and human resources is linked to an accumulation of deprivation on the lower rungs of the hierarchy. Beijing *is* exceptional, but it is an exception that reveals the character of an entire unequal system.

CAPITALIST POPULATION MANAGEMENT, INTENSIVE AND EXTENSIVE

Thus far, I have largely limited the scope of the investigation to the city, though the domestic hinterland has been a constant background presence. It would, however, be a mistake to assume that the central phenomena I have elucidated here can be fully accounted for by dynamics internal to the city. While the urbanization of people proceeds empirically at the level of the city, it is structured by phenomena organized at a variety of scales. As expounded by Henri Lefebvre and more recently taken up by Neil Brenner, a dialectical perspective on urbanization demands attention to capitalism's global implosion/explosion dynamic. "Urbanization" pertains to the implosion moment of the dialectic (i.e., that of concentration), even though it is mutually constituted by "explosion" processes of dispersion and extension within a global dynamic of uneven and combined development.[28] My aim is not to account for the development process in general, but rather the more specific problem of how power works to coordinate distributions of labor and capital in time and space. While urban China's labor market is overwhelmingly though not exclusively domestic, certainly its cities are deeply linked to global circuits of capital and commodities.

What does a global perspective achieve in accounting for the specific political strategies we have seen deployed in the Chinese city? China's incorporation into capitalism during the 1980s and 1990s came amid the broader neoliberal turn globally.

The Chinese state's approach to advancing development was to establish favorable conditions for foreign investment while pursuing export-led growth predicated on a vast and politically repressed working class. As was the case for other countries in the region, this form of development demanded labor not only in large volumes but also of relatively high quality.[29] Amid fierce global competition in the export-processing sector, key features of China's comparative advantage were its abilities not only to tightly manage the spatial distribution of labor but also to secure well-educated and healthy workers on the cheap, thanks to cities' capacity to push the costs of social reproduction onto the countryside. In other words, if we want to understand why the citizenship regime evolved as it did in the era of capitalist transition, we need to situate the urban political economy within a global context in which China's route to development was predicated on producing a workforce of the price and quality that would attract transnational capital. While this labor production and control regime has been made possible by centrally determined administrative arrangements, it has largely been up to cities to capitalize on the potential.

The state's "conveyor belt" role in global capitalism is most apparent in export-manufacturing hubs like Guangdong and the Yangzi River Delta. Local governments have played an active and indispensable role in securing land and vast quantities of labor for global capital, most spectacularly in the example of Foxconn.[30] The city of Beijing does not play a similarly critical role in global supply chains as Guangdong, and one might assume that global capital plays less of a role in shaping the city's population management regime. That is the case to a degree, and I have argued elsewhere that this accounts for some of the differences we see in practices between Beijing and Guangzhou.[31] Nonetheless, Beijing is a highly globalized

Sharma, is that postcolonial politics have resulted in a harden-
ing of borders and increased policing of movements of people
globally.[36] As evidenced by the state's incentives for Han settlement in Xinjiang and Tibet, an American-style westward
movement of people may play some role in dispersing surplus
populations, but mass emigration à la nineteenth-century
Europe is simply not possible in today's order of nation-states.
By the same token, it remains highly unlikely that the Chinese
state could bring in large volumes of foreign labor to biopolitically sustain the national population, as recently attested to by
intense public backlash against modest proposals to loosen permanent residency requirements for foreign workers.[37]

There are major implications of this vastly different, and
more constrained, global terrain for how the Chinese state
manages population. First, absent the safety valve of overseas
settler colonialism, social crises deriving from capitalist development have to be managed internally. Of course, *capital* can
and already has employed the spatial fix to escape rising wages
and labor conflict, but the state must deal with the human
beings who are left behind. This means either supplying them
with means of survival and/or devising political techniques
capable of short-circuiting revolt. Second, in the absence of a
demographically abundant and politically available racialized
other that could be sourced externally and incorporated into
capitalist production, the Chinese state inserted a social break
within the Han race. But while this surplus population is subjected to similar kinds of dehumanization and exploitation
associated with European biological racism, the key difference
is that in China it is space, rather than race, that is the key axis
of differentiation. In other words, the biopolitical problematic
of dividing up and distributing living labor in a spatiotemporal
matrix in relationship to capital is, in the case of contemporary

China, internalized within a single country and largely within a single race. The exercise of biopower in China is socially and spatially *intensive*.[38] Cities are the decisive political unit at which the sorting and management of this population proceeds. The urbanization of people is therefore profoundly influenced by this highly constrained global landscape.

REVIVAL FOR WHOM?

The social break within the Han race is at odds with the state's own increasingly assertive rhetoric of national unity and pride. For many years it has been clear that the state needed to develop alternatives to the performance-based legitimacy on which it had long relied, as the previous three decades of stupendous growth could not persist indefinitely. They key slogan associated with this ethnonationalist turn is "the great revival of the Chinese nation" (*zhonghua minzu weida fuxing* 中华民族伟大复兴), which evokes a return to the imagined glory of empires past. A charitable interpretation of the slogan would suggest that all ethnicities in the PRC are included in this revival, but it is apparent enough that Han are first among equals. As Chinese state and corporate power has increased dramatically, the severe life-denying acts visited upon the surplus population, even in the symbolic core of this revival, Beijing, materially undercuts the exhortations toward ethnonational unity and rejuvenation. Indeed, in managing access to social services within the city, the basic premise is that some members of the race must be expelled so that others can flourish. This is the ethical core of the state's neo-Malthusian practices.

Might this incongruity between ideology and material reality serve as the basis of political rupture? Could demands on the part of the PRC's surplus population for equal access to means of social reproduction catalyze politicized social insurgency?[39] At the moment, it remains unlikely. While there is no empirical evidence that Chinese people are becoming *increasingly* nationalist, there is little to suggest that Xi's popularity has been negatively impacted by the state's discriminatory citizenship regime.[40] And without question there is no domestically constituted political force that could articulate a distinct and more encompassing vision of "revival." It would appear as though the long-standing dynamic of Chinese citizens framing their grievances with reference to local officialdom persists, even when centrally determined policies are the root cause.

Even though it is unlikely that a broad-based movement for equal citizenship will emerge soon, there *are* deeply felt grievances. In my own research, there was widespread dissatisfaction among migrant schoolteachers and parents with the schooling system. Interestingly, I found that it was common for critiques of educational inequality to be framed in more or less nationalistic terms. A teacher from Zhifan School expressed his dissatisfaction thus: "On this issue [education] I'm quite dissatisfied with our government. I think Chinese people, regardless of whether they are poor or rich, they are all part of our China, we're all the descendants of the dragon."[41] Mr. Fan, the migrant father and Shandong native residing in Beijing's Liwanzhuang, was even more scathing in his assessment:

These officials are just oppressing us normal folks. They know there is enough for everyone to eat, but they'll still charge you money [to get into school]. . . . As for education, our country has really not done well, it's really bad and is widely unpopular. . . . [The government] should actively help us with schooling, but instead . . . we have to beg to get into school. [The government] should treat all children's schooling as if it was their own family. [Instead] they say, "Aren't those *your* children?" They are not considered the children of the nation.[42]

Here we can see how the national-paternalistic rhetoric of the state can boomerang in the face of glaring intra-ethnic inequities.

This simmering dissatisfaction among migrants *has* on occasion catalyzed collective protest.[43] Most of this resistance is simply reactive: following the 2011 mass school demolitions, there were numerous displays of public protest, and even disruptive direct actions.[44] Subsequent demolitions have also resulted in teachers, parents, and students mobilizing against eviction, as in the case of Beijing's Huangzhuang School (discussed in chapter 5). When the Beijing municipal government dramatically increased requirements for school admissions in 2014, migrant parents who had been operating under the assumption that their children would be enrolled in the fall were outraged. A group of parents from Shusheng and other nearby schools organized a protest at the Chaoyang District Education Department offices, where they blockaded the entrance. And a number of similar protests over restrictive school admissions took place in each of the following two years, with one parent setting himself on fire in protest in front of the Changping District government offices in 2016.[45] As with other forms of social protest in China, these events remain fractured, relatively small in scale, and steadfastly focused on immediate issues. And as is the case with protesting workers or peasants, parents are sometimes able to wrest small victories, particularly in forcing the government to accommodate displaced students following demolitions.[46] Nonetheless, these protests have remained largely defensive and have not changed the basic policy direction in Beijing or other large cities. Even a socially exclusive expansion and equalization of social protection just focused on the dominant race seems unlikely. Amid a revival in national wealth and power, the struggle to live and work in the same place shows no signs of abating for millions.

FROM INTENSIVE TO EXTENSIVE GROWTH?

The Chinese government has continually set ambitious growth targets in order to realize its stated aim of national revival. While the scale and rapidity of China's economic growth over the past forty years is unparalleled in history, dozens of other countries have attained middle income status. Reaching the ranks of wealthy nations is by no means a foregone conclusion. How might China's labor recruitment and population management regime be affected by the ongoing drive to secure growth?

This is a problem that has confronted other emergent imperial powers. Every major country that has ascended to the elite tier of capitalist economies has done so either via imperial expansion and colonialism (Netherlands, the United Kingdom, France, the United States), being tightly bound militarily and economically to an existing imperial power (Israel, South Korea, Taiwan), or some historical combination thereof (Germany, Japan).[47] The motivations for imperialism are of course diverse and have been intensely debated for more than a century. But with respect to the issue of managing distributions of labor in relationship to capital, the key issues are, as elucidated earlier, securing spaces for exporting domestic surplus populations (i.e., settler colonialism) and securing highly exploitable populations that can be disposed of with minimal political disruption. Capitalist accumulation is facilitated when the state and capital can avoid paying costs associated with the formation of labor and then slough off workers who are no longer deemed useful. Racialized workforces, mobilized in the colonies or brought back to the metropole itself, have served this role for previous imperial powers.

As already indicated, China is unlikely to have the freedom to engage in imperial expansion on the scale of Euro-American powers, especially given ongoing US military preeminence. But we can see how the pressures of excess industrial capacity, slowing growth, rising business costs, and population decline among the domestic Han workforce have already pushed China in an imperial direction. The clearest example of this impetus to incorporate new subordinated groups into circuits of capital is actually internal to the borders of the PRC. This includes an expansion of "labor transfer" programs in Xinjiang and Tibet as well as mass internment and incarceration of Muslim minorities and the associated unfree labor regimes.[48] While the state sees control of territory and political domination of racialized minorities as ends in themselves, there are clearly economic incentives at play as well.[49] Long-standing labor transfers programs, the stated aim of which is to reallocate surplus rural labor, have been dramatically expanded in recent years in western China. In the context of increasingly assimilationist and repressive ethnic policies as well as strict quotas associated with the poverty eradication campaign, the state has transferred presumably inefficient and politically suspect minority groups to wage labor. Hundreds of thousands of people from just three prefectures in Xinjiang—Aksu, Hotan, and Kashgar—have been transferred to pick cotton, while more than half a million Tibetans were trained in the labor transfer program in the first seven months of

2020.[50] Under a distinct but related effort, since 2017 hundreds of thousands of Uyghurs and other Muslims deemed security threats have been sent to reeducation camps, forced to study Mandarin and undergo job training, and then transferred to nonvoluntary employment. While the bulk of the labor of former detainees is put to work in Xinjiang itself, in some cases people are put up for sale to private companies throughout China.[51] Vicky Xu and her colleagues estimate that more than 80,000 Uyghurs were sent out of Xinjiang via this forced labor regime between 2017 and 2019, and many were in factories producing goods for well-known foreign brands.[52] These labor programs are not chattel slavery—indications are that workers are given a wage, albeit a paltry one—but the workers have no capacity to bargain over the terms of their employment, nor do they even have the thin freedom to seek work elsewhere. Cut off from their communities, they are not being socially reproduced, and the wage needs only to sustain their immediate biological existence. This labor regime is justified via a straightforwardly colonial logic in which minorities are depicted as violent and uncivilized extremists who can only be made into loyal and productive subjects via coercive state intervention. But although these initiatives are similar to the racially extensive colonialism of earlier empires in a number of respects, the relative demographic weight of Muslims and Tibetans in China remains small. In other words, while these unfree labor regimes may be profitable, ethnic minority labor within the PRC is too limited to serve as the social foundation of a new racial capitalism.

At present, significant obstacles remain to securing large volumes of super-exploitable labor overseas.[53] Bringing constrained guest workers into China on the model of numerous small countries (e.g., Taiwan, Singapore, the United Arab Emirates, Qatar)

may play a marginal role, but given the country's vast population, it is unlikely that such programs could serve as a fundamental element in the social organization of production. Certainly, both the private and state variants of Chinese capital have
been increasingly venturing abroad to shore up profitability. In
addition to the massive construction projects associated with the
Belt and Road Initiative that have captured headlines, Chinese
manufacturers have increasingly relocated to elsewhere in Asia
as well as Africa. According to McKinsey, by 2017 Chinese firms
were responsible for up to 12 percent of Africa's industrial production.[54] While other parts of Asia and Africa certainly provide abundant workers who could one day be funneled into a
super-exploitative regime capable of sustaining Chinese capital,
this would require large-scale exertion of political force—one
that could intensify conflict with other regional powers or the
United States. It is likely in the years to come that China will
continue to strive to construct overseas supply chains linking
huge volumes of highly exploitable labor to Chinese capital, but
this is by no means a simple political and institutional process.

Given this relatively constrained global context, it appears
that the *intensive* mode of managing the population will remain
paramount for some time, as China attempts to become a high-
income country and assert political dominance in Asia and
beyond. Xi Jinping's "two circulations" principle announced in
2020 suggests that China is intent on reducing exposure to
global uncertainty by increasing internal economic "circulation."[55] This is to be accomplished by expanding domestic consumption and strengthening domestically centered production
networks. In order for this China-anchored system of production to be competitive in global capitalism, the state will continue to tightly manage the movements, aspirations, and lives

of its overwhelmingly Han workforce. Given the socially and spatially intensive nature of this biopolitics, China's cities will persist as a critical site for discerning the fate not just of an emerging working class, but indeed of an entire emergent empire.

METHODOLOGICAL APPENDIX

My position as a white thirtysomething man hailing from a well-known university in the United States inevitably affected the collection of ethnographic and interview data. Although many of the schools I studied had hosted international visitors, students were often captivated by my presence. In school after school, I would be greeted by dozens of children gathering excitedly around me in the yard, asking for my autograph or my QQ number so we could chat online. In one school I visited in Chengdu, school officials took numerous photos during my visit. On a follow-up trip the next year, I was surprised to see these photos in the school's promotional materials with the somewhat misleading description that a professor from Cornell was teaching the class. Nonetheless, I found that the spectacle of my presence would fade rather quickly, and I could go about observing classes and speaking with teachers and parents in a relaxed manner.

As has been the case throughout my research career, I often received the advice that Chinese people would be unwilling to share their honest opinions with a foreigner, either out of general distrust or a more specific concern about airing their nation's dirty laundry. While of course I cannot verify which

thoughts people did *not* share with me, I did not find such reti-
cence in the field. At Mingxin and Zhenhua schools, I successfully gained access by simply walking up to the front entrance
and asking if I could speak with the principal. In fact, being a
white American quite plausibly facilitated this access—amid
high tensions over the Senkaku/Diaoyu Islands, the principal
of Zhenhua volunteered that he would not have let me in if
I were Japanese. It would be pointless to speculate about how the
study would be different if I were someone else, but there is no
question people were eager to tell their stories to me despite (or
perhaps *because* of) our social distance. That is, it often appeared
as if people were willing to divulge personal details because
that distance between us created a safe container for this information. In general, I found both teachers and parents to be
incredibly forthcoming, and I quickly lost track of the number
of times that people broke down in tears while relating intimate
details of their life experiences.

My gender mattered in terms of the kinds of settings where
I would interact with informants. While the large majority
of my interviews were with women, it was only the handful of
male teachers who ever invited me to socialize outside of the
school. These interactions with other men certainly helped add
greater texture to my understanding of their social world, and
in that sense they created something of a gendered imbalance
in the study. Nonetheless, female teachers and mothers were
still forthcoming about matters of relevance to the study (as
I believe is fully apparent particularly in chapters 4 and 6). The
supervised interviews in Chengdu, Guizhou, and Guangzhou
were conducted by ethnically Han women, and the gender of
the interviewer did not have any discernible impact on the data.

As acknowledged in the introduction, I believe my social
position *did* impose real limitations on my interactions with

children. I did not feel as though I had the cultural sensitivity or the social accountability to be able to broach potentially traumatic experiences with children as young as six. Whether children would have been willing to speak to me is another issue; I preempted this by deciding to forgo interviews with them altogether. This is a weakness of the project, but I could not ethically justify subjecting children to the risk of retraumatization for the sake of enhanced data collection. It is plausible that a researcher more culturally proximate to the community would have been able to handle this issue more adroitly.

I planned this project as a workplace study, with data collection to be based on direct observation in the classroom as well as interviews with teachers and administrators. In most schools I visited I taught at least one English class, but this was not structured as participant observation as such. Although I do think I gained some insights from these experiences, I did not presume that my own experience would ever be adequately deep for it to serve as a meaningful source of "data." Rather, teaching classes was primarily a means to ingratiate myself to my hosts and to build rapport with students, parents, and teachers. From the outset, I knew I wanted to visit multiple schools in multiple cities, and given this breadth/depth trade-off, interviews would serve as my primary source of data. As described in the introduction, I chose my primary research sites in Beijing (Yinghong, Shusheng, and Zhifan) to try to capture the range of possibility within the city's migrant schools. Although many of the details of the schools appear in the empirical chapters, it is worth providing a concise description here.

I was introduced to the "low-end" school, Yinghong, through an NGO that provided supplementary arts classes to the students. Yinghong was in Changping District outside the Sixth Ring Road, an area far to the north of the urban core.

The school was in an "urban village," but given its remoteness from the center, it felt relatively less pressure from increasing rent and the threat of demolition. As in other such urban villages, the community was overwhelmingly nonlocal. Yinghong did not have an operating license and received no subsidies from the government while charging 550 yuan per semester in 2012. Forty students in the school had received "poverty relief" grants of 500 yuan from a Hong Kong foundation, but this did not affect the school's finances, since it was directly transferred to the students. Yinghong had fewer than six hundred students, and their parents hailed from every province of China except Guangdong and Guangxi. I did the majority of my interviews at Yinghong in late 2011 and the summer of 2012, with follow-up interviews in 2014.

Shusheng was the "mid-tier" school in my study, and the place where I spent the most time and did the most interviews. Shusheng was in the eastern part of Chaoyang District, between the Fifth and Sixth Ring Roads. Although it was in an urban village, the area was under much greater redevelopment pressure than was the case for Yinghong. Chaoyang is a more prosperous part of the city, and the eastward expansion of infrastructure and real estate development had a major impact on the community. Indeed, the school and its surrounding areas had been under the threat of demolition for many years. The primary school student body was just over 550, and when I first visited in 2011 the school charged 520 yuan per semester. The school had received its initial startup funds for securing space from a foundation, and it maintained close relations with various civil society groups. This included Teach Future China, which sent recent college graduates to teach in the school. Nonetheless, it received relatively little in terms of ongoing financial support from foundations. I first visited

Shusheng in late 2011 and made a number of return visits through 2014.

The "high-end" school, Zhifan, was in the northern part of Daxing District, inside the Sixth Ring Road. As noted in chapter 5, Zhifan had been forced to relocate further into the urban periphery several times in the early 2000s before receiving its operating license. When I visited in the summer of 2012, its location was remote from the urban core, and there were no immediate threats of demolition. Nonetheless, in the subsequent years Daxing came to be the site of some high-profile cases of migrant community dislocation. This included the mass expulsion of migrants following a fire in an informal settlement in 2017, as well as huge dislocations associated with the construction of Daxing International Airport. Zhifan was larger than the other two schools, enrolling 930 students at the time of my fieldwork. Zhifan charged 700 yuan per semester and had received millions in foundation support in recent years. I spent less time at Zhifan than the other schools, in part because it represented such an outlier with respect to its financial resources. Nonetheless, it was important to include in the study to assess the best possible scenario for migrant schools.

As noted in the preface, my study was originally focused on the workplace but gradually morphed into a project on urbanization, and I had to adjust my approach accordingly. In my quest to better understand astonishing levels of student turnover—a workplace problem from the perspective of teachers—I needed to expand my pool of informants to include parents. I decided to focus my interviews on parents from a single school, Shusheng. In part this was out of convenience, since I had the best connections there and most families lived in relative proximity to the school. It was quite important for parents to feel at ease in speaking to me about the often anguished and very personal challenges they encountered in Beijing. Since I had made visits to Shusheng over the previous three years, I had established a strong degree of trust with teachers and administrators that I leaned on in connecting with parents. One consequence, however, is that my interviews with parents do not perfectly "match" my data on teachers and schools, in that they are drawn from a single case.

I similarly had to expand my pool of informants as I tried to better understand the impact of school closures and demolitions. While Shusheng and Zhifan schools had either been forced to relocate earlier or were dealing with threats of closure—an issue discussed in many of my interviews—I needed additional cases to really unpack the contours of urban redevelopment. As a result, I did interviews and collected publicly available information on schools that had quite recently been demolished or closed (Jingwei and Huangzhuang schools) as well as schools slated for imminent demolition (Mingxin and Zhenhua) amid redevelopment of their neighborhood. My interviews in 2014 at Mingxin, Zhenhua, and the new location of Jingwei were thus more focused on the issue of demolition than was the case at my primary sites. All three of these schools were in the Dongxiaokou neighborhood of southern Changping District (though Jingwei's post-demolition location was in a neighborhood further to the north). Information on the Huangzhuang case comes entirely from publicly available digital sources. This 2017 case allowed me to clarify how the politics of school closure and urban redevelopment evolved over the course of the 2010s.

I conducted semi-structured interviews at all sites. The content of the interviews varied dependent on whether I was interviewing school administrators, teachers, or parents. Nearly all interviews with administrators and teachers were carried out in schools. I endeavored to interview teachers out of earshot from students and school administrators, though this was not always possible. I interviewed a diverse group of teachers based on gender, years of experience, and level of instruction. I met with parents in a variety of settings, including in schools, on the street in front of schools, and at their homes and places of work. I personally conducted all but one of the interviews in Beijing. Research assistants conducted a handful of interviews in Guangzhou and Chengdu. Christine Wen, a PhD student in city and regional planning at Cornell, conducted all thirty-five interviews in Guizhou. Nearly all interviews were recorded and transcribed by research assistants, and I coded the interviews using ATLAS.ti. In the few instances that I was unable to record, I took notes by hand, which I supplemented with additional details as soon as feasible. In addition to interviews, I took detailed field notes to record my observations of schools and teacher interactions, conditions within the community, as well as my own experiences teaching classes. I also took photographs at all schools and did extensive video documentation in Dongxiaokou (where Jingwei, Zhenhua, and Mingxin schools were located).

NOTES

INTRODUCTION

1. It is remarkable how rapidly this cliché has been inverted, thereby revealing its ideological character. Amid a declining birthrate, there is now considerable official angst that China does not have *enough* people.
2. This was true not just in domestic, but also foreign media. Ian Johnson, "China Releases Plan to Incorporate Farmers Into Cities," *New York Times*, March 17, 2014.
3. Use of the term "human capital" throughout must not be interpreted as affirmation of human capital theory. Rather, it is used to underline the labor market–centric metrics the state has developed to sort the population.
4. Fulong Wu, Fangzhu Zhang, and Chris Webster, *Rural Migrants in Urban China: Enclaves and Transient Urbanism* (New York: Routledge, 2013), 53.
5. It is important to note that the Chinese term used here is *chengqu renkou* 城区人口, or "urban district population." There is much confusion in measuring urban populations in China, in part due to ambiguity between *chengqu* ("urban districts") and *shi* ("cities" or "prefectures"), since the latter includes rural populations as well. See Kam Wing Chan, "Measuring the Urban Millions," *China Economic Quarterly* 1 (2009): 21–26.
6. "Beijing shiwei shuji Guo Jinlong: wailai changzhu renkou jin yiwu ye gai xiangshou fuwu" [Beijing party secretary Guo Jinlong: migrant

permanent population that fulfills obligations should enjoy services], *Xin Jing Bao*, January 17, 2014.

7. Susan Greenhalgh and Edwin A. Winckler, *Governing China's Population: From Leninist to Neoliberal Biopolitics* (Stanford, CA: Stanford University Press, 2005).

8. Leta Hong Fincher, *Leftover Women: The Resurgence of Gender Inequality in China* (London: Zed Books, 2016).

9. Tian Zhao, "Shanghai Official Urges More Couples to Have Second Child," *Caixin*, January 28, 2015.

10. In speaking of the West, Silvia Federici has argued, "the collapse of the birth rate and increase in the number of divorces could be read as instances of resistance to the capitalist discipline of work"; that is, as women are increasingly pulled into wage labor, they refuse to take on excess reproductive labor. There are some clear resonances with contemporary urban China. Silvia Federici, *Revolution at Point Zero: Housework, Reproduction, and Feminist Struggle* (Oakland, CA: PM Press, 2012), 97.

11. This is a reference to, and inversion of, David Harvey's question in *The Urbanization of Capital*: "How does capital become urbanized, and what are the consequences of that urbanization?" Whereas Harvey is interested in how capital urbanizes in order to maintain profitability, I approach the question from the perspective of workers and ask how people are urbanized and how it structures survival. David Harvey, *The Urbanization of Capital: Studies in the History and Theory of Capitalist Urbanization* (Baltimore, MD: Johns Hopkins University Press, 1985), 185.

12. Kam Wing Chan, *Cities with Invisible Walls: Reinterpreting Urbanization in Post-1949 China* (Oxford: Oxford University Press, 1994); George C. S. Lin, "Chinese Urbanism in Question: State, Society, and the Reproduction of Urban Spaces," *Urban Geography* 28, no. 1 (2007): 7–29; Lynette H. Ong, "State-Led Urbanization in China: Skyscrapers, Land Revenue and 'Concentrated Villages,'" *The China Quarterly* 217 (2014): 162–79.

13. You-tien Hsing, *The Great Urban Transformation: Politics of Land and Property in China* (Oxford: Oxford University Press, 2010).

14. This is not to deny the important role industrialization plays in the urbanization process. Rather, it is to make a distinction in the locus of accumulation: with the former, value production is centered in the factory, while with the later the city itself is a force of production, both with respect to capitalizing space and in facilitating value production in the "social factory." Mario Tronti, *Workers and Capital* (London: Verso, 2019).

15. Kerry Liu, "Chinese Manufacturing in the Shadow of the China–US Trade War," *Economic Affairs* 38, no. 3 (2018): 307–24.

16. You-tien Hsing, *The Great Urban Transformation: Politics of Land and Property in China* (Oxford: Oxford University Press, 2010); George C. S. Lin and Fangxin Yi, "Urbanization of Capital or Capitalization on Urban Land? Land Development and Local Public Finance in Urbanizing China," *Urban Geography* 32, no. 1 (2011): 50–79; George C. S. Lin and Amy Y. Zhang, "China's Metropolises in Transformation: Neoliberalizing Politics, Land Commodification, and Uneven Development in Beijing," *Urban Geography* 38, no. 5 (2017): 643–65; Hyun Bang Shin, "Economic Transition and Speculative Urbanisation in China: Gentrification versus Dispossession," *Urban Studies* 53, no. 3 (2016): 471–89; Yifei Wu, Xun Li, and George C. S. Lin, "Reproducing the City of the Spectacle: Mega-Events, Local Debts, and Infrastructure-Led Urbanization in China," *Cities* 53 (2016): 51–60.

17. Meg E. Rithmire, *Land Bargains and Chinese Capitalism: The Politics of Property Rights Under Reform* (New York: Cambridge University Press, 2015).

18. Ngai Pun and Jenny Wai-ling Chan, "Global Capital, the State, and Chinese Workers: The Foxconn Experience," *Modern China* 38, no. 4 (May 2012): 383–410; Eli Friedman, "Teachers' Work in China's Migrant Schools," *Modern China* 43, no. 6 (April 2017): 559–89; Anita Chan and Kaxton Siu, "Analyzing Exploitation: The Mechanisms Underpinning Low Wages and Excessive Overtime in Chinese Export Factories," *Critical Asian Studies* 42, no. 2 (2010): 167–90; Kaxton Siu, "Continuity and Change in the Everyday Lives of Chinese Migrant Factory Workers," *The China Journal* 74 (2015): 43–65.

19. The view that this migrant workforce is becoming increasingly self-aware and politically focused has generated debate, see Ngai Pun and Huilin Lu, "Unfinished Proletarianization: Self, Anger, and Class Action among the Second Generation of Peasant-Workers in Present-Day China," *Modern China* 36, no. 5 (July 2010): 493–519; Ching Kwan Lee, "Precarization or Empowerment? Reflections on Recent Labor Unrest in China," *The Journal of Asian Studies* 75, no. 2 (May 2016): 317–33. Ivan Franceschini, Kaxton Siu, and Anita Chan, "The 'Rights Awakening' of Chinese Migrant Workers: Beyond the Generational Perspective," *Critical Asian Studies* 48, no. 3 (2016): 422–42.

20. Justin Yifu Liu, *Demystifying the Chinese Economy* (Cambridge: Cambridge University Press, 2011).

21. Kam Wing Chan, "The Chinese Hukou System at 50," *Eurasian Geography and Economics* 50, no. 2 (2009): 197–221.

22. See https://data.worldbank.org/indicator/SP.URB.TOTL.IN.ZS?locations=CN (accessed June 17, 2020).

23. Zhuoni Zhang and Xiaogang Wu, "Occupational Segregation and Earnings Inequality: Rural Migrants and Local Workers in Urban China," *Social Science Research* 61 (2017): 57–74; Li Zhang, *Strangers in the City: Reconfigurations of Space, Power, and Social Networks within China's Floating Population* (Stanford, CA: Stanford University Press, 2001); Li Zhang, "Migrant Enclaves and Impacts of Redevelopment Policy in Chinese Cities," *Restructuring the Chinese City: Changing Society, Economy and Space*, ed. Laurence J. C. Ma and Fulong Wu (New York: Routledge, 2005), 218–33; Weiping Wu, "Outsiders in the City: Migrant Housing and Settlement Patterns," in *Rural Migrants in Urban China: Enclaves and Transient Urbanism*, ed. Fulong Wu, Fangzhu Zhang, and Chris Webster (New York: Routledge, 2014), 51–66; Biliang Hu and Tony Saich, "Developing Social Citizenship? A Case Study of Education and Health Services in Yantian Village of Guangdong Province," *China & World Economy* 20, no. 3 (May 2012): 69–87; Yeqing Huang, Fei Guo, and Yiming Tang, "Hukou Status and Social Exclusion of Rural–Urban Migrants in Transitional China," *Journal of Asian Public Policy* 3, no. 2 (2010): 172–85; Holly H. Ming, *The Education of Migrant Children and China's Future: The Urban Left Behind* (New York: Routledge, 2013); Charlotte Goodburn, "Growing Up in

(and Out of) Shenzhen: The Longer-Term Impacts of Rural-Urban Migration on Education and Labor Market Entry," *The China Journal* 83, no. 1 (2020): 495–504.

24. Chan, "The Chinese Hukou System at 50"; Chan, *Cities with Invisible Walls*; Shaohua Zhan, "What Determines Migrant Workers' Life Chances in Contemporary China? Hukou, Social Exclusion, and the Market," *Modern China* 37, no. 3 (February 2011): 243–85.

25. Pei-chia Lan, "Segmented Incorporation: The Second Generation of Rural Migrants in Shanghai," *The China Quarterly* 217 (2014): 243–65. There is some debate about the trajectory of exclusion; Chris Webster sees "many indicators of progressive social, economic and even political integration of migrant workers." Wu, Zhang, and Webster, *Rural Migrants in Urban China*, 291. See also Kam Wing Chan, "Fundamentals of China's Urbanization and Policy," *The China Review* 10, no. 1 (2010): 63–94; Shaohua Zhan and Lingli Huang, "Rural Roots of Current Migrant Labor Shortage in China: Development and Labor Empowerment in a Situation of Incomplete Proletarianization," *Studies in Comparative International Development* 48, no. 1 (2013): 81–111; Chenchen Zhang, "Governing Neoliberal Authoritarian Citizenship: Theorizing Hukou and the Changing Mobility Regime in China," *Citizenship Studies* 22, no. 8 (2018): 869.

26. Cindy Fan, "Settlement Intention and Split Households: Findings from a Survey of Migrants in Beijing's Urban Villages," *China Review* 11, no. 2 (2011): 11–41; Minhua Ling, "Returning to No Home: Educational Remigration and Displacement in Rural China," *Anthropological Quarterly* 90, no. 3 (2017): 715–42.

27. Mingqiong Zhang, Cherrie Jiuhua Zhu, and Chris Nyland, "The Institution of Hukou-based Social Exclusion: A Unique Institution Reshaping the Characteristics of Contemporary Urban China," *International Journal of Urban and Regional Research* 38, no. 4 (2014): 1437–57.

28. Sandro Mezzadra and Brett Neilson, "Between Inclusion and Exclusion: On the Topology of Global Space and Borders," *Theory, Culture & Society* 29, nos. 4–5 (2012): 58–75; Sandro Mezzadra and Brett Neilson, *Border as Method, or, the Multiplication of Labor* (Durham, NC: Duke University Press, 2013).

29. Mary Gallagher has used a similar approach in linking workplace dynamics to broader processes of urbanization, arguing, "The workplace is the setting in which the state transforms rural people into urban citizens." Mary E. Gallagher, *Authoritarian Legality in China: Law, Workers, and the State* (Cambridge: Cambridge University Press, 2017), 10.

30. Michel Foucault, *"Society Must Be Defended": Lectures at the Collège de France, 1975–1976* (New York: Picador, 2003), 242.

31. Barbara Laslett and Johanna Brenner also identify the double meaning of social reproduction, employing the term "societal reproduction" for what I call here "class reproduction." Barbara Laslett and Johanna Brenner, "Gender and Social Reproduction: Historical Perspectives," *Annual Review of Sociology* 15, no. 1 (1989): 381–404.

32. Marx's understanding of "reproduction" also includes this more capacious meaning of the reproduction of society, although it is less central to the analysis than is the case for Bourdieu. Tithi Bhattacharya, "How Not to Skip Class: Social Reproduction of Labor and the Global Working Class," in *Social Reproduction Theory: Remapping Class, Recentering Oppression*, ed. Tithi Bhattacharya (London: Pluto Press, 2017), 76.

33. Pierre Bourdieu and Jean Claude Passeron, *Reproduction in Education, Society and Culture* (London: Sage Publications, 1977).

34. Paul E. Willis, *Learning to Labour: How Working Class Kids Get Working Class Jobs* (Farnborough, UK: Saxon House, 1977).

35. Louis Althusser, "Ideology and Ideological State Apparatuses," In *Lenin and Philosophy* (New York: Monthly Review Press, 1971).

36. Yan Gu, "Compulsory Education for Children of Migrant Workers: Is Hukou the Biggest Obstacle?" in *Challenges in the Process of China's Urbanization*, ed. Karen Eggleston, Jean C. Oi, and Yiming Wang (Stanford, CA: Walter H. Shorenstein Asia-Pacific Research Center, 2017); Shaohua Zhan, "What Determines Migrant Workers' Life Chances in Contemporary China?"

37. Joel Andreas and Shaohua Zhan, "Hukou and Land: Market Reform and Rural Displacement in China," *Journal of Peasant Studies* 43, no. 4 (2016): 798–827.

38. Chuanbo Chen and C. Cindy Fan, "China's Hukou Puzzle: Why Don't Rural Migrants Want Urban Hukou?" *China Review* 16, no. 3 (2016): 9–39.

39. Terry E. Woronov, "Learning to Serve: Urban Youth, Vocational Schools and New Class Formations in China," *The China Journal* 66 (2011): 77–99; Terry E. Woronov, *Class Work: Vocational Schools and China's Urban Youth* (Stanford, CA: Stanford University Press, 2015); Minhua Ling, "'Bad Students Go to Vocational Schools!': Education, Social Reproduction and Migrant Youth in Urban China," *The China Journal* 73 (2015): 108–31.

40. This is something of an irony, given the pervasive influence of Marxism in the field. With some important exceptions, the point of departure for much of this literature is the question of how capital maintains profits via spatial reorganization, rather than a labor-centric view that would ask how people survive.

41. The discrepancy is due to group interviews that I counted as a single interview with multiple people.

42. China Urban Construction Yearbook.

43. Beijing Municipality Master Plan (2016–2035) [北京城市总体规划 (2016 年–2035 年)]

44. A few other examples will help illustrate how this categorization works. If we consider sources of funding, Zhifan had regular, substantial support from a well-endowed foundation, whereas Shusheng had received some initial financial support and regularly had teachers provided to them by a nonprofit organization. Yinghong, on the other hand, was entirely funded by tuition. Zhifan had received extensive media coverage and awards in recognition of their achievements—certainly not true for Yinghong. And Shusheng had been under constant threat of closure and demolition, suggesting that the government did not hold it in particularly high esteem.

45. All of the interviews in Guizhou were conducted by a research assistant. A smaller subset of interviews in Guangzhou and Chengdu and a single interview in Beijing were conducted by assistants as well.

46. There was indeed a degree of variation between districts in Beijing, a matter I address in subsequent chapters. Nonetheless, the various districts in Beijing share much more in common with each other than they do with any district in, for example, Guangzhou.

47. This evokes Xuefei Ren's idea of "territorial politics," a "mode of governance anchored in subnational territorial authorities and institutions . . . [that has] led to an uneven distribution of rights and benefits

across localities." Xuefei Ren, *Governing the Urban in China and India: Land Grabs, Slum Clearance, and the War on Air Pollution* (Princeton, NJ: Princeton University Press, 2020), 10.

48. The language of vulnerability is drawn from Ruth Wilson Gilmore's influential conceptualization of racism, an issue to which I return in chapter 1. Ruth Wilson Gilmore, *Golden Gulag: Prisons, Surplus, Crisis, and Opposition in Globalizing California* (Berkeley: University of California Press, 2007).

1. CONCEPTUALIZING THE POLITICS OF URBANIZATION

1. Portions of this chapter previously appeared in Eli Friedman, "Just-in-Time Urbanization? Managing Migration, Citizenship, and Schooling in the Chinese City," *Critical Sociology*, 44 no. 3 (2018): 503–18.

2. Michel Foucault, *"Society Must Be Defended": Lectures at the Collège de France, 1975–1976* (New York: Picador), 241.

3. Foucault, *Society Must Be Defended*, 242.

4. See Greg Bird's call to "seriously address the intertwinement of the political and the economic in biopolitics." Greg Bird, "The Biopolitical Economy of Guest Worker Programs," *Biopolitical Governance: Race, Gender and Economy* (London: Rowman & Littlefield, 2018), 99–120.

5. Michel Foucault, *The History of Sexuality* (New York: Pantheon Books, 1978), 141.

6. Foucault, *The History of Sexuality*, 144.

7. I present a very different take on biopolitics and capitalism than Hardt and Negri, perhaps the best-known exponents of this theoretical synthesis. They see "biopolitical production" as an emerging tendency within capitalism, under which it is life itself that comes to form the substance of value creation. I credit Hardt and Negri for their early efforts to bring together Marxist and Foucauldian analyses, even while significantly differing in my interpretation of biopolitics. Michael Hardt and Antonio Negri, *Empire* (Cambridge, MA: Harvard University Press, 2000); Michael Hardt and Antonio Negri, *Multitude: War and Democracy in the Age of Empire* (New York: Penguin Press, 2004).

8. Jason Read, "Primitive Accumulation: The Aleatory Foundation of Capitalism," *Rethinking Marxism* 14, no. 2 (2002): 24–49.

9. Scholars of governmentality may notice my lack of engagement with this concept and what might be interpreted as an overemphasis on the state. This is by no means to discount the exercise of more horizontal or capillary forms of power in Chinese society. Indeed, I am quite attentive to the effects of the market, and I speculate to some extent on the impact of state-designed biopolitical efforts for self-governance and neoliberal forms of subjectivity. Nonetheless, managing human movement remains largely the dominion of the state, and it evinces an ambition and capacity that are worthy of sustained attention.

10. David Harvey, *A Brief History of Neoliberalism* (New York: Oxford University Press, 2005); Tania Murray Li, "To Make Live or Let Die? Rural Dispossession and the Protection of Surplus Populations," *Antipode* 41, no. 1 (2010): 66–93.

11. Mike Davis, *Planet of Slums* (New York: Verso, 2007).

12. Michelle Yates, "The Human-as-Waste: The Labor Theory of Value and Disposability in Contemporary Capitalism," *Antipode* 43, no. 5 (2011): 1679–95; Zygmunt Bauman, *Wasted Lives: Modernity and Its Outcasts* (Cambridge: Polity Press, 2004); Saskia Sassen, *Expulsions* (Cambridge, MA: Harvard University Press, 2014).

13. Karl Marx, *Capital*, vol. 1, *A Critique of Political Economy* (New York: Penguin Classics, 1976), 794–98; W. Arthur Lewis, "Economic Development with Unlimited Supplies of Labour," *The Manchester School* 22, no. 2 (May 1954): 139–91.

14. Michael McIntyre and Heidi J. Nast, "Bio(Necro)Polis: Marx, Surplus Populations, and the Spatial Dialectics of Reproduction and 'Race,'" *Antipode* 43, no. 5 (November 2011): 1465–88; Heather Merrill, "Migration and Surplus Populations: Race and Deindustrialization in Northern Italy," *Antipode* 43, no. 5 (2011): 1542–72.

15. Meg E. Rithmire, *Land Bargains and Chinese Capitalism: The Politics of Property Rights Under Reform* (New York: Cambridge University Press, 2015); Sally Sargeson, "Violence as Development: Land Expropriation and China's Urbanization," *Journal of Peasant Studies* 40, no. 6 (November 2013): 1063–85.

16. Philip C. Huang, "China's Neglected Informal Economy Reality and Theory," *Modern China* 35, no. 4 (2009): 405–38; Ya Ping Wang,

Yanglin Wang, and Jiansheng Wu, "Urbanization and Informal Development in China: Urban Villages in Shenzhen," *International Journal of Urban and Regional Research* 33, no. 4 (December 2009): 957–73; Fulong Wu, Fangzhu Zhang, and Chris Webster, "Informality and the Development and Demolition of Urban Villages in the Chinese Peri-Urban Area," *Urban Studies* 50, no. 10 (2013): 1919–34.

17. Ho-fung Hung, *The China Boom: Why China Will Not Rule the World* (New York: Columbia University Press, 2015); Cynthia Estlund, *A New Deal for China's Workers?* (Cambridge, MA: Harvard University Press, 2017). Chinese cities by no means have avoided slums altogether. See Jeremy L. Wallace, *Cities and Stability: Urbanization, Redistribution, and Regime Survival in China* (Oxford: Oxford University Press, 2014). Frequently, informal housing arrangements are simply less visible than is the case in other settings. Julia Gabriele Harten, Annette M. Kim, and J. Cressica Brazier, "Real and Fake Data in Shanghai's Informal Rental Housing Market: Groundtruthing Data Scraped from the Internet," *Urban Studies* 58, no. 9 (2020): 1831–45.

18. Kam Wing Chan, "A China Paradox: Migrant Labor Shortage Amidst Rural Labor Supply Abundance," *Eurasian Geography and Economics* 51, no. 4 (July 2010): 513–30; Ngai Pun and Jenny Wai-ling Chan, "Global Capital, the State, and Chinese Workers: The Foxconn Experience," *Modern China* 38, no. 4 (May 2012): 383–410.

19. Following Michael Denning, I use the term "proletarianization" not to indicate the formation of a working class but rather to refer to the destruction of nonmarket forms of reproduction, resulting in market dependence. The latter in no way guarantees that the proletarian will actually find wage labor. As suggested here, Chinese proletarians are more likely to become "workers" (in the traditional sense) than in other parts of the South. But this does not change the ontological ordering implied in Denning's work. Michael Denning, "Wageless Life," *New Left Review* 66 (2010): 79–97.

20. Foucault, *Society Must Be Defended*, 254. There is ambiguity in Foucault's work as to whether those outside of the population are "allowed" to die or "must" die. This is a major issue, and one that has been taken up by other theorists, notably Achille Mbembe.

21. Furthermore, Foucault's conception of race is so broad, including not just the "ethnic racism" associated with colonialism, but also socialist hatred of the bourgeoisie, as to be reduced to a kind of generic othering. Ann Laura Stoler, *Race and the Education of Desire: Foucault's History of Sexuality and the Colonial Order of Things* (Durham, NC: Duke University Press, 1995).

22. There is more than a century of literature analyzing this dynamic from a variety of standpoints. While it would be impossible to try to summarize this here, key issues include slavery, colonialism, the segmentation of labor markets, and neoliberal development. See W. E. B. Du Bois, *Black Reconstruction in America* (New York: Free Press, 1998); Frantz Fanon, *The Wretched of the Earth* (New York: Grove Press, 1966); Edna Bonacich, "A Theory of Ethnic Antagonism: The Split Labor Market," *American Sociological Review* 37, no. 5 (1972): 547–59; Marion Werner, "Coloniality and the Contours of Global Production in the Dominican Republic and Haiti," *Antipode* 43, no. 5 (2011): 1573–97; Michael McIntyre, "Race, Surplus Population and the Marxist Theory of Imperialism," *Antipode* 43, no. 5 (2011): 1489–1515; Achille Mbembe, "Necropolitics," *Public Culture* 15, no. 1 (2003): 11–40; Achille Mbembe, "Aesthetics of Superfluity," *Public Culture* 16, no. 3 (2004): 373–405.

23. Ruth Wilson Gilmore, *Golden Gulag: Prisons, Surplus, Crisis, and Opposition in Globalizing California* (Berkeley: University of California Press, 2007), 28.

24. Alexander G. Weheliye, *Habeas Viscus: Racializing Assemblages, Biopolitics, and Black Feminist Theories of the Human* (Durham, NC: Duke University Press, 2014).

25. Greenhalgh and Winckler raise this question as well, arguing that "Foucault's analysis is Eurocentric and needs to be amended to include alternative modes of biopolitical differentiation and 'improvement.'" However, in analyzing China's birth control policies, they suggest that racism has been replaced by sexism. Certainly sex is a key axis of biopolitical difference for their case, but it is a less salient category of differentiation in urbanization. Susan Greenhalgh and Edwin A. Winckler, *Governing China's Population: From Leninist to Neoliberal Biopolitics* (Stanford, CA: Stanford University Press, 2005), 324.

26. Ngai Pun, *Made in China: Women Factory Workers in a Global Workplace* (Durham, NC: Duke University Press, 2005).

27. Andrew Martin Fischer, "'Population Invasion' versus Urban Exclusion in the Tibetan Areas of Western China," *Population and Development Review* 34, no. 4 (2008): 631–62; Joniak-Luthi Agnieszka, "Han Migration to Xinjiang Uyghur Autonomous Region: Between State Schemes and Migrants' Strategies," *Zeitschrift für Ethnologie* 138 (2013): 155–74.

28. Ching Kwan Lee, "Raw Encounters: Chinese Managers, African Workers and the Politics of Casualization in Africa's Chinese Enclaves," *The China Quarterly* 199 (September 2009): 647–66. But for hints as to how different cities are already responding to international migrants see Adams B. Bodomo and Grace Ma, "From Guangzhou to Yiwu: Emerging Facets of the African Diaspora in China," *International Journal of African Renaissance Studies* 5, no. 2 (2010): 283–89. Clearly race is an important axis of differentiation from the perspective of Africans in Chinese cities.

29. Fanon, *The Wretched of the Earth*. My thanks to Andi Kao for bringing this formulation to my attention.

30. Foucault addresses the question of allowing some internal to the population to die, especially through war. He argues that during the nineteenth century, this came to be seen as a means of purifying the race. Parallels with China's birth control policies and *suzhi* efforts are apparent.

31. Here I follow James Tyner, who asks, "Within any given place, who lives, who dies, and who decides?" James A. Tyner, "Population Geography I: Surplus Populations," *Progress in Human Geography* 37, no. 5 (October 2013): 702.

32. Elsewhere, he is even more explicit that he is not thinking of literal death: "When I say 'killing,' I obviously do not mean simply murder as such, but also every form of indirect murder: the fact of exposing someone to death, increasing the risk of death for some people, or, quite simply, political death, expulsion, rejection, and so on." Foucault, *Society Must Be Defended*, 276.

33. Gilmore, *Golden Gulag: Prisons, Surplus, Crisis, and Opposition in Globalizing California*.

34. This life-centered conceptualization is, in a certain sense at least, more akin to Malthus than to Marx. For Malthus, a redundant population is that which cannot be sustained given the means of subsistence, and he is particularly concerned with food supply. There is little understanding of relationality and antagonism in his analysis, and it goes without saying I differ sharply from him on practical and normative orientation. T. R. Malthus, *An Essay on the Principle of Population* (Oxford: Oxford University Press, 1993), 30.

35. Salar Mohandesi and Emma Teitelman have taken a more ambitious position, arguing that it is social reproduction, rather than the traditional focus on production, that is the key to understanding the entirety of working class history. Salar Mohandesi and Emma Teitelman, "Without Reserves," in *Social Reproduction Theory: Remapping Class, Recentering Oppression*, ed. Tithi Bhattacharya (London: Pluto Press, 2017), 37–67, 2017.

36. Marx, *Capital*, 1:782.

37. Li, "To Make Live or Let Die? Rural Dispossession and the Protection of Surplus Populations," 68 (italics in the original); Mike Davis, "The Urbanization of Empire: Megacities and the Laws of Chaos," *Social Text* 22, no. 4 (2004): 9–15, at 11. Michael Denning has critiqued use of terms such as surplus and superfluity as approaching the problem of proletarianization from the perspective of capital.

38. Evelyn Nakano Glenn, *Forced to Care: Coercion and Caregiving in America* (Cambridge, MA: Harvard University Press, 2010); Saskia Sassen, "Two Stops in Today's New Global Geographies: Shaping Novel Labor Supplies and Employment Regimes," *American Behavioral Scientist* 52, no. 3 (November 2008): 457–96.

39. As we will see in chapter 5, economic motivations can also be at play in the case of expulsions of "productive" workers. The urban state may judge that the space occupied by such workers is more valuable than the labor they contribute. In any given instance, it can be quite difficult to untangle the decisive factor that motivates expulsion, though the general parameters of decision making are apparent.

40. We might consider an intermediary category of "provisional population," one that I have left out for the sake of brevity and clarity of argument. If social reproduction is, within a given territory, relatively

stable for the population and denied for the surplus population, the provisional population maintains contingent, easily revocable access. Revocation of basic reproduction may occur via loss of wages or by more direct expulsions from land or from social welfare rolls. Indeed, the majority of China's migrant workers could be classified as provisional population, given their contingent access to housing, health care, and education within the city. This intermediate category serves as a useful critique of the Agamben-influenced biopolitical literature that focuses on literal death. Indeed, racial capitalism is predicated on keeping at least some racially subordinate groups *alive*, even if only provisionally and in degraded conditions, such that they can serve as the "living labor" basis of expanded capital accumulation. This is not to deny the history of genocide, murder, and state terror under racial capitalism, but rather to indicate that the population and capital expansion more broadly are still dependent on the existence of subordinate social groups.

41. Michel Foucault, *Security, Territory, Population: Lectures at the Collège de France, 1977–1978*, ed. Michel Senellart, François Ewald, and Alessandro Fontana (New York: Picador/Palgrave Macmillan, 2009), 13.

42. Foucault, *Security, Territory, Population*, 18. Emphasis added.

43. Emblematic theorists arguing for the particularity of the South include Ranajit Guha and Dipesh Chakrabarty, while Vivek Chibber has argued passionately in favor of the continued applicability of universal concepts. Ranajit Guha, *Elementary Aspects of Peasant Insurgency in Colonial India* (Delhi: Oxford University Press, 1983); Dipesh Chakrabarty, *Rethinking Working-Class History: Bengal, 1890–1940* (Princeton, NJ: Princeton University Press, 1989); Dipesh Chakrabarty, *Provincializing Europe: Postcolonial Thought and Historical Difference* (Princeton, NJ: Princeton University Press, 2000); Vivek Chibber, *Postcolonial Theory and the Specter of Capital* (London: Verso, 2012). Much less attention has been devoted to postsocialist than postcolonial cities, though see Sonia A. Hirt, *Iron Curtains: Gates, Suburbs and Privatization of Space in the Post-Socialist City* (Malden, MA: Wiley, 2012); Stephen J. Collier, *Post-Soviet Social: Neoliberalism, Social Modernity, Biopolitics* (Princeton, NJ: Princeton University Press, 2011); and Marina Dmitrieva and Alfrun Kliems, *The Post Socialist City: Continuity and Change in Urban Space and*

Imagery (Berlin: Jovis Verlag, 2010). In the early twentieth century the city and urban problems came to be constituted as an academic object of inquiry. Studies of informality in the 1970s, followed by the emergence of postcolonial theory in the 1980s, have laid the groundwork for this more recent debate on the universality of the urban process. While this specific debate is new, questions about how to characterize urban problems certainly animated the work of nineteenth-century scholars, most notably Engels. Friedrich Engels, *The Housing Question* (New York: International Publishers, 1935); Georg Simmel, *The Metropolis and Mental Life* (New York: Free Press, 1950); Robert Ezra Park, *The City* (Chicago: University of Chicago Press, 1928).

44. A special issue of *International Journal of Urban and Regional Research* presents this debate in succinct, polemical, form. On the one side we have Allen Scott and Michael Storper, who argue that it is possible to identify "basic common denominators of urban analysis," namely agglomeration and the urban land nexus. While they are careful to note that there are myriad pathways to empirical variation, their work, "emphasizes the commonalities across all types of cities." In direct response, and building on their earlier work, Jennifer Robinson and Ananya Roy critique what they see as a proposal to view cities of the global South "as little more than variations on a universal form," stemming from "an analytical confusion between globalization and universalization and between generalization and universalization." Instead, Robinson advocates "acknowledging the locatedness of all theoretical endeavor" in developing a comparative approach to building a more global urban studies." See Allen J. Scott and Michael Storper, "The Nature of Cities: The Scope and Limits of Urban Theory," *International Journal of Urban and Regional Research* 39, no. 1 (2015): 12; Jennifer Robinson and Ananya Roy, "Debate on Global Urbanisms and the Nature of Urban Theory," *International Journal of Urban and Regional Research* 40, no. 1 (2016): 181; Jennifer Robinson, "Comparative Urbanism: New Geographies and Cultures of Theorizing the Urban," *International Journal of Urban and Regional Research* 40, no. 1 (2016): 188.

45. Walker's ambition is somewhat greater, since he claims to account for cities in general. Richard A. Walker, "Why Cities? A Response,"

International Journal of Urban and Regional Research 40, no. 1 (2016): 168.

46. David Harvey, "Cities or Urbanization?" *City* 1, no. 1–2 (1996): 38–61.

47. Notions of the "total urbanization of society" or "planetary urbanization" are helpful in drawing attention to the way in which the urban process exceeds the boundaries of particular settlements, a phenomenon that certainly holds in the Chinese case. In fact, it is precisely the glaring disjuncture between the state's formal designations of people as rural or urban and those groups' actual spatial practices that lies at the core of the migrant problem in contemporary China. The extensive focus given here to official administrative units should not be taken as confounding a reified city with urbanization more broadly—in fact, it is intended to highlight just how distinct "the city" is from the empirical reality of urbanization. Neil Brenner and Christian Schmid, "Planetary Urbanization," in *The Globalizing Cities Reader* (New York: Routledge, 2017), 479–82.

48. Xiaobo Lu and Elizabeth J. Perry, *Danwei: The Changing Chinese Workplace in Historical and Comparative Perspective* (Armonk, NY: M. E. Sharpe, 1997).

49. Dorothy J. Solinger, *States' Gains, Labor's Losses: China, France, and Mexico Choose Global Liaisons, 1980–2000* (Ithaca, NY: Cornell University Press, 2009); Sarosh Kuruvilla, Ching Kwan Lee, and Mary Elizabeth Gallagher, *From Iron Rice Bowl to Informalization: Markets, Workers, and the State in a Changing China* (Ithaca, NY: Cornell University Press, 2011); Jonathan Unger, *The Transformation of Rural China* (Armonk, NY: M. E. Sharpe, 2002).

50. David Blumenthal and William Hsiao, "Privatization and Its Discontents—The Evolving Chinese Health Care System," *New England Journal of Medicine* 353, no. 11 (September 2005): 1165–70; Yuanli Liu, William Hsiao, Qing Li, and Xingzhu Liu, "Transformation of China's Rural Health Care Financing," *Social Science & Medicine* 41, no. 8 (1995): 1085–93.

51. Tony Saich, "The Changing Role of Urban Government," In *China Urbanizes: Consequences, Strategies, and Policies*, ed. Shahid Yusuf and Anthony Saich, 181–205 (Washington, DC: World Bank, 2008).

52. Jean C. Oi, "Fiscal Reform and the Economic Foundations of Local State Corporatism in China," *World Politics* 45, no. 1 (1992): 99–126;

Barry Naughton, "Chinese Institutional Innovation and Privatization from Below," *American Economic Review* 84, no. 2 (1994): 266–270; Victor Nee and Sonja Opper, *Capitalism from Below: Markets and Institutional and Change in China* (Cambridge, MA: Harvard University Press, 2012); Andrew Walder, "Local Governments as Industrial Firms: An Organizational Analysis of China's Transitional Economy," *American Journal of Sociology* 101, no. 2 (1995): 263–301.

53. Sean Cooney, "China's Labour Law, Compliance and Flaws in Implementing Institutions," *Journal of Industrial Relations* 49, no. 5 (November 2007): 673–86; Elizabeth Economy, "Environmental Enforcement in China," in *China's Environment and the Challenge of Sustainable Development*, ed. Kristen A. Day, 102–20 (Armonk, NY: East Gate, 2005).

54. Hsing, *The Great Urban Transformation*; Ong, "State-Led Urbanization in China"; Rithmire, *Land Bargains and Chinese Capitalism*; Sargeson, "Violence as Development."

55. In Marxist terms, we might think of this as a contradiction between "labor" and "labor power." Capital requires the former for the production of value, but objectified labor can only be accessed by purchasing labor *power*, which is inalienable from its human bearer. This then entails a series of political problems associated with the production and reproduction of human life, where it will take place, under what conditions, who will underwrite it, and how it will be coordinated with demands in the labor market (not to mention complexities deriving from the long time horizon).

56. Neil Brenner, *Implosions/Explosions: Towards a Study of Planetary Urbanization* (Berlin: Jovis, 2014), 21.

57. Walker, "Why Cities? A Response;" David Harvey, *The Urbanization of Capital: Studies in the History and Theory of Capitalist Urbanization* (Baltimore, MD: Johns Hopkins University Press, 1985); Neil Smith, "Toward a Theory of Gentrification: A Back to the City Movement by Capital, Not People," *Journal of the American Planning Association* 45, no. 4 (October 1979): 538–48.

58. It is important to emphasize that this is a *perception* on the part of the state. I am not making any claim about the actual carrying capacity of the city. As Ann Anagnost has noted, concerns about overpopulation are deeply embedded in Chinese conceptions of the nation. Ann

Anagnost, *National Past-Times: Narrative, Representation, and Power in Modern China* (Durham, NC: Duke University Press, 1997).

59. Harvey, *The Urbanization of Capital*, 130.

60. Sandro Mezzadra and Brett Neilson use the term "just-in-time migration" in their *Border as Method*. I employ the term "urbanization" to draw attention to processes of capitalist transformation and the reconfiguration of the urban welfare state and politics more broadly. Ann Anagnost also refers to a "'just in time' provision of a cheap and docile labor force" in a footnote, but it is not further explicated. For whatever it is worth, I came to the term before encountering these works. Sandro Mezzadra and Brett Neilson, *Border as Method, or, the Multiplication of Labor* (Durham, NC: Duke University Press, 2013); Anagnost, "The Corporeal Politics of Quality (Suzhi)," *Public Culture* 16, no. 2: 189–208, at 194.

61. In responding to critiques of functionalism in his elaboration of the panopticon, Foucault remarked, "the Panopticon was a utopia, a kind of pure form elaborated at the end of the 18th century, intended to supply the most convenient formula for the constant, immediate and total exercising of power. . . . I immediately showed that what we are talking about is precisely a utopia which had never functioned in the form in which it existed." Methodologically, JIT urbanization plays a similar role here in that it is a critical concept intended to reveal underlying political relationships and logics of action, rather than a precise description of empirical reality. Foucault, *Foucault Live: Collected Interviews, 1961–1984*, ed. Sylvère Lotringer (New York: Semiotext(e), 1996), 257.

62. Taiichi Ohno, *Toyota Production System: Beyond Large-Scale Production* (Portland, OR: Productivity Press, 1988), 4.

63. Anagnost, *National Past-Times*; Wallace, *Cities and Stability*.

64. James P. Womack and Daniel T. Jones, *Lean Thinking: Banish Waste and Create Wealth in Your Corporation* (New York: Simon & Schuster, 2010).

65. Yasuhiro Monden wrote the definitive account of just-in-time, which was responsible for introducing the concept to an international audience. Yasuhiro Monden, *Toyota Production System: An Integrated Approach to Just-in-Time* (New York: CRC Press, 2011), 4.

66. Michelle Yates, "The Human-as-Waste: The Labor Theory of Value and Disposability in Contemporary Capitalism," *Antipode* 43, no. 5 (2011): 1679.

67. Monden, *Toyota Production System*, 311.

68. This conception is quite different from how Aihwa Ong discusses flexible citizenship in that she is concerned with how elites have become unmoored from the nation state. I am concerned with how the local provision of social services allows city governments to maintain flexibility in the distribution of the full rights of citizenship. Aihwa Ong, *Flexible Citizenship: The Cultural Logics of Transnationality* (Durham, NC: Duke University Press, 1999).

69. Franco Barchiesi, *Precarious Liberation: Workers, the State, and Contested Social Citizenship in Postapartheid South Africa* (Albany: State University of New York Press, 2011); Sandro Mezzadra and Brett Neilson, "Between Inclusion and Exclusion: On the Topology of Global Space and Borders," *Theory, Culture & Society* 29, nos. 4–5 (2012): 62.

70. Monden, *Toyota Production System*, 6.

71. Michael Storper and Richard Walker, "The Theory of Labour and the Theory of Location," *International Journal of Urban and Regional Research* 7, no. 1 (1983): 6.

72. Greenhalgh and Winckler, *Governing China's Population*; Martin King Whyte, Wang Feng, and Yong Cai, "Challenging Myths About China's One-Child Policy," *The China Journal* 74 (2015): 144–59.

73. I am operating under the assumption that rural residents want to come to the city. I recognize that this is not always the case in practice, though certainly has been the overwhelming tendency since the founding of the PRC.

74. Tamara Jacka, "Cultivating Citizens: Suzhi (Quality) Discourse in the PRC," *Positions* 17, no. 3 (2009): 523–35; Andrew Kipnis, "Suzhi: A Keyword Approach," *The China Quarterly* 186 (2006): 295–313; Andrew Kipnis, *Governing Educational Desire: Culture, Politics, and Schooling in China* (Chicago: University of Chicago Press, 2011); Yi Lin, "Turning Rurality Into Modernity: Suzhi Education in a Suburban Public School of Migrant Children in Xiamen," *The China Quarterly* 206, no. 2 (June 2011): 313–30.

75. Hairong Yan, "Neoliberal Governmentality and Neohumanism: Organizing Suzhi/Value Flow Through Labor Recruitment Networks," *Cultural Anthropology* 18, no. 4 (2003): 493–523; Anagnost, *National Past-Times*, 194.

2. URBAN DEVELOPMENTALISM AND THE INVERTED WELFARE STATE

1. Kate Xiao Zhou, *How the Farmers Changed China: Power of the People* (Boulder, CO: Westview Press, 1996); Jonathan Unger, "The Decollectivization of the Chinese Countryside: A Survey of Twenty-Eight Villages," *Pacific Affairs* (December 1985): 585–606.

2. Barry Naughton, "Chinese Institutional Innovation and Privatization from Below," *American Economic Review* 84, no. 2 (1994): 266; Jean C. Oi, *Rural China Takes Off: Institutional Foundations of Economic Reform* (Berkeley: University of California Press, 1999).

3. Victor Nee and Sonja Opper, *Capitalism from Below: Markets and Institutional and Change in China* (Cambridge, MA: Harvard University Press, 2012); Alan P. Liu, "The 'Wenzhou Model' of Development and China's Modernization," *Asian Survey* 32, no. 8 (1992): 696–711; Kristen Parris, "Local Initiative and National Reforms: The Wenzhou Model of Development," *The China Quarterly* 134 (1993): 242–63; Calvin Chen, *Some Assembly Required: Work, Community, and Politics in China's Rural Enterprises* (Cambridge, MA: Harvard University Press, 2008).

4. Dorothy J. Solinger, *States' Gains, Labor's Losses: China, France, and Mexico Choose Global Liaisons, 1980–2000* (Ithaca, NY: Cornell University Press, 2009); Sarosh Kuruvilla, Ching Kwan Lee, and Mary Elizabeth Gallagher, *From Iron Rice Bowl to Informalization: Markets, Workers, and the State in a Changing China* (Ithaca, NY: Cornell University Press, 2011); Mary Gallagher, "Time Is Money, Efficiency Is Life: The Transformation of Labor Relations in China," *Studies in Comparative International Development* 39, no. 2 (2004): 11–44.

5. Ching Kwan Lee, "The 'Revenge of History': Collective Memories and Labor Protests in North-Eastern China," *Ethnography* 1, no. 2 (2000): 217–37.

6. See Ho-fung Hung, *The China Boom: Why China Will Not Rule the World* (New York: Columbia University Press, 2015), chapter 3, for a thorough account. See also Justin Yifu Lin, *Demystifying the Chinese Economy* (New York: Cambridge University Press, 2011).

7. https://data.worldbank.org/indicator/SP.URB.TOTL.IN. ZS?locations=CN (accessed December 7, 2017); https://data.worldbank .org/indicator/SP.RUR.TOTL?locations=CN (accessed December 7, 2017).

8. https://data.worldbank.org/indicator/NY.GDP.PCAP.CD ?locations=CN (accessed December 7, 2017).

9. Amartya Sen, *Development as Freedom* (New York: Anchor, 1999), 42.

10. Feng Chen, "Union Power in China: Source, Operation, and Constraints," *Modern China* 35 (2009): 662–89; Eli Friedman, *Insurgency Trap: Labor Politics in Postsocialist China* (Ithaca, NY: Cornell University Press, 2014).

11. Kam Wing Chan, "The Chinese Hukou System at 50," *Eurasian Geography and Economics* 50, no. 2 (2009): 197–221.

12. Barry Naughton, "Implications of the State Monopoly Over Industry and Its Relaxation," *Modern China* 18, no. 1 (1992): 14–41; Kam Wing Chan, *Cities with Invisible Walls: Reinterpreting Urbanization in Post-1949 China* (Oxford: Oxford University Press, 1994).

13. C. Cindy Fan, "The Elite, the Natives, and the Outsiders: Migration and Labor Market Segmentation in Urban China," *Annals of the Association of American Geographers* 92, no. 1 (2002): 103–24; C. Cindy Fan and Wenfei Winnie Wang, "The Household as Security: Strategies of Rural-Urban Migrants in China," In *Migration and Social Protection in China*, ed. Ingrid Nielsen and Russell Smyth, 14:205–42 (Hackensack, NJ: World Scientific, 2008), 211.

14. Ngai Pun and Chris Smith, "Putting Transnational Labour Process in Its Place: The Dormitory Labour Regime in Post-Socialist China," *Work Employment and Society* 21, no. 1 (2007): 27–46; Li Zhang, *Strangers in the City: Reconfigurations of Space, Power, and Social Networks Within China's Floating Population* (Stanford, CA: Stanford University Press, 2001).

15. Jane Golley and Xin Meng, "Has China Run out of Surplus Labour?" *China Economic Review* 22, no. 4 (December 2011): 555–72.

16. Ngai Pun and Jenny Wai-ling Chan, "Global Capital, the State, and Chinese Workers: The Foxconn Experience," *Modern China* 38, no. 4 (May 2012): 383–410.

17. https://data.worldbank.org/indicator/BN.CAB.XOKA.CD ?locations=CN (accessed December 11, 2017)

18. Eli Friedman, "Getting Through the Hard Times Together? Chinese Workers and Unions Respond to the Economic Crisis," *Journal of Industrial Relations* 54, no. 4 (August 2012): 459–75; Kam Wing Chan, "The Global Financial Crisis and Migrant Workers in China: 'There Is No Future as a Labourer; Returning to the Village Has No Meaning,'" *International Journal of Urban and Regional Research* 34, no. 3 (September 2010): 659–77.

19. "Wen Jiaobao: jianchi kuoda neixu fangzhen, baochi renminbi hulü jiben wending" [Wen Jiabao: maintain direction of increasing domestic consumption, keep stable renminbi exchange rate], *Xinhua*, http://news.sina.com.cn/c/2004-03-05/09401970610s.shtml, March 5, 2004.

20. Kuznets himself likely would not assume that the "inverted U" curve, in which inequality first grows and then contracts during the course of development, would hold for a country like China. For a discussion of the limitations of the model, see Yu Xie and Yongai Jin, "Household Wealth in China," *Chinese Sociological Review* 47, no. 3 (2015): 203–29.

21. You-tien Hsing, *The Great Urban Transformation: Politics of Land and Property in China* (Oxford: Oxford University Press, 2010). Yu Xie and Yongai Jin have found that over 70 percent of household wealth in China is in housing assets. Yu Xie and Yongai Jin, "Household Wealth in China," *Chinese Sociological Review* 47, no. 3 (2015): 203–29.

22. "Top 10 Richest People in Beijing 2013: Hurun," China.org.cn, March 21, 2013, http://www.china.org.cn/top10/2013-03/21/content_28318022.htm (accessed December 12, 2017); "Top 10 Private Companies in China," *China Daily*, August 20, 2014, http://www.china.org.cn/top10/2013-03 /21/content_28318022.htm (accessed December 12, 2017).

23. Gene Hsin Chang and Josef C. Brada, "The Paradox of China's Growing Under-Urbanization," *Economic Systems* 30, no. 1 (2006): 24–40.

24. Hsing, *The Great Urban Transformation*; Siu Wai Wong, "Urbanization as a Process of State Building: Local Governance Reforms in China," *International Journal of Urban and Regional Research* 39, no. 5 (2015): 912–26; Robin Visser, *Cities Surround the Countryside: Urban Aesthetics in Postsocialist China* (Durham, NC: Duke University Press, 2010).

25. "Xi Jinping: cujin zhongguo tese xin xing chengzhenhua chixu jiankang fazhan" [Xi Jinping: promote sustainable and health development of new urbanization with Chinese characteristics], *Xinhua*, Febrary 23, 2016.

26. "Guojia xinxing chengzhenhua guihua (2014–2020)" [National New Urbanization Plan (2014–2020)], gov.cn, last modified March 16, 2014, http://www.gov.cn/zhengce/2014-03/16/content_2640075.htm.

27. "Guojia xinxing chengzhenhua guihua."

28. "Guowuyuan guanyu jin yi bu tuijin huji zhidu gaige de yijian" [State Council opnion on promoting reform of the residence system], gov.cn, last modified July 30, 2014, http://www.gov.cn/zhengce/content/2014-07/30/content_8944.htm.

29. The comparison to apartheid certainly did not appear in mainstream outlets within China. But for one example from foreign media, see Rachel Lu, "China Is Ending Its 'Apartheid.' Here's Why No One Is Happy About It," *Foreign Policy*, July 31, 2014.

30. Kam Wing Chan and Will Buckingham, "Is China Abolishing the Hukou System?" *China Quarterly*, no. 195 (2008): 582–606.

31. "Guojia xinxing chengzhenhua guihua."

32. Jeremy L. Wallace, *Cities and Stability: Urbanization, Redistribution, and Regime Survival in China* (New York: Oxford University Press, 2014).

33. "Guojia xinxing chengzhenhua guihua (2014–2020),"

34. Chongqing is a prominent outlier, with seemingly many fewer migrants than one would expect based on national trends. However, as is well known by those familiar with China's demographic patterns, the reported population of more than 28 million is due to unusual administrative arrangements and does not accurately reflect the size of the urban population.

35. At 4.94 million, Chengdu was just short of the cutoff. Along with Wuhan, it has certainly surpassed 5 million in the years that followed.

36. Figuring out what percentage of the country's internal migrants live in any given city proved to be an incredibly challenging task, since there is no single data source that reports nonlocal *hukou* residents disaggregated at the city level. The closest I and a number of my colleagues were able to find is the China Urban Construction Statistical Yearbook, which lists "temporary population." Unfortunately, and for reasons not explained, the yearbook omits data for Beijing, Shanghai, and Shenzhen—almost certainly the three top migrant destinations. The remaining extra-large cities alone—Nanjing, Chongqing, Guangzhou, and Tianjin—account for 18 percent of the country's total urban temporary population (*chengqu zanzhu renkou* 城区暂住人口).

37. Fan, "The Elite, the Natives, and the Outsiders," 108.

38. Li Zhang, "Economic Migration and Urban Citizenship in China: The Role of Points Systems," *Population and Development Review* 38, no. 3 (2012): 507.

39. For instance, in 2010, the first year of the point-based system in Zhongshan, 45 percent of applicants were awarded *hukou*. Zizhen Zheng and Jian Song, "Zhongshan Liudong Renkou de Jifenzhi Guanli Cunzai de Wenti Ji Duice Fenxi," *Nanfang Renkou* 26, no. 4 (2011): 58.

40. "Beijing shi jifen luohu guanli ban fa (shixing)," http://zhengce.beijing.gov.cn/library/192/34/738532/103061/index.html (accessed January 22, 2018)

41. This emphasis on education seems to hold for distribution of social goods in general, not just in the point plans. Sophia Woodman, "Legitimating Exclusion and Inclusion: 'Culture,' Education and Entitlement to Local Urban Citizenship in Tianjin and Lanzhou," *Citizenship Studies* 21, no. 7 (2017): 755–72.

42. 211 refers to a group of more than one hundred elite universities in China that receive additional government support. The "211" designation originally referred to the plan's aim to prepare for the twenty-first century by developing one hundred key universities.

43. For instance, in Shenzhen, an applicant can receive 100 points for the top degree, a PhD, and up to 100 points for income tax payments.

44. In Tianjin, a record of "dishonesty" results in a deduction of 30 points, equivalent to the number of points awarded for a degree from a technical college.

45. Dongguan and Shenzhen deduct 80 points, an amount equivalent to the total points awarded for a bachelor's degree.

46. A comprehensive list of such organizations and activities is not provided, but it safe to assume that this language leaves government officials with wide latitude in interpretation.

47. It is not yet clear how "green card" programs will operate in cities that also have point-based *hukou* admissions, as in Chengdu and Tianjin.

48. Viola Zhou, "How a Chinese City Has Gone All Out in the Battle for Talent," *South China Morning Post*, August 31, 2017.

49. "Quanguo zaixiao daxuesheng jin ping xueshengzheng he shenfenzheng ji ke zaixian luohu xi'an" [University students throughout China can receive Xi'an hukou by applying online with student ID and national ID], *Shaanxi Xinwen Wang*, March 23, 2018.

50. Yangpeng Zheng, "Hainan Opens Channel to Home Ownership for New Workers," *South China Morning Post*, May 14, 2018.

51. Huiyuan Wu, "The Grads Caught in the Battle for China's Best and Brightest," *Sixth Tone*, July 2, 2018.

52. Amanda Lee, "Beijing Offers 1 Million Yuan in Cash Incentives, Long-term Visas and Green Card to Attract Global Talent," *South China Morning Post*, March 23, 2018.

53. "Rencai 'lüka' ju huoli" [Human talent 'green card' gathers vitality], *Renmin Ribao*, May 10, 2018.

54. Zhang, "Economic Migration and Urban Citizenship in China."

55. Wang Fan, "Shenzhen jifen luohu xin zheng: wanquan fangkai xueli yaoqiu, 2017 nian 10000 ge zhibiao" [Shenzhen's new point-based hukou policy: eliminate the education requirement, quota of 10000 for 2017], *21 Shiji Jingji Bao*, July 17, 2017; Wei Xiao, "Zhongshan quxiao jifen ruhu, qi lei ren ke shenqing zhijie ruhu" [Zhongshan cancels point-based *hukou*, seven types of people can directly apply], *Nanfang Dushi Bao*, January 24, 2018.

56. "Beijing jifen luohu 2020 nian xin zhengce jiedu (4+2+7)" [Explaining Beijing's 2020 point-based hukou policy], *Ben Di Bao*, July 20, 2020.http://bj.bendibao.com/news/2020720/277681.shtm (accessed August 13, 2020).

57. In a statement that reflects the role of point-based systems in China's migration regime, Foucault has this to say of disciplinary power: "It individualizes bodies by a location that does not give them a fixed

position, but distributes them and circulates them in a network of relations." Michel Foucault, *Discipline and Punish: The Birth of the Prison* (New York: Vintage Books, 1979), 146.

58. Philip C. Huang, "China's Neglected Informal Economy: Reality and Theory," *Modern China* 35, no. 4 (2009): 405–38.

59. Mary Gallagher, John Giles, Albert Park, and Meiyan Wang, "China's 2008 Labor Contract Law: Implementation and Implications for China's Workers," *Human Relations* 68, no. 2 (February 2015): 197–235; Mary Gallagher, *Authoritarian Legality in China: Law, Workers, and the State* (Cambridge: Cambridge University Press, 2017).

60. China Labour Bulletin, "A Decade on, China's Labour Contract Law Has Failed to Deliver," http://www.clb.org.hk/content/decade -china%E2%80%99s-labour-contract-law-has-failed-deliver (accessed January 10, 2018).

61. Yuan Mengqiu and Li Bingbing, "nongmingong canjia yanglao baoxian, bili buzu liangcheng" [Less than 20 per cent of migrant workers participate in old age insurance], *Renmin Ribao*, August 4, 2015.

62. Youqin Huang, "Low-Income Housing in Chinese Cities: Policies and Practices," *The China Quarterly* 212 (2012): 941–64; John R. Logan, Yiping Fang, and Zhanxin Zhang, "Access to Housing in Urban China," *International Journal of Urban and Regional Research* 33, no. 4 (2009): 914–35.

63. Niny Khor, Lihua Pang, Chengfang Liu, Fang Chang, Di Mo, Prashant Loyalka, and Scott Rozelle, "China's Looming Human Capital Crisis: Upper Secondary Educational Attainment Rates and the Middle-Income Trap," *The China Quarterly* 228 (2016): 912.

64. See https://www.theatlantic.com/technology/archive/2009/07/-no-uigh urs-need-apply/21071/ (accessed October 1, 2021).

65. Björn Gustafsson and Ding Sai, "Temporary and Persistent Poverty Among Ethnic Minorities and the Majority in Rural China," *Review of Income and Wealth* 55, no. 1 (2009): 588–606.

66. Margaret Maurer-Fazio, "Ethnic Discrimination in China's Internet Job Board Labor Market," *IZA Journal of Migration* 1, no. 1 (2012): 12–12. Muslim job applicants are 50 percent less likely to receive a callback than Han applicants with the same qualifications. See Yue Hou, Chuyu Liu, and Charles Crabtree, "Anti-Muslim Bias in the

Chinese Labor Market," *Journal of Comparative Economics* 48, no. 2 (2020): 235–50.

67. Dongping Yang, "Zhongguo Liudong Ertong Jiaoyu de Fazhan He Zhengce Yanbian," [The development and policy changes for China's migrant youth education] in *Zhongguo Liudong Ertong Jiaoyu Fazhan Baogao*, ed. Dongping Yang, Hongyu Qin, and Jiayu Wei (Beijing: Social Sciences Academic Press, 2016), 4.

68. Han Zhao and Jiayu Wei, "Beijing Yiwu Jiaoyu Jieduan Liudong Ertong Jiaoyu Xianzhuang" [Current conditions for migrant youth primary education in Beijing], in Yang, Qin, and Wei, *Zhongguo Liudong Ertong Jiaoyu Fazhan Baogao*, 105–20.

69. See Article 12: http://old.moe.gov.cn//publicfiles/business/htmlfiles /moe/moe_16/200105/132.html.

70. "Guanyu jin yi bu zuohao Jincheng wugong jiuye nongmin zinü yiwu jiaoyu gongzuo yijian," http://www.gov.cn/ztzl/ywjy/content_470391 .htm.

71. Yaru Li, Wenying Sun, and Zhiping Yang, "Beijing Shi Liudong Renkou Ji Qi Zinü Jiaoyu Zhuangkuang Diaocha Yanjiu," *Journal of Capital Normal University* 2 (2003): 112.

72. Zhao and Wei, "Beijing Yiwu Jiaoyu Jieduan Liudong Ertong Jiaoyu Xianzhuang."

73. These bribes can be equivalent to more than a year's salary for many workers. The minimum wage in Beijing for 2016 was 1,720 yuan per month, which equals 20,640 yuan per year. See chapter 4.

74. Shan Jie, "One-Third of Rural Children Left Behind by Parents: Report," *Global Times*, July 24, 2017.

75. One cannot help but note the irony that the introduction of the market has resulted in much more radical reconfigurations of the family than anything accomplished during the heyday of the commune system.

76. "Liushou ertong he liudong ertong: bei shehui hongliu gongxie de 1 yi ge haizi" [Left-behind children and migrant children: 100 million children swept away in the social torrents], *Caixin*, July 26, 2017.

77. "Beijing dagong zidi xuexiao diaocha: tiaojian jianlou, banshu wu banxue zige" [Beijing migrant school investigation: poor conditions, more than half without credentials], *Fazhi Ribao*, February 24, 2009.

78. One relatively authoritative source who gave me this estimate was the director of New Citizens' Project, a well-known and highly regarded NGO in Beijing (Interview 23).

79. See http://www.xingongmin.org.cn/?p=4239 (accessed March 2, 2019); Zhao and Wei, "Beijing Yiwu Jiaoyu Jieduan Liudong Ertong Jiaoyu Xianzhuang," 119.

80. In 2004, the Beijing government proclaimed that it would strive, "within three years or so, to bring all private schools accepting migrant children up to standard," a goal it quite clearly failed to achieve. See "Beijing shi renmin zhengfu bangongting zhuanfa shi jiaowei deng bumen guanyu guanche guowuyuan bangongting jin yi bu zuohao jincheng wugong jiuye nongmin zinü yiwu jiaoyu gongzuo wenjian de tongzhi."

81. Some may object that Beijing has always been coercive toward migrants, as notably captured by the demolitions in Zhejiang village in the 1990s or in preparations for the 2008 Olympics. This has certainly been the case, but it was not until 2014 that the state's interventions were on such a scale as to dramatically slow and then reverse growth in the migrant population.

82. As it became widely referred to in China, *jiaoyu kongren*. See Han Zhao, "Beijing jinnian de 'jiaoyu kongren' you jiang lakai xumu, ranhou ne?" [The prelude to this year's 'population control via education' is about to start, what's next?], *Caixin*, February 10, 2015.

83. Employment documentation including both parent's labor contracts, social insurance records, proof of current employment, operating license from place of employment and organizational registration number; parents' marriage and birth permits, including marriage certificate, birth certificate, migrant population marriage/birth permit, child's medical birth certificate. Proof of housing in Beijing including rental lease, proof of house rental tax payment and receipt, electricity and water bills for the period of residence, ID cards for landlords (both husband and wife), and housing deed. If there is no deed, then the village committee can issue documentation with their official stamp to prove residence. See "Liudong ertong shangxue nan: fei jing ji ertong Beijing nianshu xuban 28 ge zheng" [The difficulty of enrolling for migrant children: nonlocal

children in Beijing need 28 permits to attend school], *Ban Yue Tan*, June 15, 2015.

84. This is meant in the specifically Gramscian sense: that it expresses a form of hegemony that works to obscure inequality and domination in society.

85. The information included in this section comes largely from official point-based school enrollment plans for 2014, 2015, and 2016. A research assistant collected an exhaustive national database of these plans. At the time, there were fifty-four urban districts with point-based school enrollment located in the following cities: Shanghai, Dongguan, Zhongshan, Foshan, Xiamen, Jiaxing, Ningbo, Changzhou, Guangzhou, Huizhou, Kunshan, Hangzhou, Jinan, Shenzhen, Wenling, Zhuhai, Suzhou, and Chongqing. The details of these plans, as well as the number of districts with such plans, changes year to year.

86. C. Cindy Fan, Mingjie Sun, and Siqi Zheng, "Migration and Split Households: A Comparison of Sole, Couple, and Family Migrants in Beijing, China," *Environment and Planning A* 43, no. 9 (2011): 2164–85.

87. Li Zhang and Li Tao, "Barriers to the Acquisition of Urban Hukou in Chinese Cities," *Environment and Planning A* 44, no. 12 (2012): 2883–2900.

88. Chan, "The Chinese Hukou System at 50."

89. Kyle Jaros has argued that China's large cities have excelled economically "by design," which is to say that state policy has played a critical role in generating spatial inequality. Kyle A. Jaros, *China's Urban Champions: The Politics of Spatial Development* (Princeton, NJ: Princeton University Press, 2019), 14.

90. Wallace, *Cities and Stability*.

91. It is not coincidental that Dongguan and Shenzhen are the large cities with the highest percentage of nonlocal inhabitants, since locals benefit from a massive migrant workforce that supports the tax base while remaining largely excluded from local services.

92. Jiayu Wei, "Mo rang 'xueji' chengwei ling yige 'huji!' " [Don't let 'xueji' becoming another household registration!], https://mp.weixin.qq.com/s/68H9DJxY2sanIVjZRNsG_w (accessed June 29, 2018).

93. Mun C. Tsang, "Education and National Development in China since 1949: Oscillating Policies and Enduring Dilemmas," *China Review* (2000): 579–618.

94. There have indeed been more central funds allocated to poor rural areas in the country's interior. See "Top Legislature Reviews Report on Education Equality," *Xinhua*, August 28, 2008.

95. I do not know precisely how large the effect of locality is, since people from these two cities are also disproportionally wealthy, well-educated, and with access to higher quality primary and secondary education.

96. Calculated from data available at Zhongguo Jiaoyu Zaixian, http://www.eol.cn/ (accessed February 15, 2017). I have averaged the enrollment rates for all provinces and directly administered municipalities other than the one in which the university is located. There is important variation between provinces, with applicants from the poorer and larger provinces typically facing even longer odds in admissions to universities outside their place of *hukou* registration.

97. Hongbin Li et al., "Unequal Access to College in China: How Far Have Poor, Rural Students Been Left Behind?" *The China Quarterly* 221 (2015): 185–207. The authors demonstrate that students from poor rural areas are particularly disadvantaged in college admissions.

98. Andrew G. Walder, "Markets and Inequality in Transitional Economies: Toward Testable Theories," *American Journal of Sociology* 101, no. 4 (1996): 1060–73; Yang Cao and Victor G. Nee, "Comment: Controversies and Evidence in the Market Transition Debate," *American Journal of Sociology* 105, no. 4 (2000): 1175–89; Victor Nee, "A Theory of Market Transition: From Redistribution to Markets in State Socialism," *American Sociological Review* (1989): 663–81.

99. For example, Webster suggests, "The labour market is reassuringly able to overcome an impediment to free and fair labour mobility as strong as hukou." Fulong Wu, Fangzhu Zhang, and Chris Webster, *Rural Migrants in Urban China: Enclaves and Transient Urbanism* (New York: Routledge, 2013), 279.

3. THE MIGRANT SCHOOL

1. Interview 21.
2. While family migration has certainly increased, it is important to note that ongoing obstacles to resettlement have resulted in persistent circular and split-family forms of migration. See C. Cindy Fan, "Settlement Intention and Split Households: Findings from a Survey of Migrants in Beijing's Urban Villages," *China Review* (2011): 11–41; Yiping Fang and Zhilei Shi, "Children of Migrant Parents: Migrating Together or Left Behind," *Habitat International* 76 (2018): 62–68.
3. Julia Kwong, "The Reemergence of Private Schools in Socialist China," *Comparative Education Review* 41, no. 3 (1997): 244–59; Ka-ho Mok and King-yee Wat, "Merging of the Public and Private Boundary: Education and the Market Place in China," *International Journal of Educational Development* 18, no. 3 (May 1998): 255–67; Ka Ho Mok, Yu Cheung Wong, and Xiulan Zhang, "When Marketisation and Privatisation Clash with Socialist Ideals: Educational Inequality in Urban China," *International Journal of Educational Development* 29, no. 5 (September 2009): 505–12.
4. Edward Vickers and Xiaodong Zeng, *Education and Society in Post-Mao China* (New York: Routledge, 2017), 105.
5. David Chan and Ka-Ho Mok, "Educational Reforms and Coping Strategies under the Tidal Wave of Marketisation: A Comparative Study of Hong Kong and the Mainland," *Comparative Education* 37, no. 1 (2001): 21–41, 30; Mok and Wat, "Merging of the Public and Private Boundary."
6. Raymond K. H. Chan and Ying Wang, "Controlled Decentralization: Minban Education Reform in China," *Journal of Comparative Social Welfare* 25, no. 1 (2009): 28.
7. Charlotte Goodburn, "Learning from Migrant Education: A Case Study of the Schooling of Rural Migrant Children in Beijing," *International Journal of Educational Development* 29, no. 5 (2009): 495–504; Zai Liang and Yiu Por Chen, "The Educational Consequences of Migration for Children in China," *Social Science Research* 36, no. 1 (2007): 28–47; Yiu Por Chen and Zai Liang, "Educational Attainment of Migrant Children: The Forgotten Story of China's Urbanization,"

in *Education and Reform in China*, ed. Emily Hannum and Albert Park, 117–32 (New York: Routledge, 2007).

8. Yuanyuan Chen and Shuaizhang Feng, "Access to Public Schools and the Education of Migrant Children in China," *China Economic Review* 26, no. 1 (2013): 75–88; Xiaobing Wang, Renfu Luo, Linxiu Zhang, and Scott Rozelle, "The Education Gap of China's Migrant Children and Rural Counterparts," *The Journal of Development Studies* 53, no. 11 (2017): 1865–81; Yihan Xiong, "The Broken Ladder: Why Education Provides No Upward Mobility for Migrant," *China Quarterly* 221 (2015): 161–84; T. E. Woronov, "In the Eye of the Chicken: Hierarchy and Marginality Among Beijing's Migrant Schoolchildren," *Ethnography* 5, no. 3 (2004): 289–313.

9. Mok, Wong, and Zhang, "When Marketisation and Privatisation Clash with Socialist Ideals."

10. "2014 nian nongmingong suiqian zinü zai gongban xuexiao jiuexue bili chao 80%" [More than 80 per cent of migrant children enrolled in public schools in 2014], *Zhongguo Guangbo Wang*, February 28, 2015.

11. Interview 21. Her comment that no schools had been licensed since 2001 was not true for all of Beijing. However, there is some ambiguity as to whether she is talking just about schools within Changping District. I could not verify whether any schools within Changping had been registered in this period.

12. Interview 25.

13. Shanghai distributed roughly 4,500 RMB per student to migrant schools in 2011–12. Yuanyuan Chen and Shuaizhang Feng, "Access to Public Schools and the Education of Migrant Children in China," *China Economic Review* 26, no. 1 (2013): 77. See also Holly H. Ming, *The Education of Migrant Children and China's Future: The Urban Left Behind* (New York: Routledge, 2013).

14. Interview 10.

15. At the time, the minimum wage was over 1,300 yuan per month.

16. Interview 22.

17. Interview 24b.

18. Interview 23.

19. Interview 10.

20. Interview 25.

21. Field notes, December 12, 2012.

22. Interview 10.
23. Air pollution is another major environmental hazard that is likely more severe in migrant schools. After the conclusion of my fieldwork, the Beijing municipal government bowed to pressure from parents and in 2017 agreed to install air purifiers in all public primary and middle schools.
24. Interview 26.
25. Interview 10.
26. In 2012, the school had 930 students (according to personal communication with the principal).
27. Interview 19.
28. Interview 4.
29. Interview 24b.
30. Interview 2.
31. Interview 26.
32. Teachers' lack of preparedness was more glaring in the English classes than the Chinese or math classes.
33. Interview 139.
34. This is not to suggest that public schoolteachers are without their own challenges. But relatively speaking, public school employment is a huge improvement in just about every respect.
35. Interview 22.
36. Interview 23.
37. I have attempted to be quite careful with my language to indicate that public schools are interested in students with high test scores. I am putting to the side the much more complex question of what constitutes a "quality" student or how student value should be determined. See T. E. Woronov, "Raising Quality, Fostering 'Creativity': Ideologies and Practices of Education Reform in Beijing," *Anthropology & Education Quarterly* 39, no. 4 (2008): 401–22.
38. Interview 21.
39. Minhua Ling, "Returning to No Home: Educational Remigration and Displacement in Rural China," *Anthropological Quarterly* 90, no. 3 (2017): 715–42.
40. T. E. Woronov, *Class Work: Vocational Schools and China's Urban Youth* (Stanford, CA: Stanford University Press, 2015).
41. Interview 21.

42. Yingquan Song, Yubiao Zeng, and Linxiu Zhang, "Dagong Zidi Xuexiao Xuesheng Chuzhong Hou Liuxiang Na Li? Ji Yu Beijing Shi 1866 Ming Liudong Ertong Xuesheng Changqi Genzong Diaoyan Shuju de Shizheng Fenxi," *Jiaoyu Jingji Pinglun* 3 (2017): 20–37.
43. This was certainly the case for the somewhat older vocational school students in Terry Woronov's research. T. E. Woronov, "Learning to Serve: Urban Youth, Vocational Schools and New Class Formations in China," *The China Journal*, no. 66 (2011): 77–99; Woronov, *Class Work*.
44. Jennifer Hsu, "Layers of the Urban State: Migrant Organisations and the Chinese State," *Urban Studies* 49, no. 16 (2012): 3513–30.
45. This information was provided to me by school officials.
46. Interview 13.
47. Interview 15.
48. Interview 21.

4. RENDERED SURPLUS

1. Xie Xuelin, "Fei jing ji ertong ruxue nan—kaowen Beijing renkou zhengce" [non-Beijing resident children have difficulty enrolling in school—interrogating Beijing's population policies], *Shangye Zhoukan*, May 15, 2015.
2. "Beijing Has Fewer Hukou Holders," *Xinhua*, February 27, 2018.
3. "Beijing's Population Falls Further," *Caixin*, January 23, 2019.
4. This is according to an investigation by the NGO New Citizen Program. See https://mp.weixin.qq.com/s/68H9DJxY2sanIVjZRNsG_w (accessed July 3, 2018).
5. Ms. Xu mentioned that Mr. Fan had once done home renovations for the grandson of famous twentieth-century Communist Party leader Liu Shaoqi, seemingly to indicate the success of the business.
6. Interview 140b.
7. Interview 142.
8. "Muqin wei rang erzi zai jing shangxue ban jiazheng bei zhua, dangting liulei renzui" [Mother uses fake papers to enroll son in Beijing schools, tearfully admits guilt in court], *Xin Jing Bao*, December 11, 2013.

9. Virginia Harper Ho and Qiaoyan Huang, "The Recursivity of Reform: China's Amended Labor Contract Law," *Fordham International Law Journal* 37 (2014): 1–41; Mary Gallagher, John Giles, Albert Park, and Meiyan Wang, "China's 2008 Labor Contract Law: Implementation and Implications for China's Workers," *Human Relations* 68, no. 2 (2015): 197–235.

10. 2016 nian nongmingong jiance diaocha baogao, http://www.stats .gov.cn/tjsj/zxfb/201704/t20170428_1489334.html (accessed October 3, 2021).

11. Interview 145.

12. Interview 4.

13. "Juanzi zhuxue kuan suan bu suan luan shoufei, che bu qing" [Still unclear if educational donations count as arbitrary fee collection], *Yangcheng Wan Bao*, March 19, 2013.

14. In 2016 the State Council announced a plan to grant *hukou* to all citizens who did not have one. I concluded my fieldwork before the new policy's implementation, so I was unable to see the impact on the ground. As with many of the centrally mandated rules, there is likely to be uneven local implementation. See http://www.gov.cn/xinwen /2016-01/14/content_5032915.htm (accessed June 25, 2021).

15. "Diaocha xianshi quanguo 'hei hu' 1300 wan 60% yishang wei chaosheng renyuan" [Survey reveals 13 million *hukou*-less people, more than 60% from excess births], *Yang Guang Wang*, December 12, 2015.

16. Interview 55.

17. Interview 99. This interview took place in Chengdu, but Beijing has the same *hukou* requirement for migrants wishing to access public schools.

18. The following details are derived from a special report, Ziyang Peng, "Qi zi zhi jia bei chaosheng kunzhu de rensheng" [Family of seven, a life beleaguered by excessive births], *Xin Jing Bao*, October 8, 2015.

19. The second and third were barred from taking the high school entrance exam, whereas the fourth was able to enter high school but barred from taking the university entrance exam. No reason was given for this discrepancy.

20. At the time, this was equivalent to USD $110,000.

21. Interestingly, the village authorities in Beijing where the family resides had difficulty accounting for the children during the 1990 national census. The special report notes that they had to find some workaround for reporting the extra children. Their approach is indicative of how the state views surplus children: they were reported as migrants.

22. By using this term, I am consciously drawing parallels with a similar and extensively researched topic in the United States. Nonetheless, there are significant differences between Chinese migrant workers and undocumented workers in the United States. In crude terms, the former have the legal right to sell their labor, whereas the latter have better access to public schools. In both cases, however, uneven legal statuses can result in centrifugal pressure being brought to bear on the family unit. For discussion of the US context, see Michael Fix and Wendy Zimmermann, "All Under One Roof: Mixed-Status Families in an Era of Reform," *International Migration Review* 35, no. 2 (2001): 397–419.

23. Interview 140b.

24. He Huifeng, "Shenzhen to Open Baby Hatch Where Parents Can Abandon Unwanted Infants," *South China Morning Post*, December 10, 2013.

25. Interview 144a, 144b, 144c.

26. Interview 143.

27. Yinghua Zhang, "Improving Social Protection for Internal Migrant Workers in China," International Labour Organization, 2019.

28. Stefan Schmalz, Brandon Sommer, and Hui Xu, "The Yue Yuen Strike: Industrial Transformation and Labour Unrest in the Pearl River Delta," *Globalizations* 14, no. 2 (2017): 285–97.

29. "Yixian chengshi nongmingong nan shixian baozhang jundenghua, wei jiao baoxian bili gao" [Migrants in first-tier cities have difficulty realizing equal protection, many remain without insurance], *Gongren Ribao*, February 22, 2018.

30. Interview 140a, 140b.

31. Fan Yang, "Nashui qianwan zinü wufa zai jing jiuxue; fenbi keji Zhang Xiaolong fabiao" [Paying tens of millions in taxes, children can't enroll in school in Beijing; Fenbi Technology's Zhang Xiaolong vents], *Radio Free Asia*, May 23, 2018.

32. Interview 143.
33. Interview 142.
34. Interview 143.
35. Interview 143.
36. Interview 132.
37. Interview 132.
38. Christine Wen and Jeremy L. Wallace, "Toward Human-Centered Urbanization? Housing Ownership and Access to Social Insurance Among Migrant Households in China," *Sustainability* 11, no. 13 (2019): 1–14; Yu Xie and Yongai Jin, "Household Wealth in China," *Chinese Sociological Review* 47, no. 3 (2015): 203–29.
39. Yan Song, Yves Zenou, and Chengri Ding, "Let's Not Throw the Baby out with the Bath Water: The Role of Urban Villages in Housing Rural Migrants in China," *Urban Studies* 45, no. 2 (2008): 313–30; Ya Ping Wang, Yanglin Wang, and Jiansheng Wu, "Urbanization and Informal Development in China: Urban Villages in Shenzhen," *International Journal of Urban and Regional Research* 33, no. 4 (2009): 957–73; Weiping Wu, "Outsiders in the City: Migrant Housing and Settlement Patterns," in *Rural Migrants in Urban China: Enclaves and Transient Urbanism*, ed. Fulong Wu, Fangzhu Zhang, and Chris Webster, 51–66 (New York: Routledge, 2014).
40. Fulong Wu, "Housing in Chinese Urban Villages: The Dwellers, Conditions and Tenancy Informality," *Housing Studies* 31, no. 7 (2016): 864.
41. Interview 145.
42. Luigi Tomba, "Finding China's Urban: Bargained Land Conversions, Local Assemblages, and Fragmented Urbanization," in *To Govern China: Evolving Practices of Power*, ed. Vivienne Shue and Patricia M. Thornton, 203–27 (Cambridge: Cambridge University Press, 2017).
43. Indeed, the benefits from maintaining rural land rights often times outweigh those of gaining urban *hukou* and its attendant rights. Chuanbo Chen and C. Cindy Fan, "China's Hukou Puzzle: Why Don't Rural Migrants Want Urban Hukou?" *China Review* 16, no. 3 (2016): 9–39; Joel Andreas and Shaohua Zhan, "Hukou and Land: Market Reform and Rural Displacement in China," *The Journal of Peasant Studies* 43, no. 4 (2016): 798–827.

44. Fulong Wu, Fangzhu Zhang, and Chris Webster, "Informality and the Development and Demolition of Urban Villages in the Chinese Peri-Urban Area," *Urban Studies* 50, no. 10 (2013): 1919–34.

45. Initially, home ownership was a requirement for enrolling children in a school district outside of the parents' place of *hukou* ownership. In 2018, the government announced that this approach would be extended to renters as well. While this was seen as an effective method for reducing the overheated "school district housing" (*xuequfang* 学区房) market, it predictably led to rapidly increasing rental prices in coveted school districts. See "Zu fang ruxue cuisheng xuewei zhanweifei shichang, you fangzhu jiaojia shu shiwan mai xuewei" [Rental enrollments lead to market for school registration, landlords demand hundreds of thousands], *Beijing Qingnian Bao*, June 4, 2018.

46. Lin Li, "Beijing Parents Purchasing Homes in Key Districts to Qualify for Better Education," *Global Times*, November 16, 2014.

47. Interview 148b.

48. See Minhua Ling, "Returning to No Home: Educational Remigration and Displacement in Rural China," *Anthropological Quarterly* 90, no. 3 (2017): 715–42, for a discussion of the conflicts associated with education "remigration."

49. Interview 146b.

50. Interview 140b.

51. The study took place in Jilin, Hebei, Jiangsu, Shaanxi, and Sichuan. Ziyi Huang and Li Rongde, "Two in Five Migrants Who Return Home Fail to Find Work, Study Says," *Caixin*, July 28, 2017.

52. Interview 144a.

53. Interview 142.

54. Interview 143.

55. Yuan Ren, "Guanzhu riyi yanjun de 'liuliu yi dai' wenti" [Focus on the seriously increasing 'floating and left-behind generation' problem], *The Paper*, December 26, 2018.

56. Kam Wing Chan and Yuan Ren, "Children of Migrants in China in the Twenty-First Century: Trends, Living Arrangements, Age-Gender Structure, and Geography," *Eurasian Geography and Economics* 59, no. 2 (2018): 133–63.

57. Interview 144a.

58. While this liberalization helped attract a number of migrants who had been shut out of Beijing, it is worth noting that taking the

university entrance exam in Hebei is a major downgrade. The province does not host a single one of the elite "985" group of thirty-nine universities receiving extensive government support, whereas Beijing contains eight. See https://www.dxsbb.com/news/1591.html (accessed August 10, 2018).

59. Di Yang and Ziqian Liu, "Bei Beijing 'gan' chuqu de haizi na shangxue le" [Where do children kicked out of Beijing go to school?], *Zhonguo Xinwen Zhoukan*, December 17, 2017.

60. Interview 148a.

61. Interview 148a.

62. As depicted in the documentary *After Us, The Deluge (ye cao ji* 野草集), one enterprising migrant set up a company that charged migrant parents 1,000 yuan to handle associated paperwork for enrolling their children in Hebei schools, with a focus on Hengshui.

63. "Capital" here refers to "political center" rather than economic capital. The use of the term "clearing" to refer to population management is complex but important. The character *shu* refers to dispersal or dredging (as with a river), while *jie* means to undo, dispel, or relieve. *Shujie* is difficult to translate precisely, but it suggests dispersal, enhancing of circulation, and relieving congestion, both spatial and social in nature.

64. For a discussion of "functional dispersal," see Chenchen Zhang, "Governing Neoliberal Authoritarian Citizenship: Theorizing *Hukou* and the Changing Mobility Regime in China," *Citizenship Studies* 22, no. 8 (2018): 872.

65. Interview 141b.

66. Interview 144a.

67. Interview 148a.

68. Interview 149a.

69. Interview 148b.

70. Interview 142.

5. POPULATION MANAGEMENT'S "HARD EDGE"

1. We might similarly think of this in Foucauldian terms as a discipline-punish dialectic. Those migrants who have failed to accumulate adequate points to qualify are being *punished* by the bulldozer: "The

distribution according to ranks or grade has a double role: it marks the gaps, hierarchizes qualities, skills and aptitudes; but it also punishes and rewards." There are of course differences in meaning here from the consent-coercion framing, and I have employed the Gramscian language to indicate the project of specifically classed hegemony. Michel Foucault, *Discipline and Punish: The Birth of the Prison* (New York: Vintage Books, 1979), 181.

2. I am particularly indebted in this section to Angela He, who provided an excellent literature review of urban development in China.

3. You-tien Hsing, *The Great Urban Transformation: Politics of Land and Property in China* (Oxford: Oxford University Press, 2010).

4. It should be noted that Chinese cities, and particularly Beijing, were also remade in the state socialist period, albeit according to a very different logic than was the case from the 1990s onward. See Lin Ye, "Urban Regeneration in China: Policy, Development, and Issues," *Local Economy* 26, no. 5 (2011): 337–47; Wu Hung, *Remaking Beijing: Tiananmen Square and the Creation of a Political Space* (Chicago: University of Chicago Press, 2005).

5. Shenjing He and Fulong Wu, "Property-Led Redevelopment in Post-Reform China: A Case Study of Xintiandi Redevelopment Project in Shanghai," *Journal of Urban Affairs* 27, no. 1 (2005): 1–23. (He and Wu 2005)

6. Hyun Bang Shin, "Residential Redevelopment and the Entrepreneurial Local State: The Implications of Beijing's Shifting Emphasis on Urban Redevelopment Policies," *Urban Studies* 46, no. 13 (2009): 2815–39; Lynette H. Ong, "State-Led Urbanization in China: Skyscrapers, Land Revenue and 'Concentrated Villages,'" *The China Quarterly* 217: 162–79; Ying Xu, Bo-sin Tang, and Edwin H. W. Chan, "State-Led Land Requisition and Transformation of Rural Villages in Transitional China," *Habitat International* 35, no. 1 (2011): 57–65.

7. David Harvey has commented, "The consequences [of China's urbanization] for the global economy and the absorption of surplus capital have been significant: Chile booms thanks to the high price of copper, Australia thrives and even Brazil and Argentina have recovered in part because of the strength of Chinese demand for raw materials.

Is the urbanization of China, then, the primary stabilizer of global capitalism today? The answer has to be a qualified yes." David Harvey, "The Right to the City," *New Left Review* 53 (2008): 23–40.

8. Shin, "Residential Redevelopment and the Entrepreneurial Local State"; Hyun Bang Shin, "Urban Conservation and Revalorisation of Dilapidated Historic Quarters: The Case of Nanluoguxiang in Beijing," *Cities* 27 (2010): S43–54; Li Tian, "The Chengzhongcun Land Market in China: Boon or Bane?—A Perspective on Property Rights," *International Journal of Urban and Regional Research* 32, no. 2 (June 2008): 282–304; Ya Ping Wang, Yanglin Wang, and Jiansheng Wu, "Urbanization and Informal Development in China: Urban Villages in Shenzhen," *International Journal of Urban and Regional Research* 33, no. 4 (2009): 957–73; Fulong Wu, Fangzhu Zhang, and Chris Webster, "Informality and the Development and Demolition of Urban Villages in the Chinese Peri-Urban Area," *Urban Studies* 50, no. 10 (2013): 1919–34; Li Zhang, *Strangers in the City: Reconfigurations of Space, Power, and Social Networks Within China's Floating Population* (Stanford, CA: Stanford University Press, 2001); Pu Hao, Stan Geertman, Pieter Hooimeijer, and Richard Sliuzas, "Spatial Analyses of the Urban Village Development Process in Shenzhen, China," *International Journal of Urban and Regional Research* 37, no. 6 (2013): 2177–97; Julia Chuang, "China's Rural Land Politics: Bureaucratic Absorption and the Muting of Rightful Resistance," *The China Quarterly* 219 (July 2014): 649–69; Sally Sargeson, "Violence as Development: Land Expropriation and China's Urbanization," *Journal of Peasant Studies* 40, no. 6 (2013): 1063–85; Ong, "State-Led Urbanization in China."

9. Local governments have often deployed extralegal forms of violence when they are unable to effectively displace residents via legal means. Lynette H. Ong, "'Thugs-for-Hire': Subcontracting of State Coercion and State Capacity in China," *Perspectives on Politics* 16, no. 3 (2018): 680–95; Fulong Wu, "State Dominance in Urban Redevelopment: Beyond Gentrification in Urban China," *Urban Affairs Review* 52, no. 5 (2016): 631–58; Hyun Bang Shin, "Economic Transition and Speculative Urbanisation in China: Gentrification Versus Dispossession," *Urban Studies* 53, no. 3 (2016): 471–89.

10. Shin, "Residential Redevelopment and the Entrepreneurial Local State"; Ran Liu and Tai-Chee Wong, "Urban Village Redevelopment in Beijing: The State-Dominated Formalization of Informal Housing," *Cities* 72 (2018): 160–72; Nick R. Smith, "Living on the Edge: Household Registration Reform and Peri-Urban Precarity in China," *Journal of Urban Affairs* 36, no. 1 (2016): 369–83.

11. Tai-Chee Wong and Ran Liu, "Developmental Urbanism, City Image Branding and the 'Right to the City' in Transitional China," *Urban Policy and Research* 35, no. 2 (2017): 210–23.

12. Xuefei Ren, "A Genealogy of Redevelopment in Chinese Cities," in *Urbanization and Urban Governance in China*, ed. Lin Ye (New York: Palgrave Macmillan, 2018), 93–108.

13. George C. S. Lin, "The Redevelopment of China's Construction Land: Practising Land Property Rights in Cities Through Renewals," *The China Quarterly* 224 (2015): 865–87.

14. This is quite common in Chinese cities, as represented most starkly in the expansive worker dormitories surrounding labor intensive industries as well as on-site construction worker dormitories. Ngai Pun and Chris Smith, "Putting Transnational Labour Process in Its Place: The Dormitory Labour Regime in Post-Socialist China," *Work Employment and Society* 21, no. 1 (2007): 27–46; Sarah Swider, *Building China: Informal Work and the New Precariat* (Ithaca, NY: Cornell University Press, 2016), 44–47. There are a growing number of boarding schools in small cities and towns, and these efforts have been promoted by the Ministry of Education. Following dwindling enrollments and fiscal capacity of rural schools, boarding schools have emerged as a method for housing the remaining rural children who cannot follow their parents to large cities.

15. Yi Hu, Pieter Hooimeijer, Gideon Bolt, and Dongqi Sun, "Uneven Compensation and Relocation for Displaced Residents: The Case of Nanjing," *Habitat International* 47 (2015): 83–92.

16. "Resident" here refers to officially recognized residents.

17. This is not to comment one way or the other on the terms of the compensation, which certainly vary widely.

18. Interview 23.

19. Before 2010, I was only able to find sporadic reports of school demolitions.

20. I estimated the absent observations by averaging the number of impacted students from the fifty-seven observations with complete data and then assigning this value to the remaining nineteen incomplete observations.

21. "Beijing jiang jin yi bu jiaqiang dui liudong renkou ziban xuexiao de guanli" [Beijing to strengthen management over migrant population self-run schools], *Xinhua*, October 10, 2005.

22. According to the estimate of the principal of Yuhui School, only one in five were approved. See "Wo de xia yige jiangtai zai na li?" [Where is my next classroom?], *Xin Jing Bao*, May 6, 2009.

23. Jie Liu and Zhao Ying, "Beijing Changping dagong zidi xuexiao bei po tingban diaocha" [Report of migrant school shut down in Beijing's Changping District], *Jinghua Shibao*, September 12, 2007.

24. Han Zhao and Jiayu Wei, "Beijing Yiwu Jiaoyu Jieduan Liudong Ertong Jiaoyu Xianzhuang" [Conditions for migrant youth compulsory education in Beijing], in *Zhongguo Liudong Ertong Jiaoyu Fazhan Baogao*, ed. Dongping Yang, Hongyu Qin, and Jiayu Wei (Beijing: Social Sciences Academic Press, 2016): 119.

25. This English-language account is from an official history of the school, published in 2011. I would note that it seems as though two of the incidents reported here were *both* closures and moves, that is, there were seven incidents in total, five of which resulted in moving the school.

26. For detail on the evolution and dispossession of recycling in Dongxiaokou and elsewhere in Beijing, see Carlo Inverardi-Ferri, "The Enclosure of 'Waste Land': Rethinking Informality and Dispossession," *Transactions of the Institute of British Geographers* 43, no. 2 (2018): 230–44.

27. The information in this paragraph comes from Yuanjie Tang, Chang Huaishen, Li Qingguo, Zhao Jingping, "Beijing: chengxiang shuangying de fazhan zhuanxing 50 ge zhongdian cun jianshe jishi" [Beijing: win-win urban-rural development transformation, report from construction in 50 focus villages], *Nongmin Ribao*, February 23, 2012.

28. Interview 123.

29. "Dagong zidi xuexiao mianlin chaiqian, 700 duo ming haizi handong ai dong shangke" [Migrant school faces demolition and relocation, more than 700 students endure the cold to attend class], *Keji Ribao*, January 9, 2014.

30. "Dagong zidi xuexiao mianlin chaiqian."

31. Interview 118.

32. The government's urgency to remove the children from the school was curious. When I visited the site in June 2014, six months after it had its power cut, the school remained undemolished amid extensive debris (see figure 5.1), and no further construction had proceeded. Satellite images from Baidu Maps accessed in 2019 showed the area where Jingwei had once stood to *still* consist of nothing but rubble and fields, with no indication of construction in process.

33. It is quite plausible that the extensive media coverage of the demolition had something to do with seemingly favorable outcomes.

34. Interview 123.

35. This parallels the growth of boarding schools in rural townships, owing to the closure and consolidation of village-level schools. Rachel Murphy, "Study and School in the Lives of Children in Migrant Families: A View from Rural Jiangxi, China," *Development and Change* 45, no. 1 (2014): 29–51.

36. Andrew Jacobs, "China Takes Aim at Rural Influx," *New York Times*, August 29, 2011.

37. "Beijing accommodates children of migrant workers as new school term begins," *Xinhua*, September 1, 2011; Jiana Pan, "For Migrants, Beijing School Bells Fall Silent," *Caixin*, August 10, 2011.

38. Pan, "For Migrants, Beijing School Bells Fall Silent."

39. From the documentary *After Us, The Deluge*, https://www.youtube.com/watch?v=LsXDcFCAyhk&feature=youtu.be (accessed February 25, 2019).

40. The following information largely comes from an open letter signed by the school's teachers and students, entitled *Shijingshan qu huangzhuang xuexiao xiangxi qingkuang, haizi mianlin shixue* 石景山区黄庄学校详细情况，孩子面临失学 [Details on Shijingshan District's Huangzhuang School, students facing loss of school].

41. Beijing chengjian jituan 北京城建集团.

42. See note 40.

43. Congzhi Zhang, "Beijing shijingshan huangzhuang xuexiao xiaoyuan bei feng: dagong zidi lu zai he fang?" [Beijing Shijingshan

Huangzhuang School is sealed up: what is the way forward for migrant school?], *San Lian Shenghuo Zhoukan*, September 13, 2018.

44. "Zai jing jianshou 20 nian, huangzhuang zhe suo dagong zidi xuexiao shifou yongyou mingtian?" [After persisting for 20 years, does Huangzhuang migrant school have a tomorrow?], *Jiemodui*, July 23, 2018, https://zhuanlan.zhihu.com/p/40359627 (accessed March 29, 2018).

45. Interview 140b.

46. Interview 140a.

47. Interview 130.

48. Tom Phillips, "The Gentrification of Beijing: Razing of Migrant Villages Spells End of China Dream," *The Guardian*, December 7, 2017.

49. Nancy Fraser has noted that "capitalism's orientation to unlimited accumulation tends to destabilize the very processes of social reproduction on which it relies." Nancy Fraser, "Crisis of Care? On the Social-Reproductive Contradictions of Contemporary Capitalism," in *Social Reproduction Theory: Remapping Class, Recentering Oppression*, ed. Tithi Bhattacharya (London: Pluto Press, 2017), 22.

50. Yuan Yang and Xinniang Liu, "Beijing Migrant 'Clean-Out' Hits China Ecommerce Sector," *The Financial Times*, December 2, 2017.

51. http://gongyi.baidu.com/map/dagongxuexiao.html (accessed February 22, 2013).

52. Interview 23.

53. Interview 145.

54. See *Beijing shi renmin zhengfu bangongting zhuanfa shi jiaowei deng bumen guanyu guanche guowuyuan bangongting jin yi bu zuohao jincheng wugong jiuye nongmin zinü yiwu jiaoyu gongzuo wenjian de tongzhi* 北京市人民政府办公厅转发市教委等部门关于贯彻国务院办公厅进一步做好进城务工就业农民子女义务教育工作文件意见的通知, http://www.beijing.gov.cn/zhengce/zfwj/zfwj/bgtwj/201905/t20190523_74855.html (accessed October 7, 2021).

55. Shi, Minglei, Wang Jialin, and Du Ding, "Beijing 30 suo dagong zidi xiao shou guanting tongzhi yingxiang 30 wan ming xuesheng" [30 migrant schools receive closure notification, 30,000 students impacted], *Xinlang Wang*, August 16, 2011.

56. The following information comes from, New Citizen Program. "Chaoyang qu diyi xin gong min xuexiao xuesheng fenliu diaocha baogao"

[Chaoyang District number 1 Xin Gong Ming School Student Resettlement Investigative Report], 2012.

57. Shi, Jialin, and Ding, "Beijing 30 suo dagong zidi xiao shou guanting tongzhi yingxiang 30 wan ming xuesheng."

58. "Dagong zidi xin xiaoyuan chengzaili bijin jixian" [Migrant children's new schools approach the limit of their carrying capacity], *Jinghua Shibao*, August 30, 2011.

59. "Dagong zidi xin xiaoyuan chengzaili bijin jixian."

60. "Dagong zidi xin xiaoyuan chengzaili bijin jixian."

61. Interview 24b.

62. Interview 27.

63. This is an affective state associated with "transient urbanism," a term used by Fulong Wu, Fangzhu Zhang, and Chris Webster in *Rural Migrants in Urban China: Enclaves and Transient Urbanism* (New York: Routledge, 2013).

64. Cecilie Andersson, "Situating Translocality in Flux Landscapes: Migrants and Urban Villages in the City of Guangzhou," in *Rural Migrants in Urban China*, ed. Fulong Wu, Fangzhu Zhang, and Chris Webster, 108–22 (New York: Routledge, 2013).

65. Interview 21.

66. Interview 140a.

67. Interview 133.

68. Interview 130.

6. REPRODUCTIVE SHOCK ABSORBERS

1. The following section is adapted from my article "Teachers' Work in China's Migrant Schools," *Modern China* 43, no. 6 (2017): 559–89.

2. Xiaoge Shen and Guoqiang Zhou, "Guangzhou Shi Liudong Renkou Zinü Yiwu Jiaoyu Wenti Fenxi Yu Duice," *Xiandai Jiaoyu Luncong* 5 (2005): 16. This is because a greater share of migrant schools themselves are registered in Guangzhou, as the municipal government has taken an approach characterized by marketization and regularization of migrant education.

3. Interview 3.

4. Interview 13.

5. Interview 24b.

6. Interview 10.
7. Interview 11.
8. Interview 24a.
9. Interview 25.
10. Interview 148b.
11. Teacher pensions vary by region and are frequently insufficient to support a comfortable retirement. Indeed, dissatisfaction with pension arrangements has been a major source of conflict for public schoolteachers in some areas. See https://clb.org.hk/content/teachers-china-are-prepared-take-stand-against-pension-reform (accessed October 9, 2021).
12. Interview 14.
13. "Beijing dagong zidi xuexiao diaocha: tiaojian jianlou, banshu wu banxue zige" [Beijing migrant school investigation: poor conditions, more than half without credentials], *Fazhi Ribao*, February 24, 2009.
14. I spoke to one teacher in my Beijing research who was satisfied with the wages. He was the art teacher at Zhifan and apparently appreciated the stability and opportunity to do his own art: "I earn a bit more than 1,000 yuan . . . but this school is special: they give me an art studio, I have a space" (Interview 15). As a result, he had stayed at the school for six years, much longer than the average.
15. Interview 24b.
16. Interview 13.
17. Interview 25.
18. "Dong Dandan: bian mai yumi bian jiao ke ben" [Dong Dandan: selling corn and teaching at the same time], *Jinghua Shibao*, November 15, 2011.
19. Interview 10.
20. Interview 26.
21. Interview 123.
22. Interview 14. Note: elsewhere I have translated 流动性 as "turnover" in reference to students. In this passage the teacher refers to the 流动性 of parents' work. Since "turnover" doesn't really capture the phenomenon of job loss and relocation, I've translated it here as "fluidity."
23. Taiichi Ohno, *Toyota Production System: Beyond Large-Scale Production* (Portland, OR: Productivity Press, 1988), 4.
24. Interview 3.

25. Huisheng Tian, Ni Wu, Ningjuan Zhang, and Xiaoqiang Li, "Jincheng Wugong Nongmin Suiqian Zinü Jiaoyu Zhuangkuang Diaoyan Baogao" [Investigative report on education conditions for children of migrant workers in the cities], *Jiaoyu Yanjiu* 4 (2008): 17.

26. Zhangjiakou is an area in Hebei just to the northwest of Beijing.

27. Interview 24b.

28. Interview 21.

29. Interview 22.

30. Interview 11.

31. Interview 3.

32. Interview 26.

33. Friedman, "Teachers' Work in China's Migrant Schools."

34. Interview 24b.

35. Changchang Xu, "Jincheng Wugong Renyuan Suiqian Zinü Xinli Jiankang Zhuangkuang de Bijiao Yanjiu," *Sixiang Lilun Jiaoyu*, no. 10 (2010): 62–68; Hongwei Hu, Shuang Lu, and Chien-Chung Huang, "The Psychological and Behavioral Outcomes of Migrant and Left-Behind Children in China," *Children and Youth Services Review* 46 (2014): 1–10. Research has demonstrated the entirely predictable outcome that left-behind children also suffer emotionally. This is relevant here in that many migrant children in cities have spent some time in the countryside without one or either of their parents. Shaobing Su et al., "Psychological Adjustment among Left-Behind Children in Rural China: The Role of Parental Migration and Parent–Child Communication," *Child: Care, Health and Development* 39, no. 2 (2013): 162–70.

36. Interview 21.

37. Interview 3.

38. Susan Greenhalgh and Edwin A. Winckler, *Governing China's Population: From Leninist to Neoliberal Biopolitics* (Stanford, CA: Stanford University Press, 2005), 238.

39. Interview 15.

40. Interview 148a.

41. Field notes, June 9, 2012.

42. I am referring here to Arlie Russell Hochschild's classic study of emotional labor among flight attendants and customer service

representatives, *The Managed Heart: Commercialization of Human Feeling* (Berkeley: University of California Press, 1983).

43. Interview 14.

44. I do not have any reason to believe that being in Guangzhou would have an impact on her experience. Indeed, my interviews with teachers in Beijing, Guangzhou, and Chengdu revealed no discernible variation in terms of the qualities of affective labor.

45. http://blog.sina.com.cn/s/blog_ac6936e301016wh9.html (accessed February 6, 2020).

46. Interview 26.

47. Personal communication.

48. Nancy Fraser, "Crisis of Care? On the Social-Reproductive Contradictions of Contemporary Capitalism," In *Social Reproduction Theory: Remapping Class, Recentering Oppression*, ed. Tithi Bhattacharya, (London: Pluto Press, 2017), 22.

49. There is an open question as to whether this crisis tendency is internal to capital. As I have argued throughout, the expulsionary forces at work in urban politics, that is, those interventions that destabilize social reproduction, emanate from a more or less autonomous political logic. Expulsion may benefit real estate capital at the expense of labor-intensive forms of employment, but certainly state action cannot be read as mechanistically responding to the needs of an undifferentiated "capital."

50. Tithi Bhattacharya, "How Not to Skip Class: Social Reproduction of Labor and the Global Working Class," In *Social Reproduction Theory: Remapping Class, Recentering Oppression*, ed. Tithi Bhattacharya (London: Pluto Press, 2017), 74–75.

51. Micah Uetricht, *Strike for America: Chicago Teachers Against Austerity* (New York: Verso, 2014).

CONCLUSION

1. This is intended to evoke Polanyi's use of the phrase with reference to the self-regulating market. Karl Polanyi, *The Great Transformation: The Political and Economic Origins of Our Time* (Boston: Beacon Press, 1944).

2. Han Zhao and Jiayu Wei, "Beijing Yiwu Jiaoyu Jieduan Liudong Ertong Jiaoyu Xianzhuang" [Conditions for migrant youth compulsory education in Beijing], in *Zhongguo Liudong Ertong Jiaoyu Fazhan Baogao*, ed. Dongping Yang, Hongyu Qin, and Jiayu Wei, 105–20, at 110 (Beijing: Social Sciences Academic Press, 2016); see also http://www.hukouwang.com/archives/5415 (accessed June 8, 2020).

3. Interview 46a.

4. Yihua Yue, "Tamen shi waimaiyuan, kuaidi yuan, jiazhenggong, dan tamen de haizi zai chengshi zhao bu dao yi zhang ke zhuo" [They are food delivery workers, couriers, and domestic workers, but their children cannot find a school desk in the city], *Xin Gongmin Jihua*, October 18, 2020.

5. I have written a more in-depth comparison of teacher working conditions in Beijing and Guangzhou. Eli Friedman, "Teachers' Work in China's Migrant Schools," *Modern China* 43, no. 6 (April 2017): 559–89.

6. Guangfu is a pseudonym. The information comes from a group interview with three administrators (Interview 54a, 54b, and 54c) as well as my own direct observation.

7. This is as described on an introductory display inside the school.

8. The only indicator I could get on the class background of the student body was that 60 percent had rural *hukou*. In other words, a very large minority were nonlocal from other cities. This is quite different from what I found in Beijing's migrant schools were nearly all of the students had nonlocal rural *hukou*.

9. An administrator noted that they received 200,000 yuan from the Education Department when they registered. I am not certain of the scale of ongoing support.

10. http://edu.dg.gov.cn/jyzx/jygk/content/mpost_80398.html (accessed November 17, 2020); "Guanyu jiejue Shenzhen shi suiqian zinü yiwu jiaoyu 'ruxue nan' wenti de jianyi" [A proposal for addressing difficulty in primary school enrollments for migrant children in Shenzhen], *Hugai Guancha*, January 1, 2018.

11. This section on Guizhou is largely based on data from supervised interviews conducted by Christine Wen, a former PhD student in Cornell's Department of City and Regional Planning.

12. This index is composed of hukou application criteria through the summer of 2017. For details on Macro Polo's methodology and links to the data, see https://macropolo.org/digital-projects/on-the-road/about-on-the-road/ (accessed October 9, 2021).

13. http://stjj.guizhou.gov.cn/tjsj_35719/tjxx_35728/201705/t20170524_24414633.html (accessed October 9, 2021).

14. See https://macropolo.org/wp-content/uploads/2018/05/Guiyang.pdf (accessed October 9, 2021).

15. Interview 164.

16. Qinghua Xiao, *Nongcun Liushou Yu Liudong Ertong de Jiaoyu* (Beijing: Zhongguo shehui kexue chubanshe, 2012), 62.

17. http://gz.people.com.cn/n/2014/0327/c358161-20873589.html.

18. Dongwei Wang, "Dao 2020 nian guiyang suiqian zinv jiudu gongban xuexiao jiang da 85% yi shang" [Guiyang migrant children enrollment in public schools to reach 85 per cent by 2020], *Guiyang Ribao*, July 18, 2019.

19. The following is based on publicly available admissions policies. Yunyan District (2018): http://www.yunyan.gov.cn/zwfw/bmlqfw/jypx/jyzx/201808/t20180830_11128698.html; Nanming District (2018): http://www.guiyang.gov.cn/bsfw/bsfwztfw/bsfwztfwjyfw/bsfwztfwjyfwwlrkbdjdfw/201810/t20181025_8158488.html; Guanshanhu District (2016): http://www.guiyang.gov.cn/bsfw/bsfwztfw/bsfwztfwjyfw/bsfwztfwjyfwwlrkbdjdfw/201509/t20150902_8158480.html.

20. 2016 nian nongminggong jiance diaocha baogao, http://www.stats.gov.cn/tjsj/zxfb/201704/t20170428_1489334.html (December 12, 2021).

21. Interview 187a.

22. It is important to note that this refers to education spending in relationship to the total urban population, *not* spending per student. The respective values for Beijing, Guangzhou, and Guiyang were 7,097, 4,503, and 477 yuan. Source: *China Data Online* (China City Statistics).

23. I was unable to find a reliable count of migrant schools. As in Beijing, there are many informal schools that are not reflected in the official numbers. Mr. Liu, the NGO worker, estimated there were around two hundred migrant schools in Guiyang in 2016, but that number is impressionistic.

24. Interviews 204b and 204c.
25. Interview 152c.
26. Interview 182b. "CW" refers to Christine Wen (see note 11).
27. Interview 164.
28. My view differs somewhat from that of Brenner and Schmid, who subsume both the implosion and explosion moments within a "planetary urbanization" framework. While I do not deny the mutual constitution of these diametric movements, it is unclear to me how implosion-explosion, when viewed as a totality, is distinct from what is typically called "capitalist development." A more analytically precise approach is to distinguish urbanization as pertaining to the implosion movement, whereas explosion corresponds roughly to "globalization." Without this distinction I fear "urbanization" loses analytical traction. Neil Brenner and Christian Schmid, "Planetary Urbanization," in *The Globalizing Cities Reader*, ed. Xuefei Ren and Roger Keil (New York: Routledge, 2017), 479–82.
29. As Kaoru Sugihara has argued with respect to labor-intensive development elsewhere in East Asia, "labour functioned, not like capital, but rather like land: the value of which has changed, depending on whether its quality was improved, maintained or depleted." Kaoru Sugihara, "Labour-Intensive Industrialization in Global History: An Interpretation of East Asian Experiences," in *Labour-Intensive Industrialization in Global History*, ed. Gareth Austin and Kaoru Sugihara (New York: Routledge, 2013), 43.
30. Ngai Pun and Jenny Wai-ling Chan, "Global Capital, the State, and Chinese Workers: The Foxconn Experience," *Modern China* 38, no. 4 (May 2012): 383–410.
31. Friedman, "Teachers' Work in China's Migrant Schools."
32. Walden Bello, *China: An Imperial Power in the Image of the West?* (Bangkok: Focus on the Global South, 2019), 55.
33. I am less familiar with the Japanese experience. But in the nineteenth and early twentieth centuries there were processes of "internal" colonialism both northward into Hokkaido and southward to the Ryuku Islands, as well as substantial outmigration to colonies in Asia. Eiichiro Azuma, *Between Two Empires: Race, History, and Transnationalism in Japanese America* (Oxford: Oxford University

Press, 2005), 19. After 1885, smaller numbers of Japanese migrated to Hawaii and the US mainland, and later to South America.

34. Utsa Patnaik, "Agrarian Distress," *Frontline*, June 17, 2011.

35. Kanishka Goonewardena, "The Country and the City in the Urban Revolution," in *Implosions/Explosion: Towards a Study of Planetary Urbanization*, ed. Neil Brenner (Berlin, Jovis, 2014), 218–34. Here she cites David Harvey, *The New Imperialism* (New York: Oxford University Press, 2005).

36. Nandita Sharma, *Home Rule: National Sovereignty and the Separation of Natives and Migrants* (Durham, NC: Duke University Press, 2020).

37. Matteo Giovannini, "China's Proposal of a Revised Permanent Residency Law for Foreigners Is Causing Debate," *CGTN*, March 4, 2020.

38. The intensive/extensive contrast with Euro-American empire should not be read as absolute. Of course, English capitalists dispossessed English peasants and exploited English workers, so there is an intensive dynamic at play. But from the very beginning, incorporation of other races and places was part of capitalist expansion, with the Irish emigrés to English factory towns forming a critical piece of the industrial proletariat. And the British Empire was already drawing in raw commodities on uneven terms and forcing its manufactured goods back out onto the world market. China, too, is a nation built on violent incorporation of new races and spaces, as its vast territory makes apparent. The difference is that this extensive dynamic has historically not been capitalist in nature; to the extent that capitalism developed in imperial China, it was also intensive in nature. See Andrew B. Liu, *Tea War: A History of Capitalism in China and India* (New Haven, CT: Yale University Press, 2020).

39. It should be noted that, from an ethical standpoint, this kind of movement could very easily take on a fascist character, that is, one that valorized life for the dominant race, but not for anyone else.

40. Alastair Iain Johnston, "Is Chinese Nationalism Rising? Evidence from Beijing," *International Security* 41, no. 3 (2017): 7–43. A survey of public opinion has found increasing levels of satisfaction with government under Xi Jinping, *especially* for poor and marginalized people. Edward Cunningham, Tony Saich, and Jesse Turiel, *Understanding*

CCP Resilience: Surveying Chinese Public Opinion Through Time (Cambridge, MA: Harvard Kennedy School, 2020).

41. Interview 15.

42. Interview 140a.

43. On the other hand, Min Yu has shown how migrants have engaged in low-key activism, even if it does not generally rise to the level of overt collection action. See Min Yu, "Rethinking Migrant Children Schools in China: Activism, Collective Identity, and Guanxi," *Comparative Education Review* 62, no. 3 (2018): 429–48.

44. Long Qiao, "Beijing nongmingong zidi xuexiao you bei guan, wang feng yuan fei jian qian xiao guoren que shixue" [More migrant schools closed in Beijing, internet mocks school construction in Africa while Chinese people forced to drop out], *Radio Free Asia*, August 17, 2011.

45. "Fei jing ji haizi ruxue shouzhi, 300 jiazhang chixu kangyi" [Non-Beijing resident children face constraints enrolling in school, 300 parents continue to protest], *Radio Free Asia*, May 15, 2015; "Fei jing jin xuesheng ruxue nan, jiazhang kangyi dushu yao shexian" [Non-Beijing resident students have difficulty enrolling, parents protest restrictions on education], *Radio Free Asia*, May 20, 2016; "Haizi shangxue wu wang, fei jing ji jiazhang zifen" [Child has no hope of enrolling, non-Beijing resident parent self-immolates], *Radio Free Asia*, May 22, 2016.

46. This was the case for a domestic worker in Beijing's Haidian District that I interviewed. She told me how she helped organize more than two hundred parents to protest at the district Education Department. They were incensed that their children's school was to be demolished and that there had been no announcement of resettlement. Following the protest, the government did indeed arrange for the children to enroll elsewhere. She commented, "They made good school arrangements for the kids, we didn't have to pay any fees, or textbook fees, nothing. When the public takes care of the children, of course I'm satisfied" (Interview 27).

47. I am intentionally leaving imperial Russia and the Soviet Union out of this formulation, since neither were fully capitalist. This is not to deny potentially similar pressures toward extensive empire for the feudal/precapitalist and Stalinist states; nonetheless, the dynamics are sufficiently distinct that it seems prudent to bracket this question.

The role of oil in the Gulf States gives them something of different character. Nonetheless, they are in general tightly linked to US military power, as is the case for the Asian Tigers, Japan, and Germany. With the exception of Saudi Arabia, the other states (the United Arab Emirates, Qatar, Kuwait, Bahrain) have quite small populations, which, like city-states Hong Kong and Singapore, has pushed them to be highly dependent on brutal foreign guest worker programs as a source of labor.

48. This evokes earlier debates about "internal colonies" in the Americas, and there are important parallels to the situation in Xinjiang. See Ramón A. Gutiérrez, "Internal Colonialism: An American Theory of Race," *Du Bois Review* 1, no. 2 (2004): 281; Donald J. Harris, "The Black Ghetto as Colony: A Theoretical Critique and Alternative Formulation," *The Review of Black Political Economy* 2, no. 4 (1972): 3–33.

49. As with Cedric Robinson's conceptualization of racial capitalism in Europe, in China anti-Muslim racism precedes capitalist exploitation of Muslims, both historically and ontologically. Darren Byler, "Spirit Breaking: Uyghur Dispossession, Culture Work and Terror Capitalism in a Chinese Global City," PhD diss., 2018; Cedric J Robinson, *Black Marxism: The Making of the Black Radical Tradition* (Chapel Hill: University of North Carolina Press, 2000).

50. Adrian Zenz, "Coercive Labor in Xinjiang: Labor Transfer and the Mobilization of Ethnic Minorities to Pick Cotton," *Newlines Institute*, 2020; Cate Cadell, "China Sharply Expands Mass Labor Program in Tibet," *Reuters*, September 22, 2020.

51. Amy K. Lehr and Mariefaye Bechrakis, *Connecting the Dots in Xinjiang: Forced Labor, Forced Assimilation, and Western Supply Chains*, Center for Strategic & International Studies, 2019.

52. Vicky Xiuzhong Xu, Danielle Cave, James Leibold, Kelsey Munro, and Nathan Ruser, "Uyghurs for Sale," https://www.aspi.org.au /report/uyghurs-sale (accessed December 29, 2020).

53. I am using "super-exploitation" as an analytical term to denote a labor regime where wages do not satisfy worker subsistence. Benjamin Selwyn, *The Struggle for Development* (Cambridge: Polity Press, 2017), 51.

54. Jevans Nyabiage, "China Finds Manufacturing Opportunities in Low-Wage Africa," *South China Morning Post*, June 1, 2020.

55. While this remains speculative, there is a noteworthy contradiction in China's political economy that I believe is reflected in the ambivalence of the "two circulations." In addition to building domestic supply chains, the policy has renewed emphasis on increasing domestic consumption, which has been a priority of the state since 2004, and there has been only minor success thus far. The Keynesian response would require allowing wages to rise and increasing social welfare protection, which in turn would impose costs on Chinese capital and undercut its global competitiveness. The second "circulation" is to maintain connections to foreign markets and to continue to advance free trade as an outlet for Chinese-produced goods. This in turn suggests an acknowledgment that China will indeed maintain dependence on exports—the very thing the "two circulations" aims to ameliorate.

BIBLIOGRAPHY

Althusser, Louis. 1971. "Ideology and Ideological State Apparatuses." In *Lenin and Philosophy*, 85–132. New York: Monthly Review Press.

Anagnost, Ann. 2004. "The Corporeal Politics of Quality (Suzhi)." *Public Culture* 16, no. 2: 189–208.

——. 1997. *National Past-Times: Narrative, Representation, and Power in Modern China*. Durham, NC: Duke University Press.

Andersson, Cecilie. 2013. "Situating Translocality in Flux Landscapes: Migrants and Urban Villages in the City of Guangzhou." In *Rural Migrants in Urban China*, edited by Fulong Wu, Fangzhu Zhang, and Chris Webster, 108–22. New York: Routledge.

Andreas, Joel, and Shaohua Zhan. 2016. "Hukou and Land: Market Reform and Rural Displacement in China." *Journal of Peasant Studies* 43, no. 4: 798–827.

Azuma, Eiichiro. 2005. *Between Two Empires: Race, History, and Transnationalism in Japanese America*. New York: Oxford University Press.

Barchiesi, Franco. 2011. *Precarious Liberation: Workers, the State, and Contested Social Citizenship in Postapartheid South Africa*. Albany: State University of New York Press.

Bauman, Zygmunt. 2004. *Wasted Lives: Modernity and Its Outcasts*. Cambridge: Polity Press.

Bello, Walden. 2019. *China: An Imperial Power in the Image of the West?* Bangkok: Focus on the Global South.

Bhattacharya, Tithi. 2017. "How Not to Skip Class: Social Reproduction of Labor and the Global Working Class." In *Social Reproduction Theory:*

Remapping Class, Recentering Oppression, edited by Tithi Bhattacharya, 68–93. London: Pluto Press.

Bird, Greg. 2018. "The Biopolitical Economy of Guest Worker Programs." In *Biopolitical Governance: Race, Gender and Economy*, 99–120. London: Rowman & Littlefield.

Blumenthal, David, and William Hsiao. 2005. "Privatization and Its Discontents: The Evolving Chinese Health Care System." *New England Journal of Medicine* 353, no. 11: 1165–70.

Bodomo, Adams B., and Grace Ma. 2010. "From Guangzhou to Yiwu: Emerging Facets of the African Diaspora in China." *International Journal of African Renaissance Studies* 5, no. 2: 283–89.

Bonacich, Edna. 1972. "A Theory of Ethnic Antagonism: The Split Labor Market." *American Sociological Review* 37, no. 5: 547–59.

Bourdieu, Pierre, and Jean Claude Passeron. 1977. *Reproduction in Education, Society and Culture*. London: Sage Publications.

Brenner, Neil, ed. 2014. *Implosions/Explosions: Towards a Study of Planetary Urbanization*. Berlin: Jovis.

Brenner, Neil, and Christian Schmid. 2017. "Planetary Urbanization." In *The Globalizing Cities Reader*, edited by Xuefei Ren and Roger Keil, 479–82. New York: Routledge.

Byler, Darren. 2018. "Spirit Breaking: Uyghur Dispossession, Culture Work and Terror Capitalism in a Chinese Global City." PhD dissertation, University of Washington.

Cao, Yang, and Victor G. Nee. 2000. "Comment: Controversies and Evidence in the Market Transition Debate." *American Journal of Sociology* 105, no. 4: 1175–89.

Chakrabarty, Dipesh. 2000. *Provincializing Europe: Postcolonial Thought and Historical Difference*. Princeton, NJ: Princeton University Press.

——. 1989. *Rethinking Working-Class History: Bengal, 1890–1940*. Princeton, NJ: Princeton University Press.

Chan, Anita, and Kaxton Siu. 2010. "Analyzing Exploitation: The Mechanisms Underpinning Low Wages and Excessive Overtime in Chinese Export Factories." *Critical Asian Studies* 42, no. 2: 167–90.

Chan, David, and Ka-Ho Mok. 2001. "Educational Reforms and Coping Strategies Under the Tidal Wave of Marketisation: A Comparative Study of Hong Kong and the Mainland." *Comparative Education* 37, no. 1: 21–41.

Chan, Kam Wing. 2010. "A China Paradox: Migrant Labor Shortage Amidst Rural Labor Supply Abundance." *Eurasian Geography and Economics* 51, no. 4: 513–30.

———. 2009. "The Chinese Hukou System at 50." *Eurasian Geography and Economics* 50, no. 2: 197–221.

———. 1994. *Cities with Invisible Walls: Reinterpreting Urbanization in Post-1949 China*. Oxford: Oxford University Press.

———. 2010. "Fundamentals of China's Urbanization and Policy." *The China Review* 10, no. 1: 63–94.

———. 2010. "The Global Financial Crisis and Migrant Workers in China: 'There Is No Future as a Labourer; Returning to the Village Has No Meaning.'" *International Journal of Urban and Regional Research* 34, no. 3: 659–77.

———. 2009. "Measuring the Urban Millions." *China Economic Quarterly* 1: 21–26.

Chan, Kam Wing, and Will Buckingham. 2008. "Is China Abolishing the Hukou System?" *China Quarterly* 195: 582–606.

Chan, Kam Wing, and Yuan Ren. 2018. "Children of Migrants in China in the Twenty-First Century: Trends, Living Arrangements, Age-Gender Structure, and Geography." *Eurasian Geography and Economics* 59, no. 2: 133–63.

Chan, Raymond K. H., and Ying Wang. 2009. "Controlled Decentralization: Minban Education Reform in China." *Journal of Comparative Social Welfare* 25, no. 1: 27–36.

Chang, Gene Hsin, and Josef C. Brada. 2006. "The Paradox of China's Growing Under-Urbanization." *Economic Systems* 30, no. 1: 24–40.

Chen, Calvin. 2008. *Some Assembly Required: Work, Community, and Politics in China's Rural Enterprises*. Cambridge, MA: Harvard University Press.

Chen, Chuanbo, and C. Cindy Fan. 2016. "China's Hukou Puzzle: Why Don't Rural Migrants Want Urban Hukou?" *China Review* 16, no. 3: 9–39.

Chen, Feng. 2009. "Union Power in China: Source, Operation, and Constraints." *Modern China* 35: 662–89.

Chen, Yiu Por, and Zai Liang. 2007. "Educational Attainment of Migrant Children: The Forgotten Story of China' Urbanization." In *Education and Reform in China*, edited by Emily Hannum and Albert Park, 117–32. New York: Routledge.

Chen, Yuanyuan, and Shuaizhang Feng. 2013. "Access to Public Schools and the Education of Migrant Children in China." *China Economic Review* 26, no. 1: 75–88.

Chibber, Vivek. 2012. *Postcolonial Theory and the Specter of Capital*. London: Verso.

Chuang, Julia. 2014. "China's Rural Land Politics: Bureaucratic Absorption and the Muting of Rightful Resistance." *The China Quarterly* 219: 649–69.

Collier, Stephen J. 2011. *Post-Soviet Social: Neoliberalism, Social Modernity, Biopolitics*. Princeton, NJ: Princeton University Press.

Cooney, Sean. 2007. "China's Labour Law, Compliance and Flaws in Implementing Institutions." *Journal of Industrial Relations* 49, no. 5: 673–86.

Cunningham, Edward, Tony Saich, and Jesse Turiel. 2020. *Understanding CCP Resilience: Surveying Chinese Public Opinion Through Time*. Cambridge, MA: Ash Center for Democratic Governance and Innovation, Harvard University.

Davis, Mike. 2006. *Planet of Slums*. London: Verso.

——. 2004. "The Urbanization of Empire: Megacities and the Laws of Chaos." *Social Text* 22, no. 4: 9–15.

Denning, Michael. 2010. "Wageless Life." *New Left Review* 66: 79–97.

Dmitrieva, Marina, and Alfrun Kliems. 2010. *The Post Socialist City: Continuity and Change in Urban Space and Imagery*. Berlin: Jovis Verlag.

Du Bois, W. E. B. 1998. *Black Reconstruction in America*. New York: Free Press.

Economy, Elizabeth. 2005. "Environmental Enforcement in China." In *China's Environment and the Challenge of Sustainable Development*, edited by Kristen A. Day, 102–20. Armonk, NY: East Gate.

Engels, Friedrich. 1935. *The Housing Question*. New York: International Publishers.

Estlund, Cynthia. 2017. *A New Deal for China's Workers?* Cambridge, MA: Harvard University Press.

Fan, C. Cindy. 2002. "The Elite, the Natives, and the Outsiders: Migration and Labor Market Segmentation in Urban China." *Annals of the Association of American Geographers* 92, no. 1: 103–24.

——. 2011. "Settlement Intention and Split Households: Findings from a Survey of Migrants in Beijing's Urban Villages." *China Review* 11, no. 2: 11–41.

Fan, C. Cindy, Mingjie Sun, and Siqi Zheng. 2011. "Migration and Split Households: A Comparison of Sole, Couple, and Family Migrants in Beijing, China." *Environment and Planning A* 43, no. 9: 2164–85.

Fan, C. Cindy, and Wenfei Winnie Wang. 2008. "The Household as Security: Strategies of Rural-Urban Migrants in China." In *Migration and Social Protection in China*, edited by Ingrid Nielsen and Russell Smyth, 14:205–42. Hackensack, NJ: World Scientific.

Fang, Yiping, and Zhilei Shi. 2018. "Children of Migrant Parents: Migrating Together or Left Behind." *Habitat International* 76: 62–68.

Fanon, Frantz. 1966. *The Wretched of the Earth*. New York: Grove Press.

Federici, Silvia. 2012. *Revolution at Point Zero: Housework, Reproduction, and Feminist Struggle*. Oakland, CA: PM Press.

Fincher, Leta Hong. 2016. *Leftover Women: The Resurgence of Gender Inequality in China*. London: Zed Books Ltd.

Fischer, Andrew Martin. 2008. "'Population Invasion' versus Urban Exclusion in the Tibetan Areas of Western China." *Population and Development Review* 34, no. 4: 631–62.

Fix, Michael, and Wendy Zimmermann. 2001. "All Under One Roof: Mixed-Status Families in an Era of Reform." *International Migration Review* 35, no. 2: 397–419.

Foucault, Michel. 1979. *Discipline and Punish: The Birth of the Prison*. New York: Vintage Books.

——. 1996. *Foucault Live: Collected Interviews, 1961–1984*. Edited by Sylvère Lotringer. New York: Semiotext(e).

——. 1978. *The History of Sexuality*. 1st ed. New York: Pantheon Books.

——. 2009. *Security, Territory, Population: Lectures at the Collège de France, 1977–1978*. Edited by Michel Senellart, François Ewald, and Alessandro Fontana. New York: Picador/Palgrave Macmillan.

——. 2003. *"Society Must Be Defended": Lectures at the Collège de France, 1975–1976*. New York: Picador.

Franceschini, Ivan, Kaxton Siu, and Anita Chan. 2016. "The 'Rights Awakening' of Chinese Migrant Workers: Beyond the Generational Perspective." *Critical Asian Studies* 48 no.3: 422–42.

Fraser, Nancy. 2017. "Crisis of Care? On the Social-Reproductive Contradictions of Contemporary Capitalism." In *Social Reproduction Theory: Remapping Class, Recentering Oppression*, edited by Tithi Bhattacharya, 21–36. London: Pluto Press.

Friedman, Eli. 2012. "Getting Through the Hard Times Together? Chinese Workers and Unions Respond to the Economic Crisis." *Journal of Industrial Relations* 54, no. 4: 459–75.

——. 2014. *Insurgency Trap: Labor Politics in Postsocialist China*. Ithaca, NY: Cornell University Press.

——. 2018. "Just-in-Time Urbanization? Managing Migration, Citizenship, and Schooling in the Chinese City." *Critical Sociology* 44, no. 3: 503–18.

——. 2017. "Teachers' Work in China's Migrant Schools." *Modern China* 43, no. 6: 559–89.

Gallagher, Mary E. 2017. *Authoritarian Legality in China: Law, Workers, and the State*. Cambridge: Cambridge University Press.

——. 2004. "Time Is Money, Efficiency Is Life: The Transformation of Labor Relations in China." *Studies in Comparative International Development* 39, no. 2: 11–44.

Gallagher, Mary, John Giles, Albert Park, and Meiyan Wang. 2015. "China's 2008 Labor Contract Law: Implementation and Implications for China's Workers." *Human Relations* 68, no. 2: 197–235.

Gilmore, Ruth Wilson. 2007. *Golden Gulag: Prisons, Surplus, Crisis, and Opposition in Globalizing California*. Berkeley: University of California Press.

Glenn, Evelyn Nakano. 2010. *Forced to Care: Coercion and Caregiving in America*. Cambridge, MA: Harvard University Press.

Golley, Jane, and Xin Meng. 2011. "Has China Run out of Surplus Labour?" *China Economic Review* 22, no. 4: 555–72.

Goodburn, Charlotte. 2020. "Growing Up in (and Out of) Shenzhen: The Longer-Term Impacts of Rural-Urban Migration on Education and Labor Market Entry." *The China Journal* 83, no. 1: 129–47.

——. 2009. "Learning from Migrant Education: A Case Study of the Schooling of Rural Migrant Children in Beijing." *International Journal of Educational Development* 29, no. 5: 495–504.

Goonewardena, Kanishka. 2014. "The Country and the City in the Urban Revolution." In *Implosions/Explosion: Towards a Study of Planetary Urbanization*, edited by Neil Brenner, 218–34. Berlin: Jovis.

Greenhalgh, Susan, and Edwin A. Winckler. 2005. *Governing China's Population: From Leninist to Neoliberal Biopolitics*. Stanford, CA: Stanford University Press.

Gu, Yan. 2017. "Compulsory Education for Children of Migrant Workers: Is Hukou the Biggest Obstacle?" In *Challenges in the Process of China's Urbanization*, edited by Karen Eggleston, Jean C. Oi, and Yiming Wang, 113–37. Stanford, CA: Walter H. Shorenstein Asia-Pacific Research Center.

Guha, Ranajit. 1983. *Elementary Aspects of Peasant Insurgency in Colonial India*. Delhi: Oxford University Press.

Gustafsson, Björn, and Ding Sai. 2009. "Temporary and Persistent Poverty Among Ethnic Minorities and the Majority in Rural China." *Review of Income and Wealth* 55, no. 1: 588–606.

Gutiérrez, Ramón A. 2004. "Internal Colonialism: An American Theory of Race." *Du Bois Review* 1, no. 2: 281.

Hao, Pu, Stan Geertman, Pieter Hooimeijer, and Richard Sliuzas. 2013. "Spatial Analyses of the Urban Village Development Process in Shenzhen, China." *International Journal of Urban and Regional Research* 37, no. 6: 2177–97.

Hardt, Michael, and Antonio Negri. 2000. *Empire*. Cambridge, MA: Harvard University Press.

——. 2004. *Multitude: War and Democracy in the Age of Empire*. New York: Penguin Press.

Harris, Donald J. 1972. "The Black Ghetto as Colony: A Theoretical Critique and Alternative Formulation." *The Review of Black Political Economy* 2, no. 4: 3–33.

Harten, Julia Gabriele, Annette M. Kim, and J. Cressica Brazier. 2020. "Real and Fake Data in Shanghai's Informal Rental Housing Market: Groundtruthing Data Scraped from the Internet." *Urban Studies* 58, no. 9: 1831–45.

Harvey, David. 2005. *A Brief History of Neoliberalism*. New York: Oxford University Press.

——. 1996. "Cities or Urbanization?" *City* 1, no. 1–2: 38–61.

——. 2005. *The New Imperialism*. New York: Oxford University Press.

——. 2008. "The Right to the City." *New Left Review* 53: 23–40.

——. 1985. *The Urbanization of Capital: Studies in the History and Theory of Capitalist Urbanization*. Baltimore, MD: Johns Hopkins University Press.

He, Shenjing, and Fulong Wu. 2005. "Property-Led Redevelopment in Post-Reform China: A Case Study of Xintiandi Redevelopment Project in Shanghai." *Journal of Urban Affairs* 27, no. 1: 1–23.

Hirt, Sonia. 2012. *Iron Curtains: Gates, Suburbs, and Privatization of Space in the Post-Socialist City.* Hoboken, NJ: Wiley.

Ho, Virginia Harper, and Qiaoyan Huang. 2014. "The Recursivity of Reform: China's Amended Labor Contract Law." *Fordham International Law Journal* 37: 1–41.

Hochschild, Arlie Russell. 1983. *The Managed Heart: Commercialization of Human Feeling.* Berkeley: University of California Press.

Hou, Yue, Chuyu Liu, and Charles Crabtree. 2019. "Anti-Muslim Bias in the Chinese Labor Market." *Journal of Comparative Economics* 48, no. 2: 235–50.

Hsing, You-tien. 2010. *The Great Urban Transformation: Politics of Land and Property in China.* Oxford: Oxford University Press.

Hsu, Jennifer. 2012. "Layers of the Urban State: Migrant Organisations and the Chinese State." *Urban Studies* 49, no. 16: 3513–30.

Hu, Biliang, and Tony Saich. 2012. "Developing Social Citizenship? A Case Study of Education and Health Services in Yantian Village of Guangdong Province." *China & World Economy* 20, no. 3: 69–87.

Hu, Hongwei, Shuang Lu, and Chien-Chung Huang. 2014. "The Psychological and Behavioral Outcomes of Migrant and Left-Behind Children in China." *Children and Youth Services Review* 46: 1–10.

Hu, Yi, Pieter Hooimeijer, Gideon Bolt, and Dongqi Sun. 2015. "Uneven Compensation and Relocation for Displaced Residents: The Case of Nanjing." *Habitat International* 47: 83–92.

Huang, Philip C. 2009. "China's Neglected Informal Economy Reality and Theory." *Modern China* 35, no. 4: 405–38.

Huang, Yeqing, Fei Guo, and Yiming Tang. 2010. "Hukou Status and Social Exclusion of Rural–Urban Migrants in Transitional China." *Journal of Asian Public Policy* 3, no. 2: 172–85.

Huang, Youqin. 2013. "Low-Income Housing in Chinese Cities: Policies and Practices." *The China Quarterly* 212: 941–64.

Hung, Ho-fung. 2015. *The China Boom: Why China Will Not Rule the World.* New York: Columbia University Press.

Hung, Wu. 2005. *Remaking Beijing: Tiananmen Square and the Creation of a Political Space.* London: Reaktion Books.

Inverardi-Ferri, Carlo. 2018. "The Enclosure of 'Waste Land': Rethinking Informality and Dispossession." *Transactions of the Institute of British Geographers* 43, no. 2: 230–44.

Jacka, Tamara. 2009. "Cultivating Citizens: Suzhi (Quality) Discourse in the PRC." *Positions* 17, no. 3: 523–35.

Jaros, Kyle A. 2019. *China's Urban Champions: The Politics of Spatial Development*. Princeton, NJ: Princeton University Press.

Johnston, Alastair Iain. 2017. "Is Chinese Nationalism Rising? Evidence from Beijing." *International Security* 41, no. 3: 7–43.

Joniak-Luthi, Agnieszka. 2013. "Han Migration to Xinjiang Uyghur Autonomous Region: Between State Schemes and Migrants' Strategies." *Zeitschrift für Ethnologie* 138: 155–74.

Khor, Niny, Lihua Pang, Chengfang Liu, Fang Chang, Di Mo, Prashant Loyalka, and Scott Rozelle. 2016. "China's Looming Human Capital Crisis: Upper Secondary Educational Attainment Rates and the Middle-Income Trap." *The China Quarterly* 228: 905–26.

Kipnis, Andrew. 2006. 2011. *Governing Educational Desire: Culture, Politics, and Schooling in China*. Chicago: University of Chicago Press.

——. "Suzhi: A Keyword Approach." *The China Quarterly* 186: 295–313.

Kuruvilla, Sarosh, Ching Kwan Lee, and Mary Elizabeth Gallagher. 2011. *From Iron Rice Bowl to Informalization: Markets, Workers, and the State in a Changing China*. Ithaca, NY: Cornell University Press.

Kuznets, Simon. 1955. "Economic Growth and Income Inequality." *The American Economic Review* 45, no. 1: 1–28.

Kwong, Julia. 1997. "The Reemergence of Private Schools in Socialist China." *Comparative Education Review* 41, no. 3: 244–59.

Lan, Pei-chia. 2014. "Segmented Incorporation: The Second Generation of Rural Migrants in Shanghai." *The China Quarterly* 217: 243–65.

Laslett, Barbara, and Johanna Brenner. 1989. "Gender and Social Reproduction: Historical Perspectives." *Annual Review of Sociology* 15, no. 1: 381–404.

Lee, Ching Kwan. 2016. "Precarization or Empowerment? Reflections on Recent Labor Unrest in China." *The Journal of Asian Studies* 75, no. 2 (May): 317–33.

——. 2009. "Raw Encounters: Chinese Managers, African Workers and the Politics of Casualization in Africa's Chinese Enclaves." *The China Quarterly* 199: 647–66.

——. 2000. The 'Revenge of History': Collective Memories and Labor Protests in North-Eastern China." *Ethnography* 1, no. 2: 217–37.

Lehr, Amy K., and Mariefaye Bechrakis. *Connecting the Dots in Xinjiang: Forced Labor, Forced Assimilation, and Western Supply Chains.* Washington, DC: Center for Strategic & International Studies, 2019.

Lewis, W. Arthur. 1954. "Economic Development with Unlimited Supplies of Labour." *The Manchester School* 22, no. 2: 139–91.

Li, Hongbin, Prashant Loyalka, Scott Rozelle, Binzhen Wu, and Jieyu Xie. 2015. "Unequal Access to College in China: How Far Have Poor, Rural Students Been Left Behind?" *The China Quarterly* 221: 185–207.

Li, Tania Murray. 2010. "To Make Live or Let Die? Rural Dispossession and the Protection of Surplus Populations." *Antipode* 41, no. 1: 66–93.

Li, Yaru, Wenying Sun, and Zhiping Yang. 2003. "Beijing Shi Liudong Renkou Ji Qi Zinü Jiaoyu Zhuangkuang Diaocha Yanjiu." *Journal of Capital Normal University*, no. 2: 118–22.

Liang, Zai, and Yiu Por Chen. 2007. "The Educational Consequences of Migration for Children in China." *Social Science Research* 36, no. 1: 28–47.

Lin, George C. S. 2007. "Chinese Urbanism in Question: State, Society, and the Reproduction of Urban Spaces." *Urban Geography* 28, no. 1: 7–29.

——. 2015. "The Redevelopment of China's Construction Land: Practising Land Property Rights in Cities through Renewals." *The China Quarterly* 224: 865–87.

Lin, George C. S., and Fangxin Yi. 2011. "Urbanization of Capital or Capitalization on Urban Land? Land Development and Local Public Finance in Urbanizing China." *Urban Geography* 32, no. 1: 50–79.

Lin, George C. S., and Amy Y Zhang. 2017. "China's Metropolises in Transformation: Neoliberalizing Politics, Land Commodification, and Uneven Development in Beijing." *Urban Geography* 38, no. 5: 643–65.

Lin, Justin Yifu. 2011. *Demystifying the Chinese Economy.* New York: Cambridge University Press.

Lin, Yi. 2011. "Turning Rurality Into Modernity: Suzhi Education in a Suburban Public School of Migrant Children in Xiamen." *The China Quarterly* 206, no. 2: 313–30.

Ling, Minhua. 2015. "'Bad Students Go to Vocational Schools!': Education, Social Reproduction and Migrant Youth in Urban China." *The China Journal* 73: 108–31.

———. 2017. "Returning to No Home: Educational Remigration and Displacement in Rural China." *Anthropological Quarterly* 90, no. 3: 715–42.

Liu, Alan P. 1992. "The 'Wenzhou Model' of Development and China's Modernization." *Asian Survey* 32, no. 8: 696–711.

Liu, Andrew B. 2020. *Tea War: A History of Capitalism in China and India*. New Haven, CT: Yale University Press.

Liu, Kerry. 2018. "Chinese Manufacturing in the Shadow of the China–US Trade War." *Economic Affairs* 38, no. 3: 307–24.

Liu, Ran, and Tai-Chee Wong. 2018. "Urban Village Redevelopment in Beijing: The State-Dominated Formalization of Informal Housing." *Cities* 72: 160–72.

Liu, Yuanli, William Hsiao, Qing Li, and Xingzhu Liu. 1995. "Transformation of China's Rural Health Care Financing." *Social Science & Medicine* 41, no. 8: 1085–93.

Logan, John R., Yiping Fang, and Zhanxin Zhang. 2009. "Access to Housing in Urban China." *International Journal of Urban and Regional Research* 33, no. 4: 914–35.

Malthus, T. R. 1993. *An Essay on the Principle of Population*. Oxford: Oxford University Press.

Marx, Karl. 1976. *Capital*. Vol. 1, *A Critique of Political Economy*. New York: Penguin Classics.

Maurer-Fazio, Margaret. 2012. "Ethnic Discrimination in China's Internet Job Board Labor Market." *IZA Journal of Migration* 1, no. 1: 12.

Mbembe, Achille. 2004. "Aesthetics of Superfluity." *Public Culture* 16, no. 3: 373–405.

———. 2003. "Necropolitics." *Public Culture* 15, no. 1: 11–40.

McIntyre, Michael. 2011. "Race, Surplus Population and the Marxist Theory of Imperialism." *Antipode* 43, no. 5: 1489–515.

McIntyre, Michael, and Heidi J. Nast. 2011. "Bio(Necro)Polis: Marx, Surplus Populations, and the Spatial Dialectics of Reproduction and 'Race.'" *Antipode* 43, no. 5: 1465–88.

Merrill, Heather. 2011. "Migration and Surplus Populations: Race and Deindustrialization in Northern Italy." *Antipode* 43, no. 5: 1542–72.

Mezzadra, Sandro, and Brett Neilson. 2012. "Between Inclusion and Exclusion: On the Topology of Global Space and Borders." *Theory, Culture & Society* 29, nos. 4–5: 58–75.

——. 2013. *Border as Method, or, the Multiplication of Labor*. Durham, NC: Duke University Press.

Ming, Holly H. 2013. *The Education of Migrant Children and China's Future: The Urban Left Behind*. New York: Routledge.

Mohandesi, Salar, and Emma Teitelman. 2017. "Without Reserves." In *Social Reproduction Theory: Remapping Class, Recentering Oppression*, edited by Tithi Bhattacharya, 37–67. London: Pluto Press.

Mok, Ka-Ho, and King-yee Wat. 1998. "Merging of the Public and Private Boundary: Education and the Market Place in China." *International Journal of Educational Development* 18, no. 3: 255–67.

Mok, Ka-Ho, Yu Cheung Wong, and Xiulan Zhang. 2009. "When Marketisation and Privatisation Clash with Socialist Ideals: Educational Inequality in Urban China." *International Journal of Educational Development* 29, no. 5: 505–12.

Murphy, Rachel. 2014. "Study and School in the Lives of Children in Migrant Families: A View from Rural Jiangxi, China." *Development and Change* 45, no. 1: 29–51.

Naughton, Barry. 1994. "Chinese Institutional Innovation and Privatization from Below." *American Economic Review* 84, no. 2: 266.

——. 1992. "Implications of the State Monopoly Over Industry and Its Relaxation." *Modern China* 18, no. 1: 14–41.

Nee, Victor. 1989. "A Theory of Market Transition: From Redistribution to Markets in State Socialism." *American Sociological Review* 54, no. 5: 663–81.

Nee, Victor, and Sonja Opper. 2012. *Capitalism from Below: Markets and Institutional Change in China*. Cambridge, MA: Harvard University Press.

Ohno, Taiichi. 1988. *Toyota Production System: Beyond Large-Scale Production*. Portland, OR: Productivity Press.

Oi, Jean C. 1992. "Fiscal Reform and the Economic Foundations of Local State Corporatism in China." *World Politics* 45, no. 1: 99–126.

——. 1999. *Rural China Takes Off: Institutional Foundations of Economic Reform*. Berkeley: University of California Press.

Ong, Aihwa. 1999. *Flexible Citizenship: The Cultural Logics of Transnationality*. Durham, NC: Duke University Press.

Ong, Lynette H. 2014. "State-Led Urbanization in China: Skyscrapers, Land Revenue and 'Concentrated Villages.'" *The China Quarterly* 217: 162–79.

——. 2018. "'Thugs-for-Hire': Subcontracting of State Coercion and State Capacity in China." *Perspectives on Politics* 16, no. 3: 680–95.

Park, Robert Ezra. 1928. *The City.* Chicago: University of Chicago Press.

Parris, Kristen. 1993. "Local Initiative and National Reforms: The Wenzhou Model of Development." *The China Quarterly* 134: 242–63.

Perry, Elizabeth, and Xiaobo Lu. 1997. Danwei: *The Changing Chinese Workplace in Historical and Comparative Perspective.* Armonk, NY: M. E. Sharpe.

Polanyi, Karl. 1944. *The Great Transformation: The Political and Economic Origins of Our Time.* Boston: Beacon Press.

Pun, Ngai. 2005. *Made in China: Women Factory Workers in a Global Workplace.* Durham, NC: Duke University Press.

Pun, Ngai, and Jenny Wai-ling Chan. 2012. "Global Capital, the State, and Chinese Workers: The Foxconn Experience." *Modern China* 38, no. 4 (May): 383–410.

Pun, Ngai, and Huilin Lu. 2010. "Unfinished Proletarianization: Self, Anger, and Class Action Among the Second Generation of Peasant-Workers in Present-Day China." *Modern China* 36, no. 5 (July): 493–519.

Pun, Ngai, and Chris Smith. 2007. "Putting Transnational Labour Process in Its Place: The Dormitory Labour Regime in Post-Socialist China." *Work Employment and Society* 21, no. 1: 27–46.

Read, Jason. 2002. "Primitive Accumulation: The Aleatory Foundation of Capitalism." *Rethinking Marxism* 14, no. 2: 24–49.

Ren, Xuefei. 2018. "A Genealogy of Redevelopment in Chinese Cities." In *Urbanization and Urban Governance in China*, 93–108. Springer.

——. 2020. *Governing the Urban in China and India: Land Grabs, Slum Clearance, and the War on Air Pollution.* Princeton, NJ: Princeton University Press.

Rithmire, Meg E. 2015. *Land Bargains and Chinese Capitalism: The Politics of Property Rights Under Reform.* New York: Cambridge University Press.

Robinson, Cedric J. 2000. *Black Marxism: The Making of the Black Radical Tradition.* Chapel Hill: University of North Carolina Press.

Robinson, Jennifer. 2016. "Comparative Urbanism: New Geographies and Cultures of Theorizing the Urban." *International Journal of Urban and Regional Research* 40, no.1: 187–99.

Robinson, Jennifer, and Ananya Roy. 2016. "Debate on Global Urbanisms and the Nature of Urban Theory." *International Journal of Urban and Regional Research* 40, no. 1: 181–86.

Saich, Tony. 2008. "The Changing Role of Urban Government." In *China Urbanizes: Consequences, Strategies, and Policies*, edited by Shahid Yusuf and Anthony Saich, 181–205. Washington, DC: World Bank.

Sargeson, Sally. 2013. "Violence as Development: Land Expropriation and China's Urbanization." *Journal of Peasant Studies* 40, no. 6: 1063–85.

Sassen, Saskia. 2014. *Expulsions*. Cambridge, MA: Harvard University Press.

———. 2008. "Two Stops in Today's New Global Geographies: Shaping Novel Labor Supplies and Employment Regimes." *American Behavioral Scientist* 52, no. 3: 457–96.

Schmalz, Stefan, Brandon Sommer, and Hui Xu. 2017. "The Yue Yuen Strike: Industrial Transformation and Labour Unrest in the Pearl River Delta." *Globalizations* 14, no. 2: 285–97.

Scott, Allen J., and Michael Storper. 2015. "The Nature of Cities: The Scope and Limits of Urban Theory." *International Journal of Urban and Regional Research* 39, no. 1: 1–15.

Selwyn, Benjamin. 2018. *The Struggle for Development*. Cambridge: Polity Press.

Sen, Amartya. 1999. *Development as Freedom*. New York: Anchor.

Sharma, Nandita. *Home Rule: National Sovereignty and the Separation of Natives and Migrants*. Durham, NC: Duke University Press, 2020.

Shen, Xiaoge, and Guoqiang Zhou. 2005. "Guangzhou Shi Liudong Renkou Zinü Yiwu Jiaoyu Wenti Fenxi Yu Duice." *Xiandai Jiaoyu Luncong* 5: 15–22.

Shin, Hyun Bang. 2016. "Economic Transition and Speculative Urbanisation in China: Gentrification Versus Dispossession." *Urban Studies* 53, no. 3: 471–89.

———. 2009. "Residential Redevelopment and the Entrepreneurial Local State: The Implications of Beijing's Shifting Emphasis on Urban Redevelopment Policies." *Urban Studies* 46, no. 13: 2815–39.

———. 2010. "Urban Conservation and Revalorisation of Dilapidated Historic Quarters: The Case of Nanluoguxiang in Beijing." *Cities* 27: S43–54.

Simmel, Georg. 1950 (1903). *The Metropolis and Mental Life.* New York: Free Press.

Siu, Kaxton. 2015. "Continuity and Change in the Everyday Lives of Chinese Migrant Factory Workers." *The China Journal* 74: 43–65.

Smith, Neil. 1979. "Toward a Theory of Gentrification: A Back to the City Movement by Capital, Not People." *Journal of the American Planning Association* 45, no. 4: 538–48.

Smith, Nick R. 2016. "Living on the Edge: Household Registration Reform and Peri-Urban Precarity in China." *Journal of Urban Affairs* 36, no. 1: 369–83.

Solinger, Dorothy J. 2009. *States' Gains, Labor's Losses: China, France, and Mexico Choose Global Liaisons, 1980–2000.* Ithaca, NY: Cornell University Press.

Song, Yan, Yves Zenou, and Chengri Ding. 2008. "Let's Not Throw the Baby out with the Bath Water: The Role of Urban Villages in Housing Rural Migrants in China." *Urban Studies* 45, no. 2: 313–30.

Song, Yingquan, Yubiao Zeng, and Linxiu Zhang. "Dagong Zidi Xuexiao Xuesheng Chuzhong Hou Liuxiang Na Li? Ji Yu Beijing Shi 1866 Ming Liudong Ertong Xuesheng Changqi Genzong Diaoyan Shuju de Shizheng Fenxi." *Jiaoyu Jingji Pinglun* 3 (2017): 20–37.

Stoler, Ann Laura. 1995. *Race and the Education of Desire: Foucault's History of Sexuality and the Colonial Order of Things.* Durham, NC: Duke University Press.

Storper, Michael, and Richard Walker. 1983. "The Theory of Labour and the Theory of Location." *International Journal of Urban and Regional Research* 7, no. 1: 1–43.

Su, Shaobing, Xiaolo Li, Danhua Lin, Xiaoyenan Xu, and Maoling Zhu. 2013. "Psychological Adjustment Among Left-Behind Children in Rural China: The Role of Parental Migration and Parent-Child Communication." *Child: Care, Health and Development* 39, no. 2: 162–70.

Sugihara, Kaoru. 2013. "Labour-Intensive Industrialization in Global History: An Interpretation of East Asian Experiences." In *Labour-Intensive Industrialization in Global History,* edited by Gareth Austin and Kaoru Sugihara, 34–78. New York: Routledge.

Swider, Sarah. 2016. *Building China: Informal Work and the New Precariat.* Ithaca, NY: Cornell University Press.

Tian, Huisheng, Ni Wu, Ningjuan Zhang, and Xiaoqiang Li. 2008. "Jincheng Wugong Nongmin Suiqian Zinü Jiaoyu Zhuangkuang Diaoyan Baogao." *Jiaoyu Yanjiu* 4:13–21.

Tian, Li. 2008. "The Chengzhongcun Land Market in China: Boon or Bane?—A Perspective on Property Rights." *International Journal of Urban and Regional Research* 32, no. 2: 282–304.

Tomba, Luigi. 2017. "Finding China's Urban: Bargained Land Conversions, Local Assemblages, and Fragmented Urbanization." In *To Govern China: Evolving Practices of Power*, edited by Vivienne Shue and Patricia M. Thornton, 203. Cambridge: Cambridge University Press.

Tronti, Mario. 2019. *Workers and Capital*. London: Verso.

Tsang, Mun C. 2000. "Education and National Development in China since 1949: Oscillating Policies and Enduring Dilemmas." *China Review*, 579–618.

Tyner, James A. 2013. "Population Geography I: Surplus Populations." *Progress in Human Geography* 37, no. 5: 701–11.

Uetricht, Micah. 2014. *Strike for America: Chicago Teachers Against Austerity*. New York: Verso.

Unger, Jonathan. 1985. "The Decollectivization of the Chinese Countryside: A Survey of Twenty-Eight Villages." *Pacific Affairs* 58, no.4: 585–606.

——. 2002. *The Transformation of Rural China*. Armonk, NY: M. E. Sharpe.

Vickers, Edward, and Xiaodong Zeng. 2017. *Education and Society in Post-Mao China*. New York: Routledge.

Visser, Robin. 2010. *Cities Surround the Countryside: Urban Aesthetics in Postsocialist China*. Durham, NC: Duke University Press.

Walder, Andrew. 1995. "Local Governments as Industrial Firms: An Organizational Analysis of China's Transitional Economy." *American Journal of Sociology* 101, no. 2: 263–301.

——. 1996. "Markets and Inequality in Transitional Economies: Toward Testable Theories." *American Journal of Sociology* 101, no. 4: 1060–73.

Walker, Richard A. 2016. "Why Cities? A Response." *International Journal of Urban and Regional Research* 40, no. 1: 164–80.

Wallace, Jeremy L. 2014. *Cities and Stability: Urbanization, Redistribution, and Regime Survival in China*. New York: Oxford University Press.

Wang, Xiaobing, Renfu Luo, Linxiu Zhang, and Scott Rozelle. 2017. "The Education Gap of China's Migrant Children and Rural Counterparts." *Journal of Development Studies* 53, no. 11: 1865–81.

Wang, Ya Ping, Yanglin Wang, and Jiansheng Wu. 2009. "Urbanization and Informal Development in China: Urban Villages in Shenzhen." *International Journal of Urban and Regional Research* 33, no. 4: 957–73.

Weheliye, Alexander G. 2014. *Habeas Viscus: Racializing Assemblages, Biopolitics, and Black Feminist Theories of the Human.* Durham, NC: Duke University Press.

Wen, Christine, and Jeremy L. Wallace. 2019. "Toward Human-Centered Urbanization? Housing Ownership and Access to Social Insurance Among Migrant Households in China." *Sustainability* 11, no. 13: 1–14.

Werner, Marion. 2011. "Coloniality and the Contours of Global Production in the Dominican Republic and Haiti." *Antipode* 43, no. 5: 1573–97.

Whyte, Martin King, Wang Feng, and Yong Cai. 2015. "Challenging Myths About China's One-Child Policy." *The China Journal*, no. 74: 144–59.

Willis, Paul E. 1977. *Learning to Labour: How Working Class Kids Get Working Class Jobs.* Farnborough, UK: Saxon House.

Womack, James P., and Daniel T. Jones. 2010. *Lean Thinking: Banish Waste and Create Wealth in Your Corporation.* New York: Simon & Schuster.

Wong, Siu Wai. 2015. "Urbanization as a Process of State Building: Local Governance Reforms in China." *International Journal of Urban and Regional Research* 39, no. 5: 912–26.

Wong, Tai-Chee, and Ran Liu. 2017. "Developmental Urbanism, City Image Branding and the 'Right to the City' in Transitional China." *Urban Policy and Research* 35, no. 2: 210–23.

Woodman, Sophia. 2017. "Legitimating Exclusion and Inclusion: 'Culture,' Education and Entitlement to Local Urban Citizenship in Tianjin and Lanzhou." *Citizenship Studies* 21, no. 7: 755–72.

Woronov, T. E. 2015. *Class Work: Vocational Schools and China's Urban Youth.* Stanford, CA: Stanford University Press.

——. 2004. "In the Eye of the Chicken: Hierarchy and Marginality Among Beijing's Migrant Schoolchildren." *Ethnography* 5, no. 3: 289–313.

——. 2011. "Learning to Serve: Urban Youth, Vocational Schools and New Class Formations in China." *The China Journal* 66: 77–99.

———. 2008. "Raising Quality, Fostering 'Creativity': Ideologies and Practices of Education Reform in Beijing." *Anthropology & Education Quarterly* 39, no. 4: 401–22.

Wu, Fulong. 2016a. "Housing in Chinese Urban Villages: The Dwellers, Conditions and Tenancy Informality." *Housing Studies* 31, no. 7: 852–70.

———. 2016b. "State Dominance in Urban Redevelopment: Beyond Gentrification in Urban China." *Urban Affairs Review* 52, no. 5: 631–58.

Wu, Fulong, Fangzhu Zhang, and Chris Webster. 2013. "Informality and the Development and Demolition of Urban Villages in the Chinese Peri-Urban Area." *Urban Studies* 50, no. 10: 1919–34.

———. 2013. *Rural Migrants in Urban China: Enclaves and Transient Urbanism*. New York: Routledge.

Wu, Weiping. 2014. "Outsiders in the City: Migrant Housing and Settlement Patterns." In *Rural Migrants in Urban China: Enclaves and Transient Urbanism*, edited by Fulong Wu, Fangzhu Zhang, and Chris Webster, 51–66. New York: Routledge.

Wu, Yifei, Xun Li, and George C. S. Lin. 2016. "Reproducing the City of the Spectacle: Mega-Events, Local Debts, and Infrastructure-Led Urbanization in China." *Cities* 53: 51–60.

Xiao, Qinghua. 2012. *Nongcun Liushou Yu Liudong Ertong de Jiaoyu*. Beijing: Zhongguo shehui kexue chubanshe.

Xie, Yu, and Yongai Jin. 2015. "Household Wealth in China." *Chinese Sociological Review* 47, no. 3: 203–29.

Xiong, Yihan. 2015. "The Broken Ladder: Why Education Provides No Upward Mobility for Migrant." *China Quarterly* 221: 161–84.

Xu, Changchang. 2010. "Jincheng Wugong Renyuan Suiqian Zinü Xinli Jiankang Zhuangkuang de Bijiao Yanjiu." *Sixiang Lilun Jiaoyu* 10: 62–68.

Xu, Vicky Xiuzhong, Danielle Cave, James Leibold, Kelsey Munro, and Nathan Ruser. 2020. "Uyghurs for Sale." *Australian Strategic Policy Institute* 26.

Xu, Ying, Bo-sin Tang, and Edwin H. W. Chan. 2011. "State-Led Land Requisition and Transformation of Rural Villages in Transitional China." *Habitat International* 35, no. 1: 57–65.

Yan, Hairong. 2003. "Neoliberal Governmentality and Neohumanism: Organizing Suzhi/Value Flow Through Labor Recruitment Networks." *Cultural Anthropology* 18, no. 4: 493–523.

Yang, Dongping. 2016. "Zhongguo Liudong Ertong Jiaoyu de Fazhan He Zhengce Yanbian." In *Zhongguo Liudong Ertong Jiaoyu Fazhan Baogao*, edited by Dongping Yang, Hongyu Qin, and Jiayu Wei, 1–20. Beijing: Social Sciences Academic Press.

Yates, Michelle. 2011. "The Human-as-Waste: The Labor Theory of Value and Disposability in Contemporary Capitalism." *Antipode* 43, no. 5: 1679–95.

Ye, Lin. 2011. "Urban Regeneration in China: Policy, Development, and Issues." *Local Economy* 26, no. 5: 337–47.

Yu, Min. 2018. "Rethinking Migrant Children Schools in China: Activism, Collective Identity, and Guanxi." *Comparative Education Review* 62, no. 3: 429–48.

Zhan, Shaohua. 2011. "What Determines Migrant Workers' Life Chances in Contemporary China? Hukou, Social Exclusion, and the Market." *Modern China* 37, no. 3: 243–85.

Zhan, Shaohua, and Lingli Huang. 2013. "Rural Roots of Current Migrant Labor Shortage in China: Development and Labor Empowerment in a Situation of Incomplete Proletarianization." *Studies in Comparative International Development* 48, no. 1: 81–111.

Zhang, Chenchen. 2018. "Governing Neoliberal Authoritarian Citizenship: Theorizing *Hukou* and the Changing Mobility Regime in China." *Citizenship Studies* 22, no. 8: 855–81.

Zhang, Li. 2012. "Economic Migration and Urban Citizenship in China: The Role of Points Systems." *Population and Development Review* 38, no. 3: 503–33.

——. 2005. "Migrant Enclaves and Impacts of Redevelopment Policy in Chinese Cities." In *Restructuring the Chinese City: Changing Society, Economy and Space*, edited by Laurence J. C. Ma and Fulong Wu, 218–33. New York: Routledge.

——. 2001. *Strangers in the City: Reconfigurations of Space, Power, and Social Networks Within China's Floating Population*. Stanford, CA: Stanford University Press.

Zhang, Li, and Li Tao. 2012. "Barriers to the Acquisition of Urban Hukou in Chinese Cities." *Environment and Planning A* 44, no. 12: 2883–900.

Zhang, Mingqiong, Cherrie Jiuhua Zhu, and Chris Nyland. 2014. "The Institution of Hukou-based Social Exclusion: A Unique Institution

Reshaping the Characteristics of Contemporary Urban China." *International Journal of Urban and Regional Research* 38, no. 4: 1437–57.

Zhang, Yinghua. 2019. "Improving Social Protection for Internal Migrant Workers in China." International Labour Organization.

Zhang, Zhuoni, and Xiaogang Wu. 2017. "Occupational Segregation and Earnings Inequality: Rural Migrants and Local Workers in Urban China." *Social Science Research* 61: 57–74.

Zhao, Han, and Jiayu Wei. 2016. "Beijing Yiwu Jiaoyu Jieduan Liudong Ertong Jiaoyu Xianzhuang." In *Zhongguo Liudong Ertong Jiaoyu Fazhan Baogao*, edited by Dongping Yang, Hongyu Qin, and Jiayu Wei, 105–20. Beijing: Social Sciences Academic Press.

Zheng, Zizhen, and Jian Song. 2011. "Zhongshan Liudong Renkou de Jifenzhi Guanli Cunzai de Wenti Ji Duice Fenxi." *Nanfang Renkou* 26, no. 4: 57–64.

Zhou, Kate Xiao. 1996. *How the Farmers Changed China: Power of the People.* Boulder, CO: Westview Press.

INDEX

Page references in *italics*, followed by *f*, refer to figures.

to, 43–44; in point-based *hukou*
admission, 57; point-based
school enrollment, 72–77;
population control via, 107–8,
119–23; public school enrollment
in Beijing, 69–72, 70f;
regulation of, in Beijing,
159–60; of rural workforce, 62;
spending, per capita, on, in
cities, 80–81, 80f. *See also*
schools
education donations, 114–15
education registration (*xueji*),
123–27, 132
English (language), instruction
in, 98

Fan (Mr.), 109–10; on children's
hukou, 117–18; on demolitions of
workplaces, 173–74; government
criticized by, 237–38; on social
insurance requirement, 122–23
fast track policies, 59
Federici, Silvia, 254n10
Feng Huai, 112, 128–29, 178
forged documents, 111
Foucault, Michel, 9, 264n30; on
biopolitics, 24–25; on biopower,
21–22; on China's point-based
hukou admission, 277–78n57; on
discipline-punish dialectic,
291–92n1; on panopticon, 36,
270n61; on population, 26–27,
264n32; on race and racism,
263n21; on urbanization, 29
Fraser, Nancy, 215, 297n49
Fudan University, 82

Gallagher, Mary, 258n29
Gilmore, Ruth Wilson, 25, 260n48
globalization, 304n28
Goonewardena, Kanishka, 234
green card policies, 59
Greenhalgh, Susan, 209, 263n25
Gu (teacher), 102, 194
Guangdong, 225, 232
Guangfu School (pseudonym),
224–25
Guangzhou: *hukou* ranking of, 226;
migrant schools in, 92, 230,
298n2; point-based *hukou*
admission in, 61; point-based
school enrollment in, 72, 74, 76;
urbanization in, 222–24
Guiyang, 222, 225–30
Guo (teacher), 91, 98, 205
Guo Jinlong, 3, 105

Haidian District, 181–82
Hainan, talent programs in, 60
Han (people), 236
Hardt, Michael, 260n7
Harvey, David, 234; on capitalist
accumulation in China, 23; on
just-in-time urbanization,
35–36; on urbanization in
China, 292–93n7; on
urbanization of capital, 254n11
Hebei Province, 137–39
heterosexual couples, in point-based
school enrollment, 75–76
higher education, 78; "211"
universities, 57; university
admissions, 82
high school entrance exams, 100

GPSR Authorized Representative: Easy Access System Europe, Mustamäe tee 50, 10621 Tallinn, Estonia, gpsr.requests@easproject.com

www.ingramcontent.com/pod-product-compliance
Lightning Source LLC
Chambersburg PA
CBHW022135020426
42334CB00015B/904